50 0488642 4

D0635419

323.6
OOM

Citizenship, Nationality
and Ethnicity

To Josephine for her 'grudging' co-operation!

UWE BRISTOL
WITHDRAWN
LIBRARY SERVICES

Citizenship, Nationality and Ethnicity
Reconciling Competing Identities

T. K. Oommen

UWE, BRISTOL

-7 APR 1997

Library Services

Polity Press

Copyright © T. K. Oommen 1997

The right of T. K. Oommen to be identified as author of this work has been
asserted in accordance with the Copyright, Designs and Patents Act 1988.

First published in 1997 by Polity Press
in association with Blackwell Publishers Ltd.

Editorial office:
Polity Press
65 Bridge Street
Cambridge CB2 1UR, UK

Marketing and production:
Blackwell Publishers Ltd
108 Cowley Road
Oxford OX4 1JF, UK

Published in the UK by
Blackwell Publishers Inc.
238 Main Street
Cambridge, MA 02142, USA

All rights reserved. Except for the quotation of short passages for the
purposes of criticism and review, no part of this publication may be
reproduced, stored in a retrieval system, or transmitted, in any form or by
any means, electronic, mechanical, photocopying, recording or otherwise,
without the prior permission of the publisher.

Except in the United States of America, this book is sold subject to the
condition that it shall not, by way of trade or otherwise, be lent, re-sold,
hired out, or otherwise circulated without the publisher's prior consent in
any form of binding or cover other than that in which it is published and
without a similar condition including this condition being imposed on the
subsequent purchaser.

ISBN 0-7456-1619-4
ISBN 0-7456-1620-8 (pbk)

A CIP catalogue record for this book is available from the British Library
and the Library of Congress.

Typeset in 10 on 12 pt Palatino
by Puretech
Printed in Great Britain by Hartnolls Ltd, Victoria Square, Bodmin,
Cornwall, England.

This book is printed on acid-free paper.

Contents

Acknowledgements

The idea of writing this book was first suggested to me by Anthony Giddens in the course of our correspondence in 1994, but for which this book would not have been written. Therefore he deserves my gratitude above all.

A book of this sort cannot be written all of a sudden. I have been thinking about and writing on this theme for the past decade. However, one needs substantial time and concentration unencumbered by the distractions of routine work to put the ideas together. An invitation from Collegium Budapest, Institute of Advanced Studies (Hungary), to spend the academic year 1994–5 therefore came at the most opportune moment, as I had already accepted Giddens's suggestion. The extremely cordial atmosphere and the facilities provided by the Collegium, under the exuberant leadership of its Rector, Professor (Dr) Lajos Vekas and his team of dedicated staff, provided the required acceleration to write the book. The stay at Budapest was made pleasant in numerous ways by the help and co-operation of Professor (Dr) Rudolf Andorka, Rector of the Budapest University of Economic Sciences and his wife Mrs Judith Andorka. I thank them for their many acts of kindness.

It is one thing to get an invitation for an academic assignment but quite another to avail oneself of it. The writing of this book was facilitated by the Vice-Chancellor of Jawaharlal Nehru University Dr Y. K. Alagh who sanctioned my sabbatical leave within record time and by my colleagues at the Centre for the Study of Social Systems of the School of Social Sciences at JNU who shared out between them my teaching responsibilities and my research supervisions.

I must record my deep sense of gratitude to members of my family. My two sons, Koshy Oommen and Johnny Oommen, had to live by themselves and put up with numerous discomforts to which they were not accustomed as their mother accompanied me to Hungary. I am grateful for their understanding. My wife Josephine Oommen took leave for a year from her onerous responsibility of administering a school in New Delhi to be with me. The writing of this book would not have been completed so quickly but for her doing the required computer work to prepare the manuscript. As a token of my appreciation for her sacrifices, I dedicate this book to her.

Two persons contributed enormously to improve the quality of the manuscript. One is the anonymous reader of Polity Press who made several useful suggestions. The other is Ms Bela Butalia by her dedicated and deft editing.

Finally, I want to thank Dr George Mathew, Director, Institute of Social Sciences, New Delhi for making the infrastructural facilities of the Institute available and Mr P. N. Kuttappan for his help and cooperation in finalizing the manuscript. The conventional disclaimer stands.

Part I
The Conceptual Kit

The Search for Clarity

1

Introducing the Argument

To begin with, a word of justification for writing a new short book on an old vast theme so frequently and fully discussed in contemporary social science. This book is about three concepts – citizenship, nationality and ethnicity – and their applicability to a variety of empirical situations. While concepts in themselves are not a substitute for description or explanation, conceptualization has profound significance for apprehending reality, theory construction, formulation of social policy and even for averting or increasing human misery. Therefore, those who formulate and use concepts have a great responsibility. Ernest Barker noted:

> The conception of the scholar, perverted by the publicist, and then harnessed to political objects by the politician may thus become dynamite for the explosion of an existing system of states. There is all the more reason that the scholar should keep his conception pure and undefiled; that he should watch its use and rebuke its abuse. The scholar who gives birth to an idea can never divest himself of responsibility for its career. (*1948: 25*)

While conception and conceptualization are not the same, the two are intimately related. The latter is often influenced by the former. Our conceptualization is firmly anchored to our conception of reality.

Even a quick perusal of the social science writings on themes such as nation and nationalism unfolds the widespread prevailing ambiguity. For example, nationalism is qualified by the following terms: autonomist, anti-colonial, bureaucratic, black, bourgeois, civic, colonial, communist, colour, cultural, conservative, developmental, dynastic, dynamic, diaspora, economic, ecclesiastical, elite, ethnic, ethnocratic, fissiparous, geographic, historic, insular, integral, irredentist, linguistic, liberal, mass, Marxist, military, modern, melting-pot, messianic, neo-, old, official, organic, pan-, political, proletarian, poly-centric, politico-religious, populist, racial, reactive, reform, regional, renewal, romantic, religious, separatist, sub-, supra-, sacred, socialist, secessionist, secular, settler, territorial, Third World, and traditionalist. Even this list is not exhaustive. Some consider fascism, Nazism, imperialism, populism, racism and the like to be different forms of nationalism. These qualifying terms, which indirectly imply a large variety of nations, are utterly confusing, to put it rather mildly. Needless to say, much of this confusion emanates from the inappropriate conceptualizations involved.

Concepts in general and social science concepts in particular emanate out of particular situations in order to capture and mirror the nature of reality in a summary form. The large number of qualifying terms of nationalism listed above is in fact a reflection of the anxiety to capture the essence of the changing empirical scene. The end of the twentieth century seems to be an appropriate time to redefine the concepts that I propose to deal with in this book. The idea of nation-state was initiated by the Treaty of Westphalia concluded in 1648 in Germany, and within three centuries it became a near universal ideal, relentlessly pursued in all parts of the world. But the lack of fit between concept and reality was often forgotten, and all forms of states – uni-national, multi-national, poly-ethnic – invariably came to be designated as nation-states. In the meantime, Western Europe, the birthplace of the nation-state, has become or is becoming its graveyard, with the emergence of the European Union. On the other hand, multi-national socialist states are being dismantled in Europe. The first 'new nation', the United States of America, has become a veritable multi-cultural and poly-ethnic state. The Union of Indian States continues to be a stupendous multi-national entity. Clearly, the concept of nation-state has become an inadequate, even inappropriate one to describe the multitude of entities that we are encountering.

A word of caution should be added here. I am not suggesting for a moment that the content and meaning of concepts that we are discussing have not changed over a period of time. Indeed, they have. In fact, the concept of nation has had a spectacular career. Zernatto (1944: 351–66), for example, notes that the term *natio*, the Latin word for nation, was used by the ancient Romans to refer to foreigners, the exact opposite of what the term stands for today. Later, it was used to refer to the assembly of nobles and clergy drawn from particular peoples. But all people did not have this component. Thus, in 1731 when John Innocent Micu, a bishop, referred to the right of the Walachian nation (Rumanian people) to be represented in the Transylvanian Parliament, his words met with the cry: 'There is no Walachian nation, there is only a Walachian plebs.' Once again, the idea of equating nation with elites or assuming that only some nations are privileged to have elites is totally at variance with the contemporary impulse. Today, the nation is viewed as the totality of a people of the same religion, race or language, although there is no consensus on the specificity of the attribute. In fact, Greenfeld identifies five different phases through which the meaning of nation has passed. These are a group of foreigners, a community of opinion, an elite, a sovereign people and a unique people (1992: 9).

I suggest that we should think of a nation as a totality comprising all those who consider the nation as their homeland, irrespective of their background. Incidentally, such a view is in accord with the original sense of the term citizen: the residents of a city. Such a perspective is an imperative, given the substantial relocation of peoples, thanks to the creation of the New World and the ongoing process of modernization and globalization. This also calls for a re-thinking of the meaning of citizenship. As for the meaning of ethnicity, the notion has become something like beauty, which is said to be located in the eye of the observer. Each analyst has attached a different meaning to the term. It is precisely the ambiguity of these concepts that calls for their reformulation; they deserve to be firmed up.

Clarity of concepts is a prerequisite for theory construction, that is, explanation. Unless we are clear about the nature of the object that is being explained – the explanandum – the explanation will not only be unsatisfactory, but misleading. A wide variety of factors has been invoked to explain the emergence of nationalism and, consequently, modern nation formation. The more important of these are capitalism, democracy, industrialization, and the quest for equality and modernization. Such explanations gain wide currency partly because the critical minimum elements of nation have not been identified. This remark is also true of citizenship and ethnicity. To be useful, conceptualization has to be undertaken so as to capture the difference between the empirical phenomena that the different concepts purport to describe and explain.

Why need we reconceptualize?

I have already indicated three reasons why these concepts need careful scrutiny. First, their imprecise usage and the consequent implication for description and analysis. Second, the substantial changes in their meanings over time. Third, the fundamental alterations in the empirical situations to which they are being applied. But there are several other reasons why the concepts of citizenship, nationality and ethnicity need to be re-examined. While these concepts are invariably used either interchangeably (as in the case of twin concepts, such as citizenship and nationality, or nationality and ethnicity) or independently, they can be more meaningfully employed as a trio that will unfold the dynamic and processual relationships between them. This is so because it is more rewarding to situate them in an interactional context, as their relationships vary depending on the property of the situation.

In mono-national states citizenship and nationality co-exist and coalesce, while ethnics are invariably non-citizens. In multi-national and poly-ethnic states a variety of combinations emerges and exists. But persons or a collectivity cannot be nationals and ethnics at the same time in the same locale, in that these are mutually exclusive identities. The case of citizenship is different. One can either be a citizen and a national, a citizen and an ethnic, or an ethnic and a non-citizen in such societies. What I am suggesting is that the three identities are of different types and the possibilities of different permutations and combinations exist depending upon the property of the situation and the attributes of the individuals. Clearly, I am not using these concepts in the prevalent senses, and I seek the patience of the reader till I explain them.

The second reason for the re-examination of these concepts is the importance of another dimension of what I have called the property of the situation. Categorization of social phenomena is purposive; one categorization may not be suited for all purposes. The categorization of the world into three – the First, the Second and the Third – has been in wide currency and was useful to understand the differences in the levels of development and patterns of political arrangements. But the categorization has serious limitations when situating the concepts of citizenship, nationality and ethnicity. This is not because of the recent momentous transformation leading to the virtual eclipse of the Second World. In fact some of the states (e.g. China and Cuba) are still in that category because they are not yet multi-party democracies.

The tripartite division of the world is not a useful one for situating the concepts of nationality and ethnicity, because the ideas of nations and nationality cannot be unequivocally applied to the New World – the Americas, Australia and New Zealand – at any rate in the sense in which they are applicable to the Old World. In my reckoning, the Old World is not confined to Europe alone, but also includes Asia and

Africa. All three worlds include parts of the Old and the New. The difference between the old societies and the new settler-majority countries is fundamental, particularly for the applicability of the notions of nationality and ethnicity and perhaps even for citizenship (which I hope to demonstrate eventually). Therefore, the categorization into old societies and settler countries is more appropriate for empirically anchoring the discussion of these concepts. Ignoring this vital distinction, enormous amounts of research have been done and the results published under headings such as 'Nationalism in the Third World', 'Ethnicity in the First World', 'Citizenship in the Second World', etc. By using the blanket terms 'First World' (that is, the West) while referring to the developed countries drawn from Western Europe, North America, Australia, New Zealand, etc. (parts of the Old and New Worlds); 'Third World', which again includes the New (Latin America) and Old Worlds (Asia and Africa); and 'Second World', which also include both New (Cuba) and Old (East Europe) – aspects of reality significant to our understanding of nationality, ethnicity and citizenship have been swept under the carpet. Further, the West/non-West dichotomy has led to facile generalizations on both. 'The fundamental framework of non-Western politics is a communal one, and all political behavior is strongly colored by considerations of communal identification', wrote Pye in the late fifties (1958: 469). The same idea is echoed in a volume edited by Geertz (1963). Although Diamant argued (1959: 126) that there is nothing like a specific non-Western political process, it largely went unnoticed. However, by the 1970s ethnic conflict in the West came to be recognized as a ubiquitous phenomenon (Esman 1977). Indeed it is time for us to recover from this analytical anomie.

Three broad geographical regions, whose total population makes for the majority of humanity, together make up the entity designated as the Third World, although racially and culturally they are different from each other. The first is Latin America, which in both respects is close to the First World. Predominantly Christian and Catholic, most Latin American states have a European language – Spanish or Portuguese – as their official language. At its core, Latin America is an extension and a cultural reproduction of what used to be the European periphery (Spain and Portugal). Most Latin American countries today are settler-majority or mestizo countries. The second is Africa, which is racially distinct or mixed (e.g., South Africa) and which consists of countries with a cultural amalgam of natives and the alien-colonial West. Of the fifty African states, 80 per cent have one of the European languages (English, French or Portuguese) as their official language, and the dominant religions – Islam and Christianity –

have been transplanted through conquest and colonialism. There is no settler-majority country – not even South Africa – in the African continent. The third geographical region is Asia, which is the homeland of two major civilizations: the Chinese and the Indian. Of the forty states in Asia, only one is predominantly Christian (the Philippines) and, except for Hong Kong the small port-state, none has a European language as its official language. There is no country in Asia with a substantial presence of an 'alien' race. That is, the three regions put together and labelled as the Third World have hardly anything in common in their socio-cultural milieu except Western influence. And this common factor of Western derivation is, admittedly, colonialism.

However, not all Third World countries have experienced colonialism and not all ex-colonial countries have remained in the Third World. In fact, there are two types of ex-colonial countries: those that not only became incorporated into the First World (e.g. the USA, Canada, Australia, New Zealand), but which surpassed and even assumed leadership over their erstwhile masters. Further, some of the countries located in the regions traditionally identified with the Third World are very affluent today. Japan heads the list of developed countries and the development ratings of Singapore, Korea and Taiwan are quite high (UNDP 1991). The other type of ex-colonial countries are those that were thickly populated and older (Asia and Africa). Therefore, a distinction between transplantive or replicative colonialism (which reproduced the culture, society, polity and economy of the imperial power) and intrusive and oppressive colonialism (which dominated the colony, but led to the withdrawal of the imperial power) ought to be made. The cultural baggage left behind by these two colonialisms are radically different. Ignoring the basic difference between the two types, it is argued that the Asian and African leaders 'who once castigated European domination as violative of self-determination are not now prepared to recognize such a right on the part of their own minorities' (Connor 1994: 161).[1] Such sentiments were articulated by others too. It is further suggested that the colonial political-administrative divisions were kept intact by the post-colonial governments (Emerson 1964).

Two points may be noted here. There was nothing like political-administrative units in the modern sense of the word in the New World before colonialism; they needed to be created. In Asia and Africa such units and divisions did exist, based on kinship and kingship. As for the resistance to the principle of self-determination, the qualitative difference between the pre-colonial and post-colonial situations is often ignored. The colonial Europeans were distant outsiders; they had no moral claim on the land and could not instantaneously create nations in thickly populated Asia and Africa. In fact, what is happening in these continents is precisely what had happened and continues to happen in Western Europe today, as illustrated by the cases of Brittany, the Basque Country, Ireland and numerous others. Therefore, the refusal to concede the right of self-determination to smaller and weaker nations within multi-national states is common to Asia, Africa and Europe, and the situation is drastically different from that of the New World settler countries. The point I want to make at this juncture is that the categorization of the world into three is not a useful distinction when one deals with issues of identity and culture or of self-determination.

The significance of the unit of analysis is not confined to the societal level. Confusion enters not only when the differences between the types of societies are ignored, but also when the unit of analysis is shifted from the individual to the collectivity and vice versa. Modernization theorists argue (e.g., Black 1966; Deutsch 1953) that national and ethnic identities will gradually disappear with the onward march of industrial urbanization, secularization and the spread of education. On the other hand, primordialists insist not only that these identities will not wither away, but that there is a great deal of evidence to show that modernization often leads to their reinforcement, crystallization and articulation (e.g., Connor 1994; Horowitz 1985).

However, the difference between these two positions is not so basic if one notices that the units of analysis on which they focus differ. Nobody can deny that the process of modernization has led to the partial erosion of some traditional attachments and loyalties, including national and ethnic ones. But this did not happen for any collectivity as a whole, even for the most modernized of collectivities. Modernization as a process impinges on different groups and categories within nations and ethnies with varying degrees of velocity ('ethnie' is used as a noun for groups that have all the characteristics of nations, except territory; see below p. 35, 'Dissecting ethnicity'). Further, it is particular individuals in specific collectivities – industrial workers, peasants, students, elites, professionals, intellectuals – who are more or less modern. On the other hand, it is also true that modernization has prompted particular collectivities within nations and ethnic groups (linguists, poets, novelists or intellectuals in general) to pursue the cause of their collective identities more vigorously than others (Znaniecki 1952). Therefore, the differences in the two articulations at least partly arise out of the differing focus on the units of analysis. If the modernists focus on the individuals and conceive collectivity as an aggregation, the primordialists concentrate on collectivities and take an organic view of society. Thus viewed, the differences between them can be better understood and properly situated.

One of the virulent critics of the modernization theory (and of the theorists) is Connor. He argues that increased transportation and communication add to the cultural awareness of nations and individuals, thereby reinforcing their cultural identity. To clinch the argument he draws from Keys (1966: 362–9) who has shown through a field study of villages in north-east Thailand that the transistor radio has made the Lao-speaking villagers aware of the linguistic and cultural differences between them and the politically dominant Siamese-speaking people. It has also made them aware of their cultural affinity with the Lao-speaking people who live in north-east Thailand and across the Mekong river in Western Laos.

In interpreting the meaning of this research it is important to note the following. First, the Lao-speaking nation was divided between the territories of three states: Thailand, Vietnam and Laos; the Lao speech community made up 91 per cent of Thailand's population, 69 per cent of the population in Laos and 4 per cent of the population in Vietnam in the mid-1960s when the field work was done. Second, through modern communication the Lao nation is becoming 'integrated'; but, third, this 'integration' is not functional for the states into which this community is distributed. That is, what is integrative for the nation is disintegrative for the state. A statement that claims either that modernization is integrative or that it is disintegrative is incomplete; it depends on what unit of analysis is employed. In the case cited, modernization integrates the Lao nation, but it unsettles the states into which the Lao people are distributed. Once again, the unit of analysis and the particular circumstances are crucial for an understanding of the situation.

There is yet another reason for the reconceptualization of nationality, ethnicity and citizenship. Although the tripartite division of the world is not appropriate as an empirical anchorage for these concepts, its ideological orientations provide an apt moment for their reconceptualization. The bourgeois revolution gave birth to the First World, the proletarian revolution to the Second and the colonial revolution to the Third. Each of them created expectancies, all of which remain unfulfilled to this day. The liberal expectancy of the First World postulated the disappearance of primordial ties and traditional loyalties and the emergence of a democratic and rational 'man'. The radical expectancy of the Second World assumed that a 'socialist man' would emerge who would abandon narrow loyalties to the fatherland. The nationalist expectancy of the Third World presumed that the citizens of the new states would waive their particularistic identities and loyalties in favour of building the 'nation'.

But the hopes of creating a 'socialist man' have been completely shattered, and most of the socialist states themselves have been dismantled. The Third World continually experiences threats against 'national integration', and many communities within the multinational states have claimed that they – not the present artificial states created by the colonial regimes – constitute the nations. Even the First World, notwithstanding its onward march towards 'progress' and 'rationality', is witnessing an incessant search for roots. The 'new ethnicity' of the West is disparaged by some who hope that reason will prevail; others, however, have rechristened it as post-modernity. But one thing is certain: the search for identity is common to the whole of humanity. The issues are concerned with which identities will persist, for how long and why; which identities are appropriate and in which context. That is, the task involved is not only scientific (description, explanation and prediction) but also normative (evaluation and prescription). In undertaking this task, conceptual clarity is an essential first step.

I have noted above that there is a persisting tendency to conflate identities such as citizenship and nationality as well as nationality and ethnicity, ignoring the nature of the context in which they are used. There is a related problem, namely the tendency to concentrate on one identity as a master identity – be it class, race, nationality or ethnicity – and to treat other identities as secondary. Thus, both Marxists and modernists tend to concentrate on class, the peasantry or occupational identities, while primordialists focus on nationality, ethnicity or race. But it is necessary to insist that individuals and collectivities have multiple identities and that no single one can acquire primacy in all contexts.

Individuals and collectivities tend to invoke the appropriate and/or convenient element from their identity-sets, which consist of their total number of identities. It is the invoking of an identity, while ignoring the context, that creates problems and raises the issue of legitimacy. That is to say, the idea of one master identity being displaced by another master identity as society 'modernizes' or 'progresses' is the wrong way of looking at the empirical processes. What often happens is a net increase in the number of identities constituting the identity-sets, even as some of the older ones become obsolete, as societies become more complex and as inter-societal interactions increase. Many of the contentious issues in the world today are due to the invoking of identities, while ignoring the contexts.

We must identify some of the implications of the wrong application of the concepts of ethnicity, nationality and citizenship before we proceed further. Both the First Nations[2] – that is, the original inhabitants of the New World – and the guest workers in Western Europe are invariably referred to as ethnic groups, not only in the mass media but also in social science writings. The New World is new only for the settlers; for the natives it is a very old world, it is their homeland. For example, it is estimated that the Australian tribes have been living there for some twenty thousand years. But the history of guest workers is that of a few decades. To label both these categories as 'ethnic' clearly implies a serious flaw. On the other hand, the earliest European settlers who have been in the New World for barely two hundred years have become 'nationals'. This mode of conceptualization legitimizes conquest and colonialism, as those who have acquired power and dominance have become nationals, while the powerless are relegated to the background as ethnics.

The manner in which a collectivity is labelled is also significant in legitimizing or delegitimizing it. Two communities, the Jews and Muslims, are invariably identified by their religion. Thus, in the context of the Bosnian conflict there are Serbs, Croats and Muslims. In the Philippines there are Tagalog, Ilocanos, Visayans and Muslims. Even after several centuries of being settlers in Europe the Jews have not become Europeans in the eyes of the host society. To argue that these religious communities define themselves as such does not help; there are others – Christians, Hindus, Buddhists – who also use religious labels for self-definitions in their actual or adopted homelands. To describe a collectivity as a religious category, ignoring its territorial base and linguistic identity, is to delegitimize it vis-à-vis its nations and states; it is to deny it nationality and citizenship.

There is also a difference in the adjectives used to describe similar processes when they occur in different parts of the world. The unwarranted assumption seems to be that the West European world of 'nation-states' anchored to linguistic communities is the ideal, and everybody should imitate it. When territories are divided up after intense struggles between linguistic communities in Switzerland, it is approvingly called 'cantonization', that is, democratic decentralization. Although the country has four national languages and groups, the Romansch people (with 1 per cent of the population) and Italians (with about 7 per cent of the population) scarcely figure in intergroup conflicts. These invariably take place between the French and the Germans, who are divided not only on linguistic but also on regional and religious (denominational) bases. In 1979 the Bern Canton was divided into two zones after prolonged conflicts: one French and predominantly Catholic zone, and one German and largely Protestant zone. And yet these conflicts were not described as 'communal'.

But when a similar thing happened after squabbles between religious groups in Lebanon, it gave birth to the pejorative term 'lebanonization'. Although it had a population of only two million in the mid-1970s, Lebanon had fourteen religious sects, four of which were major ones: Maronite Christians (30 per cent), Sunni Muslim (20 per cent), Shiite Muslim (18 per cent), Greek Orthodox (11 per cent). Historically, these religious segments enjoyed a certain level of autonomy even in secular matters under the *millet* system of the Ottoman Empire (see Lijphart 1980). Therefore, an insistence on the continuation of these privileges would have appeared legitimate, in spite of the changed political context.

When even the small nations insist on becoming independent states in Western Europe, it is seen as a measure of their national consciousness and their aspiration for self-determination. But when a similar event occurred in the Balkans or in the Soviet Union it was stigmatized as 'balkanization'. In the case of Africa such a process is denigrated as tribalization, and in South Asia, communalism. If cantonization, decentralization, national self-determination and the like have a positive connotation, balkanization, tribalization and communalism are all negative and regressive. I am not suggesting that there is a world conspiracy to present the happenings in Western Europe as positive and those in Eastern Europe, Asia or Africa as negative. What I want to affirm is that the widespread tendency to perceive the same events as negative or positive is based on a deeper malaise; that is, an inadequate specification of the defining criteria of the concepts such as nation and nationality, or ethnie and ethnicity.

The process of ethnification

Ethnification is a process through which the link between territory and culture is attenuated, and the possibility of a nation sustaining its integrity is put into jeopardy. There are several types of ethnification. First, a nation may continue to be in its ancestral or adopted homeland and yet it may be ethnified by the colonizing or native dominant collectivity. That is, the link between territory and culture should not be viewed merely as a physical phenomenon. There are three main variants of this: (a) Transforming the original inhabitants of a territory into a minoritized and marginalized collectivity. The most obvious example of this is the First Nations in the New World; although they continue to live in their ancestral homeland, they have been dispossessed of it. (b) Labelling a collectivity in such a way as to imply that it has no moral claim over its ancestral or adopted homeland. This is precisely what analysts do when, in labelling some collectivities, they ignore their nationality and invoke their religious identities instead. The Muslims of Bosnia, the Hindus of the Kashmir valley and the Jews in Europe are examples of 'ethnified' collectivities that have been created by wrong labelling. (c) Some nations are subjected to ethnification as a result of a division of their ancestral homeland into two or more state territories, thereby endangering their integrity as nations. This is the case with regard to Kurds, Basques, Nagas, Mizos and similar other nations.

A second type of ethnification is the denial of full-fledged participation in the economy and polity to an immigrant collectivity which had adopted a new land as its homeland. The case of indentured Indian and Chinese labour brought to the plantations and mines in colonial societies exemplifies this. It is not enough that immigrants expect to become nationals in their new homeland from the moment of arrival; their claim and aspiration ought to be respected not only by the state, but also by the original and earlier inhabitants so that their ethnic status is transformed into a national status. But this may not always happen. The Fijians of Indian origin, in spite of adopting Fiji as their homeland, are not yet full-fledged nationals. A similar situation existed in the case of the Jews, and was well captured by Hertz when he wrote (1944: 13–14) about their situation in Germany:

> An immigrant may legally . . . acquire citizenship of the country where he has founded a new home. But (he or his children) must also assimilate its social outlook and its national traditions, and even if (they) succeed in this task it is not yet sure whether they will be accepted by the national community as real nationals . . . Jews have been living in Germany for a very long time . . . and most of them were completely assimilated. Nevertheless . . . the Nazi regime branded them as aliens . . .

A third, is the the tendency on the part of a settler collectivity to identify with its ancestral homeland even after several decades, sometimes even after centuries, of immigration. This is manifested in the New World when collectivities refer to themselves as Anglo-Americans, Asian-Americans, Afro-Americans, and the like. It may be noted that the dominant ethnies' self-definition connotes only a symbolic identification with their ancestral homeland. In contrast, the dominated ethnies experience collective alienation because of continued discrimination and oppression in the land to which they have been brought, and where they have been assigned a subordinate status and a stigmatized identity. While the dominant collectivity may not question the internality of the dominated collectivity, as both are ethnies, members of the latter may not completely identify with their adopted homeland. This self-externalization is the route of their ethnification. The persistent tendency on the part of the erstwhile African slaves in the New World to describe themselves as Afro-Americans, Afro-Brazilians and so on, should be viewed in this light.

Fourth, ethnification also occurs when a state attempts to 'integrate' and homogenize the different nations in its territory into a common people. The mechanisms resorted to are physical uprooting, creation of artificial politico-administrative units, state-sponsored colonization of the territory of the weaker and smaller nations, prevention of the use of their mother tongue and the distortion of a people's national history. Both socialist multi-national states and capitalist nation-states have resorted to this, although their ideological motivations and strategic weapons have differed vastly.

Fifth, if those who migrate to alien lands are denied basic human and citizenship rights even when they become eligible for them, they are ethnified in that they are treated as strangers and outsiders. The cases of guest workers in Western Europe, particularly those from ex-colonial countries, and immigrant workers in the Middle East from Asian countries, all belong to this category.

Finally, even when immigrants are accepted as co-nationals by the host society, the former may not want that identity and might wish to return to their homeland. This ambivalence emanates partly from their assessment of the impossibility of complete acceptance in the host society, and partly from the prospects awaiting them back home. In the 1950s and 1960s Italy was a 'sending' country, but by the 1970s and 1980s she became prosperous and a 'receiving' country. Italian guest workers who had been readily accepted in some of the affluent Catholic countries gradually started returning home. On the other hand, the prospects for guest workers in Europe from Tunisia or Turkey, even if they wish to settle down, are limited, because the chances of their being accepted as full-fledged members in Western Christian countries is slim. In other words, the process of transformation of an ethnie into a nation calls for a change in the attitudes and value orientations of both collectivities, namely, the immigrants and the host society.

It is of great importance to note the following point here. While in all the different varieties of ethnies there is a weakening of the relationship between territory and culture, in most cases it is both physical

UWE, BRISTOL LIBRARY SERVICES

and psychological. But in some cases it is only a psychological phenomenon; these ethnies are aliens in their own homeland. Further, most of them are deprived collectivities, both in symbolic and material terms.

The above analysis should not be taken to mean that there is no possibility of an ethnie transforming itself into a nation. There are several possibilities. An ethnie may assert its identity as a 'nation' at the point of its arrival if it acquires sufficient resources – economic and political. Thus, European settlers became the first 'new nation': the United States of America. However, at that stage the USA only became a polity and not a nation, as most settlers still looked to Europe as their homeland. A second possibility is that an ethnie that was dispersed, even for centuries, may recover its nationhood by returning to its ancestral homeland, as exemplified by the Jewish case. But such a possibility is very slim if a dispersed ethnie is not in a position to stake its moral claim vis-à-vis any territory. This is the case even now with the gypsies. Finally, the liquidation of an earlier basis of identity (say race) and the acquisition of a new basis of identity (say culture) is possible through race mixture. Mestizos and ladinos in Latin America are products of miscegenation, and their identity is now anchored to ethnicity rather than to race. They gradually became part of the cultural mainstream and were completely identified with Latin America.

If the transformation of an ethnie into a nation is a matter of subjective perception on the part of the collectivities involved, acquisition of citizenship is a legal and individual act between particular individuals and two states, one at the point of departure and another at the point of arrival – dual citizenship is extremely uncommon. Clearly, this condition is not applicable in situations of colonization and conquest. In such cases, the state and government at the point of destination may be absent and/or may not be strong. In the case of inter-state migrations, acquiring citizenship at the point of arrival is a matter between the individuals and the two state apparatuses. Even when one has acquired citizenship through due process, that is, by renunciation of the old if required at the point of departure, and the acquisition of the new at the point of arrival, one may encounter prejudices and discriminations from the host community. Legislation is not an appropriate or adequate instrument to cope with such a situation, but education in the broadest sense of the term is. The sources of prejudice and discrimination are both a matter of visibility (physical appearance, dress pattern) as well as a product of interaction, as religious faith, style of speaking the local language or dietary preferences are soon revealed.

In the final analysis, ethnification is a process through which some collectivities are defined and perceived as outsiders. This has nothing to do with facts of history, length of residence, or degree of assimilation. There are at least four contexts in which this happens. The first is when the mainstream cultural community in a multi-national or poly-ethnic state asserts that it constitutes the nation, and that others should assimilate in the interests of the 'nation'. Waspization in the United States, Russification in the former Soviet Union, or Hanization in China are all examples of this. Second, even when a collectivity belongs to the same land, it may be perceived as an outside element because of its actual or attributed association with conquest and colonization. This is why Hindu militants view Muslims and Christians in India as outsiders. A third instance is when descendants of a people may be defined as aliens and driven out, even after they have been in a country for several centuries. This is the case of the Turks in Bulgaria. Fourth, a people may be driven out of its ancestral homeland because their religion is different. Examples of such types of ethnification are Bosnian Muslims or the Hindus of Kashmir Valley. This process is referred to as 'ethnic cleansing' in the press, the electronic media and even in social science writing. However, in terms of the conceptualization proposed in this book it is an incorrect description, because what is actually happening is the de-nationalization of a people vis-à-vis their ancestral homeland.

The reverse of ethnification is nationalization, which happens when an elective affinity is shown to people who are believed to be ancestral kin. Thus, if Germans who have lived outside Germany for several decades or centuries declare that their ancestors were Germans, they are instantly acknowledged as nationals. When they arrive in Germany, they are given the status of returnees or *Aussiedlers* (refugees). Whether or not they speak the German language and pursue the local lifestyle, they are German nationals beùcause nationality is defined by blood. This is also true of Italy and Japan, although to a lesser extent. And both the German and Italian states reinforce this conception of nationality, by conferring citizenship on those who claim to be Germans or Italians by blood. Thus, those who are in reality ethnies are instantly transformed into nationals and citizens.

It would be rewarding to examine at this juncture, albeit briefly, the processes involved in ethnies becoming nationals, and nationals being transformed into ethnies, and/or marginalized as minorities. Most immigrants (not to be confused with those who migrate for employment for brief periods, students, etc.) initially have a sojourner's attitude; they hope to return to their ancestral homeland. Whether or not the sojourner orientation persists depends upon a variety of factors, the most important being the motivating factors behind migration and the existential conditions at the points of departure and destination. As long as an ambivalence about one's homeland, old or new, persists, one is clearly an ethnie. That is, ethnicity is an outsider status, either because one is considered as such by the nationals at one's point of arrival, or because one has not made up one's mind to become a settler. Becoming a citizen often facilitates the process of overcoming the sojourner attitude, but it does not follow automatically that citizens instantly become nationals. To put it differently, to be a national is not a matter of formal definition and legal entitlements, but one of isomorphism between one's self-defini-tion and other's definition of the self. Viewed thus, it would be easy to understand why quite a sizeable proportion of sojourners are citizens but not nationals in the New World. In order to become nationals they are required to eschew their sojourner ambivalence and view the territory into which they have migrated as their new home-land; that is, they should become settlers. This process may be legitim-ately designated as nationalization. Obversely, the act of terrorizing and flushing out people from their ancestral homeland is ethnifica-tion, a process through which nationals are transformed into ethnies, and through which insiders are forced to become outsiders. This variety of ethnification entails de-territorialization of the nationals.

What I am suggesting is that the processes of nationalization and ethnification should be clearly distinguished, as their origins and their crystallizations are vastly different. More importantly, the implica-tions for the collectivities subjected to these processes vary enormous-ly in terms of achieving equality and maintaining identity. The ethnification of First Nations implies robbing them of their national land; they are in their territory but not of it. They are outsiders only symbolically. The nationalization of immigrants entails a process of acquiring identification with the land on which they have settled. In both cases the link between territory and nation is clear.

The crucial importance of territory as a social fact has been eroded substantially in recent times in the context of the much-heralded process of globalization. It needs to be rehabilitated as a crucial social reality if we are to understand the relationship between nationality and ethnicity. It takes a few generations for a re-located collectivity – be they voluntary migrants, refugees, exported labour, colonizers or conquerors, that is, an ethnic group – to feel at home as settlers. For first generation migrants, perhaps, this never happens, and they in-variably look towards the old homeland with nostalgia. Conversely, it is difficult for nationals, be they marginalized First Nations or those who have been flushed out of their territory, to become reconciled to the fact that their legitimate claim over their ancestral homeland has been eroded. They persist with their moral claim, even as their legal claim has been usurped. Nations are not simply physical entities but consist of communities to which their members have a sense of belonging. When a collectivity develops the feeling that it does not belong and/or is treated as an outsider because of its specific identity, it becomes an ethnie. Citizenship in such cases can provide at least partial succour to ethnies, because it is essentially an instrument of equality.

Towards a reformulation

I am now in a position to advance some tentative definitional proposals of nation/nationality, state/citizenship and ethnie/ethnicity. The nation is a territorial entity to which the nationals have an emotional attachment and in which they invest a moral meaning; it is a homeland – ancestral or adopted. Nationality is the collective identity that the people of the nation acquire by identifying with the nation. For a nation to be sustained, the people should be in a position to communicate with one another, that is, they should have a common language. This need not be their ancestral language, it can be an alien tongue (e.g., Bahasa Indonesia). On the other hand, it is not the case that all those who communicate in the same language necessarily make a nation. English, French, Spanish and Chinese, for example, are spoken by people inhabiting different territories in different parts of the world. It is the combination, the fusion of territory and language, that makes the nation; a nation is a community in communication in its homeland.

The state is a legally constituted institution, which provides its residents with protection from internal insecurity and external aggression. Territory is common to the nation and the state. But there is a crucial difference between national territory and state territory; the former is a moral, and the latter a legal entity. A welfare or socialist state also provides for the social well-being of its residents. A democratic state is a community of people who participate directly or indirectly in the governance of the state. If the state and the nation are coterminous, we have a nation-state. But most states today are multinational, poly-ethnic, or a combination of the two.

It is not possible to extend measures of social well-being and the right of political participation to all residents of a state, because they are of two types – citizens and non-citizens. All citizens, by definition, are entitled to welfare and participation. Therefore, a polity ought to be a community of full-fledged citizens, although often this is not the case. That is why we frequently encounter the phrase 'second-class citizens'. Residents who are nationals are invariably citizens. The non-national residents, the ethnies, could also be citizens, although they encounter several problems in acquiring citizenship. Thus, one may speak of full-fledged citizens, nominal citizens and non-citizens.

I have noted above that a common homeland is the critical minimum for the existence of a nation; the dissociation between a people (or a segment of that people) and their homeland de-nationalizes them, and they become an ethnie. Just as territory is common to the state and the nation (with a crucial difference in its meaning), language is common to nation and ethnie. In the case of the former, language and territory are in union, while in the case of the latter the two are dissociated. That is, ethnicity is a product of dissociation between territory and language, a process that takes a variety of forms and could be designated as ethnification.

The ethnie may or may not retain its 'original' language. But what is important is whether an ethnie identifies with the new territory, that is, whether it adopts the territory as a new homeland; if it does, it becomes a nation. It may or may not continue with its old language. The Spaniards, the Portuguese and the English all retained their language and basic institutions in the New World. But an ethnie may also abandon its ancestral language and acquire a new one, as did both the Germans and the Swiss when they migrated to the New World; the retention of the ancestral language is not an absolutely necessary condition for the maintenance of nationhood, although attachment to the homeland is. The Scots abandoned their written language in the seventeenth century and began to write standard English. The English language was not imposed on the Scots, it was gradually adopted by them. The Scottish priests, who were usually the youngest sons of aristocratic families, were the initial link between England and Scotland through the King James Bible (Deutsch 1969: 110). Thus, a common homeland and a common language (ancestral or adopted) are the critical minimum markers of a nation and national identity.

All three concepts that constitute the theme of this book connote identities, but there is a crucial difference between them. While nationality and ethnicity as identities are exclusive and could generate inequalities, citizenship could be essentially inclusive and equality-oriented. Identities will not wither away; if old ones disappear or recede, new ones will be invented and constructed. Human beings are identity-seeking animals, both as individuals and as collectivities. But there is an equally forceful quest that pervades the contemporary world – the pursuit of equality. The pursuit of equality and identity co-exists and competes, and the real issue is how to reconcile the two.

The problem is rendered more vexatious not only because the three identities pull in two different directions in terms of their value orientations, but also because the two units to which they are anchored vary: if nationality and ethnicity are essentially group identities, citizenship is an individual identity. But very often group identities (race, caste, religion, language, region) are invoked as the basis for acquiring citizenship identity. Reconciling these competing perspectives – the individual and group bases of citizenship – poses a durable challenge in the contemporary world.

The plan of the book

The analytical strategy that is being pursued is as follows. The remaining chapters in part I will discuss conceptual matters; part II will deal with the empirical process of ethnification; part III is concerned with the rapprochement between concepts and reality.

Historically, the process of ethnification started with the sixteenth-century geographical explorations and the consequent de-territorialization of race and religion. But the relentless march of ethnification continues even today. I propose to identify four major sources of ethnification and discuss their differing contexts and contents. These four sources are: colonialism and European expansion; proletarian internationalism and the socialist state; the nation-state and project homogenization; and immigration and the chauvinism of prosperity. They form the subject-matter of part II.

As the process of ethnification continues, the two identities of nationality and ethnicity will persist and will be in juxtaposition. However, neither race nor religion can provide authentic content to the process of nation formation and national identity as they did in the past, because they have both undergone de-territoralization. On the other hand, human beings cannot live by identity alone; they need dignity. Dignity at the level of the collectivity is possible through pluralism (which is reconceptualized in part III) and at the individual level through equality, which is realized through the instrument of citizenship, irrespective of national or ethnic backgrounds.

Let me present here the gist of my argument so that readers will know what they should expect. I propose to argue that (a) neither religion nor race is relevant to nation formation, and that the minimum conditions for a nation to emerge and exist are only a common homeland and a critical level of communication; (b) ethnicity is a product of disengagement between territory and culture; (c) identity based on nationality and ethnicity will not be eclipsed by modernization, as contemporary polities are increasingly becoming heterogeneous due to migration; (d) the issues of individual inequality and group identity can be negotiated through citizenship (entitlements irrespective of individual backgrounds); and (e) through pluralism (that is, dignified co-existence of identity groups within polities) the competing demands of equality and identity can be reconciled.

2

Rethinking Citizenship, Nationality and Ethnicity

Concepts in the social sciences are formulated on the basis of specific historical experiences and yet, unless they transcend their empirical contexts, they are of limited utility. One of the tasks of social science is to establish the link between concepts and theories vis-à-vis a variety of empirical situations in order to establish their plausibility and test their validity. This task is attended to in this chapter with special reference to three concepts, namely citizenship, nationality and ethnicity. As a prologue to this exercise I suggest that these concepts be used in precise ways so as to avoid ambiguities and overlaps. Before I begin to establish the required clarity, we must understand what the terms state, nation and ethnie mean, as the concepts of citizenship, nationality and ethnicity are inextricably bound to them and in fact emanate from them.[3]

Defining the state

In contemporary Western social science a state is defined as an entity that is endowed with political sovereignty over a clearly defined territorial area; that has a monopoly on the use of legitimate force; and that consists of citizens whose terminal loyalty is to the state. A series of empirical situations is assumed to be in existence for such a definition to be operative. For example, if a 'people' does not have its own territory, in which it can lead a settled life, it is believed to be 'stateless'. Yet, what 'leading a settled life' implies is not clear, as it is well known that settled agriculture, the starting point of a settled life, is a relatively recent phenomenon in the long span of human history.

A state can thus be conceived as a collectivity of citizens with certain civil, political and social entitlements. The civil element endows citizens with the rights of individual freedom; the political element provides them with the right to participate in the political process; the social element is essentially a series of entitlements to economic and social welfare. The developments of these separate elements took place in different centuries: the concept of equality before the law belonging to the eighteenth, equal political rights to the nineteenth and equal social rights to the twentieth (Marshall 1965). And yet, even the notion of political citizenship, that is, membership in a state with full political rights, the most universal expression of which is the franchise, was accomplished in Europe itself only by the mid-twentieth century. In fact, it was only in 1919, after World War I, that citizenship was accepted in principle in Europe; it became a sacred right all over the Continent only as recently as the 1940s. This 'contemporization' of human social reality by a 'retreat into the present', to recall the evocative phrase of Elias (1989: 223–48), has created an abysmal wedge between the past and the present.

The notion of monopoly on the use of legitimate force does not take into account the fact that a wide variety of structures – kingdoms, empires, city-states, republics and federations – are covered by the notion of state. Even the Greek city-state, widely acknowledged for its 'direct democracy', did not permit the participation of slaves and plebeians in the decision-making process. Empires and kingdoms had subjects, but not citizens. The history of ex-colonial societies is replete with instances of protest against the illegitimacy of the colonial state. The expression 'state terrorism' is frequently used today to describe the activities of authoritarian and, by the disgruntled, even of democratic states. That is to say, only in the case of democratic states – and even there as an ideal – is the attribute of legitimate force valid. The problematique of the Weberian (see Gerth and Mills 1948) definition lies in completely ignoring the question 'who is exercising force?' and, instead, in focusing exclusively on 'what is the state?'.

The terminal loyalty of a citizen to the state implies coterminality between state and nation, that is, they share common objectives; makes a mockery of the very Western notion of the autonomy and division of labour between church and state; and, in consequence, presupposes a hierarchy of loyalty, with primacy to the state. But citizens of a multi-religious and multi-lingual polity may have several basic allegiances, each having different contexts, which need not necessarily be mutually contradictory. They might, for example, feel loyalty in the religious context to an ecclesiastical authority, which may have jurisdiction over a community distributed across several states. But this need not necessarily be in conflict with one's terminal loyalty to the state as a citizen. Therefore, it is tenable to conceptualize the co-existence of a series of terminal loyalties, each of which has a different context or content.

It is useful to recall here the empirical contexts that seem to have influenced the definition of a state in the West. Basing himself on the West European experience – mostly, indeed, on Britain – Gellner (1983) has argued that language is the fulcrum on which nations (he uses states and nations as interchangeable entities) are built. This is so because, according to him, unless there exists a common medium of communication, industrial societies cannot be sustained. Such an argument does not stand up in the light of empirical facts, even from Europe itself, where there were seventy-three nations, but only twenty-four states, according to Smith (1971) when he was writing his book. The lack of coterminality between states and nations has been noted since by several writers (e.g., Eriksen 1991: 263–78; Connor 1994). The most systematic analysis of this theme was undertaken by Nielsson (1985: 27–56), who proposed a global taxonomy of states and 'nation groups', and listed twenty-eight states in Europe. But with the break-up of several multi-national socialist states in Eastern Europe in 1989 the number increased still further, although of course the number of nations remained constant.

Apart from this lack of fit between empirical reality and its conceptualization, there are several other flaws in Gellner's argument. First, a common medium of communication is necessary not only for an industrial society, but for any society; the very existence of a society implies this, even though the nature and intensity of communication may vary. Second, it is possible and true that several nations do and can co-exist in the territorial area of one state (e.g., Great Britain, India). But Gellner's argument denies the very possibility of multi-lingual states. Third, if we pursue the argument to its logical end it would mean that multi-national states would and should break up into mono-national states, and/or the dominant language, which invariably means the language of the dominant nation in the state, will have to be imposed on or accepted by other nations within the state. In the case of the Scots, the Welsh and the Irish, the language of the dominant nation within the UK, namely English, was accepted (and not imposed) as the official language. However, their own languages were relegated to the background at the time of unification. But there is evidence to the contrary. While the imposition of the Russian language on other nations in the erstwhile Soviet Union has substantially contributed to the break-up of the latter, the Indian state survives precisely because of its policy of multi-lingualism. The point is that Gellner's argument and conceptualization are based on extremely limited empirical experiences, and are not therefore valid for most of the multi-national states, of which there are quite a few cases.

There is another feature of the state, namely, a common legal system, that is believed to be a universal attribute. Once again, this description fits only culturally homogeneous and uni-religious polities. In the case of multi-religious and culturally plural societies, three different types of civil legal systems, operating at different levels and contexts, co-exist. The state legal system (SLS) applies uniformly to all citizens. But if the population of a state is drawn from different religious faiths, and if the state has not yet evolved and implemented a uniform civil code, several religious legal systems (RLS) would co-exist. While SLS is applied to fellow citizens, RLS is subscribed to by fellow religionists distributed over several states. Third, folk legal systems (FLS) exist and are often recognized, if not always administered, by the state. Thus, both in the reservations of Native Americans and in certain tribal areas in India, FLS is in existence. All three legal systems, thus, often co-exist; they are applicable to different sets of persons within a state in different permutations and combinations. The Scottish nation has its own legal system, although it exists as a unit within the British state. To put it succinctly, cultural diversity begets and sustains legal pluralism. Ignoring this fact and this possibility, it is often argued that a uniform state legal system universally applicable to all citizens is a distinguishing mark of the modern state. Such a presumption smacks of empirical innocence and conceptual claustrophobia.

There is no consensus about the nature and purpose of a state among the writers of the West. The German historian Heinrich Von Treitschke, in his lectures delivered in 1897, maintained: 'Man fulfills his moral vocation in and through the state, states realise their essence only when they come to grips with each other, war, in fact, is not barbarism but a holy ordeal which rightly determines the destiny of peoples' (cited in Aron 1966: 586). In contrast, Reinhold Niebuhr, the American theologian, views states as the very embodiment of evil. To him, the collective beings, or states, are worse than individual beings. Individuals at least occasionally practise Christian virtues, while states never do. The immorality of states is in fact greater in that they impart a legitimate feeling to the citizens, who dedicate themselves to and occasionally even sacrifice themselves for the state (see Aron 592–3). If for Treitschke man finds his moral fulfilment through the state, for Niebuhr even the individual's sacrifice for the state is immoral. In spite of these two extreme forms of divinizing and demoni-zing the state, the notion of the democratic state is that of an impartial final arbiter between citizens precisely because the source of its legit-imacy is derived from them. Therefore the democratic state ought to be viewed as a collective of citizens who enjoy judicial equality in the territory of the state, irrespective of their having identities based on race, religion, language, class or gender.

The real issue is whether the state can be an impartial arbiter when its population is heterogeneous, particularly because the state has to operate in its day-to-day functioning through the bureaucratic apparatus. The widely shared assumption not always made explicit seems to be that human frailty is such that only under conditions of cultural homogeneity can the state function impartially. After having undertaken an analysis of 114 states, Robert Dahl concluded that those with a low level of cultural pluralism are more stable compared with those with considerable or extreme levels of pluralism. Systems with marked subcultural pluralist characteristics may sometimes confront 'a set of unhappy and even tragic choices . . . the price of polyarchy may be the break up of the country. And the price of territorial unity may be a hegemonic regime' (1971: 120–1). There are two basic difficulties with such a position. First, a culturally homo-geneous democratic state can be rendered unstable by its deprived sections. Women, the youth or the proletariat, for instance, can or may successfully challenge the authority of the state, although they cannot actually break up the state. Second, even when the popu-lation of a state is substantially heterogeneous in terms of race or culture its stability may not be affected if the resources or strik-ing power of these segments is low. Therefore the important point is to specify both the nature of the segments and the intensity of the threat.

The state as an institution has to face a variety of threats, but these are not of the same intensity; in other words, a state faces a hierarchy of threats (Oommen 1990(b)). The integrity of the state is affected only when a segment of its population wants to disengage itself from the rest (secession) or wants to obtain a certain level of freedom in decision-making (autonomy). These threats are qualitatively differ-ent. Territorially dispersed groups (ethnies) cannot aspire to either situation. Nations – that is, groups with a moral claim on their territ-ory – may aspire and often demand secession or autonomy. So stab-ility is a real problem only for multi-national states and not for poly-ethnic ones. Thus, it is not a problem for a polyarchy like the United States of America, but it was a problem for the multi-national but non-polyarchic Soviet Union.

In the New World, populations of different cultural or racial backgrounds are usually dispersed within the territory of a state, and its
stability is therefore relatively unthreatened. When members of such
groups are concentrated they do pose a threat, as the antibellum South
did in the USA, Quebec does in Canada or the Spanish-speaking
community in California may do in future. The situation in multi-
national states of the Old World is quite different. A demand for secession is not a frequent occurrence in most of them. The squabbles between
the Walloons and the Flemish are well known, but they do not want
separate states, only a certain level of autonomy within the state of
Belgium. Although the People's Republic of China, the state with the
largest population in the world, has 56 'national minorities', accounting for 90 million persons inhabiting 60 per cent of its territory, only
Tibet has demanded secession or autonomy. The cultural pluralism of
India is staggering, but secessionist movements are few and far between. Ukraine, a nation of 70 million, was willing to be a part of the
Soviet Union on condition that its language was protected and the
cultural differences from the Great Russians was accepted.

The point is that the idea of citizenship as an instrument of equality
poses far fewer problems in homogeneous states in which it is fused
with nationality. We need the concept of citizenship precisely because
it is different from nationality and ethnicity. Citizenship provides the
non-national ethnic and minority populations in a multi-national
state with a sense of belonging and security. It is a partial compensation for their remaining within the state in spite of their different
identity from the mainstream, dominant nation or nationalities. Perhaps it is no accident that the notion of citizenship as a civic collectivity was originally conceived, internalized and institutionalized in
Great Britain, a multi-national state.

Understanding the nation

If the relatively simple notion of 'state' has defied a clear definition
applicable to the various empirical situations, it is perhaps hardly
surprising that the concept of 'nation', which is rather more complex,
presents even greater problems.

In its original classical Latin sense the word *nasci* meant a tribal-
ethnic group, a people born in the same place and territory; the political
dimension was not a necessary element. The emergence of the nation
as a community of citizens – that is, a political entity – was the
creation of the French Revolution. And having followed the maxim
one nation, one state, a nation becomes at once a cultural entity as well
as a political entity in Europe. It is small wonder, then, that a nation,

in fact a sub-nation, is defined as 'a people, a folk, held together by some or all of such more or less immutable characteristics as common descent, territory, history, language, religion, way of life, or other attributes that members of a group have from birth onwards' (Petersen 1975: 181), as well as 'a community of sentiment which would adequately manifest itself in a state of its own; hence a nation is a community which normally tends to produce a state of its own' (Weber in Gerth and Mills 1948: 176). Thus it came to be believed that it is not only natural for a nation to have a state, but a necessary condition if its cultural identity is to be maintained and protected.

Given the trajectory of Western history – the advocacy of intense and terminal loyalty to one's nation-state; the maxim one nation, one state; the crusades; the world wars; Nazi horrors and colonialism – nationalism is perceived both as a positive and a negative force. These views are clearly articulated by J. S. Mill and Lord Acton. Mill (cited in Anthony Smith 1971: 9) unambiguously endorsed the doctrine of national self-determination:

> It is, in general, a necessary condition of free institutions that the boundaries of government should coincide in the main with those of nationality – where the sentiment of nationality exists in any force, there is a prima facie case for uniting all the members of the nationality under the same government, and a government to themselves apart. This is merely saying that the question of government ought to be decided by the governed.

In contrast, in his essay on nationality Lord Acton (Smith p. 9) wrote: 'Nationality does not aim at either liberty or prosperity, both of which it sacrifices to the imperative necessity of making the nation the mould and measure of the state. Its course will be marked with material as well as moral ruin.'

In the voluminous writings on nation and nationalism both the positive and negative connotations of the terms are found to surface frequently. But it would be correct to say that the meanings change depending upon the historicity of context. Thus, nationalism has been viewed as a positive force in the ex- colonial countries in the context of anti-imperialist struggles. But should any of the constituent units of the multi-national colony assert that it is a separate nation and mobilize its national sentiment after the attainment of freedom, the remaining constituents, particularly the dominant nation, would invariably dispute the claim and instantly condemn the mobilization as being 'anti-national'.

It is untenable to follow the Latin sense of the term nation, which refers to a tribal-ethnic group, in the contemporary world. Before the

French Revolution, polities were either small (tribes, peasant villages, caste councils, city-states) or large (empires, federations, universal churches). Today the tendency is to establish viable polities. In fact, there are not more than 220 or 230 states in the contemporary world. But in Africa alone there are about 6,000 tribes, and in South Asia there are more than 600. Not only are a large number of these tribes too small in size to constitute viable states, they may not always have any cultural distinctiveness either. Further, if the political dimension is taken into account, many of them are either 'stateless' societies and/or are incorporated into larger polities. Therefore, Coleman's (1958: 423–4) definition, 'the tribe is the largest social group defined primarily in terms of kinship, and is normally an aggregate of clans, intermediate to nationality', is not helpful in understanding the specificity of nation and nationality because some tribes, if they have an accredited territory and a language, could be nations. That is, even if all tribes are not nations, the possibility of some tribes being considered as nations should not be ruled out. On the other hand, several tribes may conjointly constitute a nation if they have a common homeland and communication medium.

This brings us to the two definitions by Petersen and Weber. There are two problems with Petersen's definition. First, the difference between a nation and a sub-nation is left unspecified. But since the definition of a sub-nation does not mention the state as an attribute, it may be assumed that a sub-nation becomes a nation when it acquires its own state. In other words, Petersen too conflates state and nation. The second problem is the inclusion of religion and common descent in the list of characteristics compiled by Petersen to define nation. In defining an entity one should ask and answer two questions: What are the irreducible minimum conditions for that entity to exist? Will the removal of one of the attributes endanger the existence of that entity or not?

As I have suggested in chapter 1, there are only two basic prerequisites for a nation to exist: common territory and communication. Religion and common descent are attributes shared by ethnic groups also, and are not prerequisites for a nation to emerge or exist; the fact that these attributes are often pressed into service to mobilize people into collective actions in the context of nation formation should not mislead us into accepting them as attributes of nation. Religion is an irrelevant variable to define a nation because secular ideologies have also been used for the same purpose; there are several multi-religious nations; one can imagine a nation of agnostics or atheists; and there is no necessary linkage between religion and territory. The unfortunate but persisting tendency to define religious collectivities as nations has not only perpetuated conceptual confusion, but has resulted in human misery. The fact that in Europe most nations are uni-religious, nay, uni-denominational, seems to have promoted the tendency to accept religion as an attribute of nation. But this limited empirical experience is a slippery basis for constructing a viable definition. The attribute of common descent to define nation ignores the empirical reality of the entire New World in which a collection of people of differing descents live together. To insist on common descent quite simply rules out the possibility of these people becoming nationals even after their adoption of the new land as their homeland.

The main difficulty in the Weberian definition is an unwarranted assumption, namely that 'a nation is a community which normally tends to produce a state of its own'. Perhaps the reverse would be true if one nation were not subjected to discrimination, exploitation and oppression by another. That is, a nation tends to produce its state when it faces abnormal situations. Thus, none of the major nations (and there are quite a few) that constitute the Indian state, save the Tamils, has articulated any desire to produce a state of its own. The tendency to secede is confined to smaller nations located on inter-state borders, some of which face the threat of extinction because of the steps taken by the central state authority in the name of national security or 'integration'. This, however, is not to suggest that relatively bigger nations in a multi-national state would simply acquiesce. On the contrary, not only do they have the clout to resist the domination, but they usually demand, and are successful in securing, a certain level of political autonomy within a federal system.

After a critical and clinical analysis of a wide variety of authorities, Anthony Smith lists seven characteristics of a nation (1971: 318). These are size, economic integration, territorial mobility, a distinctive culture, external relationships, equal membership rights and group loyalty. A nation, according to Smith, '*is a large vertically integrated and territorially mobile group featuring common citizenship rights and collective sentiments together with one (or more) common characteristics, which differentiate its members from those of similar groups with whom they stand in relations of alliance or conflict*' (1971: 175; italics in original). It is evident that Smith is conflating state and nation as most writers do (a theme we will discuss in chapter 3), although of course he frequently refers to the need to keep the distinction between them. For example, common citizenship rights are untenable for the population of a nation if it does not have its own state. The Kurds, who are currently distributed into five different states, do not have any common citizenship rights. Indeed, they have been articulating their national sentiment for at least a century. Similarly, territorial mobility as a defining criterion becomes relevant only if a nation has its own state. As nationals, the Basques did not have had any territorial mobility within their homeland before the emergence of the European Union. If they have it now, it is as citizens of the Union and not as citizens of two states – France and Spain.

The size factor is a slippery one in that it is not possible to prescribe a minimum or maximum number for a nation; some are big, most are small. The Chinese nation, that is, the Chinese-speaking community living in their homeland, is the biggest in the world, numbering several hundred millions. The Russian and German nations are the biggest in Europe. On the other hand, scores of nations have populations of less than a million. The size factor becomes important when one views a nation as a state in which economies of scale, matters of administrative efficiency, power and prestige in the context of inter-state relations are relevant. Finally, nations do not stand in relation to each other in terms of alliance or conflict, while states do.

Given the empirical reality and ideological preference in the West, not only are the terms state and nation interchangeably used, but they are believed to be coterminous in Western social science theory. Bauman's apt observations ought to be recalled here in full:

> Sociology, as it came of age in the bosom of Western civilisation and as we know it today, is endemically national- biased. It does not recognise a totality broader than a politically organised nation: the term 'society', as used by well-nigh all sociologists regardless of their school loyalties is, for all practical purposes, a name for an entity identical in size and composition with the nationstate (1973: 42–3).
>
> Further . . . with hardly any exception, all the concepts and analytical tools currently employed by social scientists are geared to a view of the human world in which the most voluminous totality is a 'society', a notion equivalent for all practical purposes, to the concept of the 'nation-state'. (1973: 78)

This predicament and vision is largely shared by Marxist theory also. But two assumptions – the dispensability of state and the centrality of class – and an empirical fact – multi-national socialist states – have prompted the Marxists to make amends and accommodations. They simply assumed that the state, as an instrument in the hands of the dominant class, would wither away. Similarly, since the proletariat does not have a fatherland and since the notion of nationalism is a product of false consciousness, the possibility of each nation aspiring to constitute its own state was not taken seriously. But the struggle of dominated nations against imperialism was recognized and given respectability, and the possibility of 'nationalities' co-existing in the same state during the transitional period was conceded.

Nationalities are nations without states; nations that have failed to establish their own states (Worsely 1984: 247–8). In this mode of conceptualization 'nationality' is a consolation prize for a nation that has not realized its aspiration of becoming a state. In theory, a nation would aspire to achieve its goal – a vision kept under suspension – as and when it acquired the requisite striking power. But as I have noted above, this is not an empirical fact; there are numerous nations that have not staked any claim to statehood, although they have often opted for a separate administrative arrangement within a federal set-up. The notion of nationality unfolds an ambivalence in conceptualization because it shares the assumption that nations without states are untenable.

To conclude, if nations in Europe are essentially cultural entities relentlessly pursuing the establishment of their own states and intensely devoted to maintaining them if they already have them, in the colonized parts of the world, as well as in the ex-colonial countries, nations are viewed as political units. Further, most of the new nations are also culturally plural. Thus, African nations have emerged through the incorporation of many tribes which spoke different languages or dialects and followed different religious faiths. While race is the most salient common feature, even this criterion is not universal, as exemplified in the case of South Africa, which is a multi-racial state. In Asia, almost all states are multi-religious and multi-lingual. In the case of Latin America, the populations of particular states are multi-racial, multi-lingual, multi-religious, or all of these. In North America and Australia national populations are constituted predominantly by migrants from Europe speaking different languages and who belonged to different religious denominations. The meaning of the term 'nation' and the background of the national population will understandably vary across continents. The point to be noted is that it is the historicity of context which invests meanings on concepts. The 'people' of the United States of America did not have a pre-existent 'nation' (in the European sense) to latch on to their nationalism, and yet American nationalism led to the formation of a state. On the other hand, nations may not always clamour for their sovereign states, as is borne out by the experience of India.

The nationalist movements of the ex-colonial countries were explicitly political and oriented to state-building. These movements had been efforts to transform colonies into states and subjects into citizens. But at the height of anti-imperialist activity it was often forgotten that colonies were multi-national entities. The primary objective of the anti-imperialist struggle was to liberate the colonies from the foreign political yoke and establish self-governments. Understandably, though unfortunately, nations and states came to be treated as synonymous entities, creating as a consequence enormous conceptual confusion.

It is true that in Europe the ideal was the nation-state. But even in Europe before 1800 the demand for political autonomy in the name of cultural distinctiveness was confined to two specific contexts. These were, first, when empires imposed or tried to impose official religions on dissenting minorities and, second, when empires attempted to increase central control through imperial administration (Tilly 1994: 131–46). While in the last two centuries the demands for political autonomy based on cultural specificity have increased, 'only a tiny proportion of the world's distinctive religious, linguistic, and cultural groupings have formed their own states, while precious few of the world's existing states have approximated the homogeneity and commitment conjured up by the label "nationstate" ' (1994: 137). This is in spite of the stupendous efforts at homogenization of state populations (see below, chapter 7). If this really is the case, the nation-state as an aspiration and as an ideal ought to be abandoned. Perhaps the emergence of the European Union is indicative of this trend and way of thinking.

But even Tilly, an astute sociologist of nationalism who anchors his research firmly in history, does not tell the full story. In the course of his analysis of the European situation over five centuries, he notes that there were several political 'turbulences' in the British states – Scotland and Wales – before they were integrated (Tilly 1993). But Wales and Scotland were joined to England; they were not annexed. And Catalonia, the second most industrialized nation of Europe after England in the eighteenth century, did not seek a separate state. The Catalonian elite did not perceive any contradiction between maintaining a certain level of economic, political and cultural autonomy for the nation, even while forming part of the Spanish state (Pi-Sunyer 1985: 254–76). Therefore, while it covers most cases, Tilly's categorization of nationalism into two – state-led and state-seeking – leaves out some others.

In the case of state-led nationalism, rulers demanded that citizens should subordinate all other interests to those of the state, which led to the subsequent emergence of 'nations'. In state-seeking nationalism, leaders sought to create new states which could pursue the interests of distinct populations with a specific cultural identity; nationalism, in other words, created states. But there were nations and national leaderships in Europe that renounced a separate state and preferred a union within a larger polity. Wales, Scotland and Catalonia all seem to fit this description. In Indonesia all the constituent nations, save East Timor, have accepted the union. In the case of the Philippines, except for Mindanao, the other three nations all seem to have integrated well. The point is, nations do not always seek their states; some nations may renounce states. Therefore state-renouncing nationalism is an empirical fact and a conceptual possibility.

As for state-led nationalism, most states have not achieved their avowed objective of homogenization of their populations, as Tilly himself has noted. At any rate, the idea of bartering one's cultural identity for purposes of material equality does not seem to appeal to all nations. At least some do not endorse the trade-off; they want to have both identity and equality. But they seem to think that for the preservation of identity one need not have an exclusive sovereign state since it can as well be maintained within a common polity with a certain level of national autonomy. For example, 'the supreme object of ... Welsh national leaders was essentially equality within the United Kingdom and an expanding empire, not severance from it' (Morgan 1971: 165). But this can exist only in a democratic, plural set-up.

Dissecting ethnicity

In contemporary social science an ethnic group is characterized in terms of a multiplicity of attributes – religion, sect, caste, region, language, nationality, descent, race, colour and culture. These attributes, singly or in different combinations, are used to define ethnic groups and ethnicity, but one rarely comes across any specification of the crucial variable. This can only perpetuate analytical confusion.

Before I take up this discussion, it may be noted that hardly anybody, with the exception of Anthony Smith, refers to the notion of 'ethnie'. Smith lists six characteristics of an ethnie. These are: a collective name, a common myth of descent, a shared history, a distinctive shared culture, an association with a specific territory, and a sense of solidarity (1986: 24). There are two main difficulties with this characterization. First, the sixth characteristic is a product of the first five features, which conjointly produce a sense of solidarity. To invoke the product as a defining feature does not accord well with the rest of the features. The second difficulty is that this characterization fits the concept of nation equally well, although Smith may respond by saying that an ethnie becomes a nation only when it acquires its own state. Such a position creates several problems, which I will discuss in chapter 3. It will suffice for the present to note that nation and ethnie share all the features listed by Smith, except territory. That is, if and when an ethnie identifies itself with a territory, it becomes a nation. An ethnie is a cultural collectivity that is outside its ancestral territory – actual (e.g., European Jews) or imagined (e.g., gypsies). The settlers of the New World who nurse a sojourner attitude also constitute an ethnie. When they adopt the territory into which they have immigrated as their homeland they become a nation. However, to become nationals in the territory into which a group migrates is not simply a matter of that group's choice, but also its acceptance by the earlier inhabitants. This was clearly evident in the case of German Jews, as I have noted in chapter 1.

It is possible to identify at least five different senses in which an ethnic group and ethnicity are conceptualized (see Roosens 1989). First, an ethnic group is conceptualized as a relatively small one, sharing a common culture with and tracing its descent to a common ancestor, the tribe being the favourite example cited. But in today's world, societies and groups are not insulated by descent and kinship. They are constantly exposed to alien influences through migration and colonization, as well as through the mass media. This changing context has invested ethnicity and ethnic groups with new meanings, and most writers do not use these concepts in their original sense. As Gordon has noted, 'Ethnicity, as representing a special ancestral identification with some portion of mankind . . . disappeared entirely' (1964: 24), although some argue that ethnicity should be defined in terms of common descent, that is, race (Francis 1976). Second, an ethnic group is viewed as a self-defined group based on subjective factors, which are chosen by the members from their past history or present existing conditions. The cultural traits so selected provide for the creation and maintenance of a socio-cultural boundary vis-à-vis other ethnic groups with whom they interact (Barth 1969). Third, ethnic groups are viewed as interest groups competing for benefits from the welfare state (Glazer and Moynihan 1963). Racial, religious and linguistic groups are included in this definition, which views ethnicity as a resource used by deprived immigrant groups. Fourth, ethnicity is considered as an identity-seeking instrument by the peoples of multi-racial and multi-cultural societies. In this latter case ethnicity is not always instrumentally oriented (Horowitz 1985). Fifth, ethnicity is conceptualized as a device through which people seek a profound psychological unity, often based on common origin, that is, sharing common blood, actual or fictitious (see Devos and Ross 1975).

A few interesting points about these conceptualizations may be noted. One is the nature of the societies where the studies were done and the disciplinary orientations of the authors, which have clearly influenced their conceptualizations. The first definition is based on the classic field work situation of social and cultural anthropology, that is, the isolated tribal societies. Although the authors of the second and the fifth definitions are also anthropologists, their places of study are vastly different. Barth did his work in Afghanistan where different tribes lived in the same geographical area, which perhaps prompted the salience of boundary maintenance in his definition of ethnicity. In contrast, the psychological orientation is brought forth by those authors who did their work in complex multi-cultural situations in which the minority ethnic groups were experiencing a deep psychological insecurity. The third definition is formulated by sociologists in the context of a multi-ethnic United States of America. They document the way in which successive immigrant groups use their ethnic identity as a resource to improve their material conditions through democratic bargaining. Horowitz, instead, having undertaken a comparative study across Asia, Africa and the Caribbeans, finds ethnicity to be a feature even of those groups that are native to the soil – that is, nationals.

Further, definitions one and five recognize the phenotypical similarity of the ethnic group (common descent, blood), while definitions one, two, four and five focus on different dimensions of identity. The focus of definition three is on material pay-offs. If definition three is geared to emphasize the instrumental dimension, definition four concentrates on the symbolic aspect. It is clear that each author is impressed by the specificity of his particular field-work location and emphasizes it, reminding us of the famous Indian fable of five blind men trying to understand the shape of an elephant. This is so much the case that Roosens (1989: 19) has written:

> The term 'ethnic identity' can, for example, refer to origin, uniqueness, passing on of life, 'blood', solidarity, unity, security, personal integrity, independence, recognition, equality, cultural uniqueness, respect, equal economic rights, territorial integrity and so on, and these in all possible combinations, degrees of emotional content, and forms of social organization . . . It is impossible for ethnic identity to mean anything without the existence of ethnic groups or categories, for it is a relational construct.

It is necessary at this juncture to advert briefly to the controversy between the primordialists and constructionists that is frequently alluded to in current social science writings. The intellectual ancestry of primordialists can be traced to Weber. Those who pursue this perspective treat ethnicity as a latent phenomenon present everywhere, which is invoked by deprived communities at an opportune moment when they experience an erosion of existing privileges, or when they attempt to overcome long-standing denials of privileges. This contextual invocation of ethnicity does not satisfy the constructionists, who insist that ethnicity and its cultural content is invariably the result of particular historical conjunctures (see, for example, Anderson 1983; Hobsbawm and Ranger 1983). It is suggested that identities such as Yoruba, Zulu and so on (in the African context) are nineteenth-century European creations (see Comaroff 1991: 666–7). It is also the case that identities such as European and Hindu are creations, the first by the Greeks and the second by the Muslims. The important point here is not who has 'created' these identities and when, but why these labels stuck, while others (e.g., barbarians, primitives) did not. I would suggest that it is because they struck a familiar chord, fulfilled an emotional need and provided a shorthand device to communicate certain aspects shared alike by all the people under reference, be it a common homeland, religion, language or civilization. Thus, some of the constructed identities become acceptable precisely because they contain a primordial element, which is construed as 'sacred' by the collectivity concerned. The posited dichotomy between the primordialists and the constructionists is therefore a false one.

We need concepts to make sense of the complex and often confusing empirical reality. But the ways in which ethnicity is defined has led to contrary results. What we need is a reformulation, and this is to be done vis-à-vis the other two concepts – nationality and citizenship. Ethnicity, nationality and citizenship are all identities, but the bases of them differ. Citizenship is an instrument of equality in democratic states, but ethnicity and nationality are often invoked by states to confer or deny equality. This is the rationale behind viewing these concepts in a relational vein.

The terms ethnic and ethnicity are most favoured and popular in the USA, as they should be, because they aptly capture and convey the social situation there; the USA is a conglomeration of varieties of people 'uprooted' or 'dislodged' from different nations. As Yancey et al. (1976: 401) correctly observe: 'Ethnicity may have relatively little to do with Europe, Asia or Africa, but more to do with the requirements of survival and the structure of opportunity in this country', that is, the United States of America. But the equivalent concepts that are suited to describe the overall situation in Europe are nation (and nationality), given the strong attachment people have to their homelands. This is equally true of Asia, although of course these terms are scarcely used. And this reluctance should be understood in terms of the prevailing situation in Asian countries. Most Asian states incorporate several nations, and the process of state formation is not yet complete, nor the states stable, largely because of their multi-national composition. Therefore, to assert one's identity in national terms is to spell danger to the state. National identity is often de-legitimized to uphold the integrity of the state (Oommen 1990a: 163–82). Further, assertions of identity based on religion, language, region, tribe, and so on are viewed as 'communal,' 'parochial' and even 'anti-national'.

I have hinted above that the term nation-state is coined out of the limited West European experience. Terms such as 'ethno-nationalism' have also been in circulation for quite some time (see, for example, Richmond 1987: 3–18; Connor 1994) to refer to nationalisms based on primordial loyalties. Similarly, Worsely writes:

> Nationalism is also a form of ethnicity but it is a specific form. It is the institutionalisation of one particular ethnic identity by attaching it to the state. Ethnic groups do not necessarily act together except when they have special interest to secure. When those interests are to obtain a state of its own (or part of a State) the group becomes a nationality. (1984: 247)

This conceptualization, too, suffers from several difficulties. First, it attributes a specificity to ethnic groups which in fact is common to all groups. No group action, whatever may be the basis of constituting it, takes place unless it has a special interest to pursue. Second, it shares with other conceptualizations the false assumption that the linkage between nation and state is axiomatic. Third, while it recognizes instrumental ethnicity, it denies symbolic ethnicity. It seems to me that it is the combination of instrumental ethnicity emanating out of material deprivation, and symbolic ethnicity based on the anxiety to preserve one's cultural identity, that gives birth to the motive force for state formation. Deprivations emanating out of inequality or denial of identity in isolation will not lead to the crystallization of the demand for a separate state. However, such a demand is plausible only if the ethnic group can constitute itself into a nation, the prerequisites of which are common territory and language.

In order to get rid of the prevailing confusion we need to conceptualize ethnicity as interactional, as against an attributional notion. We must view ethnicity as a product of conquest, colonization and immigration and the consequent disengagement between culture and territory. It is the transformation of the 'outs' into the 'ins' that leads to the process of ethnies becoming nations.

Concepts and reality

If people with common descent, history and language lived in their ancestral territory, issues of ethnicity would not have arisen. But in the last five hundred years, largely because of colonialism and the migrations that accompanied and followed it, the situation has changed drastically. It is possible to identify three variants of colonization here. First, colonial masters withdrew from the foreign territory that they had been occupying for nearly two centuries in response to 'nationalist' movements, as in the case of Asia and most of Africa. Second, both the migrants and the natives continued to co-exist in varying proportions, as in the case of Latin America and, to a certain extent, South Africa. Third, the natives were largely exterminated and/or completely marginalized, as in the case of North America and Australia. I will discuss the specificities of these situations in chapter 5, but suffice it to state here that the state–nation–ethnie linkages manifested themselves in different ways according to the circumstances.

In those situations where the number of natives was small (due to sparsely populated territory) and/or weak (because of economic and technological backwardness), the colonial migrants established their legal claim over the territory first, through war and violence, and subsequently staked their moral claim over it as their homeland. For example, to firm up their claim on the territory, immigrants to America began by exterminating and marginalizing the First Nations, and then fought the American War of Independence to cut the umbilical cord between the British Empire and the American colony. Nevertheless, a certain amount of ambivalence continued to exist, as the first few generations of European immigrants to America continued to search for their home in Europe. The phenomenon of hyphenated Americans is a manifestation of this ambivalence. On the other hand, the trajectory of experience and status passage of later immigrants to the United States is quite different, encompassing issues such as those related to immigrant workers or students (an occupational status); the acquisition of citizenship (membership in a polity); the fight for rights and privileges as an ethnic group (interest articulation); and the adoption or acceptance of the USA as the homeland (becoming nationals). While the first two phases call for only individual actions, the latter two entail collective actions and identities. It is evident that the linkages between citizenship, nationality and ethnicity differ in the case of the initial colonizing migrants and that of the later employment-seeking migrants.

In the case of Asia and Africa, the colonial state was replaced by the national state. The populations of the two continents had for centuries consisted of the native inhabitants of the territory of the colonial state, whether it was maintained as one entity or broken into pieces, whether directly administered or indirectly controlled. What emerged out of the anti-colonial struggles in Asia and Africa were states and not nations. And yet, the new entities were instantly labelled, and believed to be, 'nations' or, at best, nations-in-the-making. It is this erroneous labelling that is at the root of a large number of the problems experienced by the 'new nations' of Asia and Africa.

Discrimination, oppression and exploitation, objectively experienced or subjectively perceived, emerge in situations of disjuncture between citizenship, nationality and ethnicity. One can identify at least five empirical situations in which such disjunctures exist. The first is when a nation is divided into two or more segments and assigned to different states. The classic cases are those of the Poles, distributed between Russia, Prussia and Austria between 1795 and 1919; and the Kurds (numbering 20 million), apportioned between Iran, Iraq, Syria and Turkey, to this day. The Nagas and Mizos of South Asia afford other examples. It is the experience of numerous nations, particularly subaltern peoples situated on inter-state borders; usually their bifurcation is done for reasons of statecraft, but is projected under the label of 'national security'. Sometimes the division of national territory across two or more states is based on religion or secular ideology. In this process, a common history, descent, collective experience and memory, common culture and lifestyle, all get relegated to the background, even disowned, and competing claims for the national territory may be made by two different states. In fact, in this process every effort is made to construct alternative visions of collective memory and history. Germany and Vietnam were, and Korea continues to be, divided on the basis of secular ideologies. The Israeli–Palestinian and India–Pakistan divisions were done on the basis of religion. In the two Punjabs and the two Bengals the issues are taken to be 'settled' and the problems 'solved'. In the two Irelands the issues are taken to be 'settled', and the problems 'solved' from the perspective of the 'winners', but they continue to persist from the angle of the 'losers'.

Second, disjuncture can be discerned where the colonization of a territory by a distinct and distant alien people results in the extermination and/or the marginalization of the native nations. There are at least four variants of this: (a) a situation in which the colonizers did not physically liquidate the native people, although they enslaved, exploited and marginalized them. In the wake of the anti-colonial movements of the twentieth century, the nationals launched their struggle, not intending to drive out the alien colonizer, but to establish a just society in which both the native population and the immigrant settlers could live as dignified partners. The most outstanding case of this type is South Africa; (b) a situation in which the immigrant population has established its hegemony and yet the native population is not entirely voiceless and works towards re-empowerment. The case of Australia proximates this situation; (c) a situation in which the initial migrants have established unequivocal dominance and the First Nations are virtually decimated, but because of the immigration policy a wide variety of ethnic groups co-exist. Thus, in the USA a poly-ethnic state, a hierarchy of ethnic layers, is formed – white Anglo-Saxon Protestants, Asian-Americans, Hispanics, Native Americans, Negroes, and so on; (d) a situation in which the migrants enter with a low status (e.g., as indentured labour), but settle down and eventually claim the territory as their adopted homeland. However, the claim may not be conceded by the native people who try to establish their hegemony over the alien elements. The cases of Malaysia and Fiji fit this description.

The internal colonization of the territory or homeland of a weak or minority nation by the dominant nation, usually sponsored by the state, leading to conflicts between nations and ethnies, constitutes a third example of disjuncture. This is usually done to render irrelevant the moral and legal claims of a nation over its homeland, in which it has a clear majority. Examples of this are Tibet in China, Tamil territory in Sri Lanka, and the Chittagong Hill Tract inhabited by Buddhist tribes in Bangladesh. Sometimes the internal colonization sponsored by the state is to control the local situation. The well-known case of Russians being assigned to different republics in the Soviet Union exemplifies this.

A fourth example is when a nation is apportioned between different administrative units within the same state. This is illustrated by the Armenian case in the USSR, and the cases of Bhils, Santals and Gonds, among others in India, each nation in this case consisting of a few million members. Through such acts of division, the possibility of a nation aspiring to an exclusive administrative unit within the federal state is attenuated, leading to 'culturocide'[4] as each of the segments assigned to different politico-administrative units are compelled to undergo a process of acculturation vis-à-vis different dominant groups.

Finally, situations of disjuncture between citizenship, nationality and ethnicity can be seen to exist where the state and the dominant nation have discriminated against ethnies in the context of economic opportunities, civil rights and political privileges, even though the latter may have been residents of the territory for decades, if not for centuries. The discrimination against ethnies who were initially enticed into several European countries as guest workers illustrates this tendency. The case of the European Jews is indeed a classic example here. The discrimination becomes acute when the ethnies belong to different physical types, or to different religious or language groups.

In the light of the empirical situations outlined above, the following propositions may be advanced. First, whatever may be the definitions of citizenship, nationality and ethnicity, there seems to be an implicit expectation that they should coincide. Where they do not, discrimination, exploitation and even oppression of weak and small nations and ethnies are likely to ensue, which is then legitimized in the name of 'national interests'. Second, once the geographical boundary of a state is fixed, irrespective of the circumstances which led to the incorporation of the different units, and ignoring the irrelevance of the rationale, the state, the political elite and the cultural mainstream (the dominant nation) will invariably disapprove, even ruthlessly suppress, any of the constituents that wish to opt out of the state. Even those who advocate the doctrine of self-determination are no exception to this. Third, there is an innate tendency on the part of the dominant nation or ethnie to establish hegemony over the smaller and weaker nations and ethnies. The hegemony of the dominant collectivity is defined by itself as nationalism, and the weaker nations and ethnies are persuaded to get assimilated. If they do not fall into line, they are labelled as parochial, chauvinistic and anti-national. Fourth, the weaker and smaller nations and ethnies tend to preserve the purity of their culture and strive to maintain their identity even when these may not be viable propositions. In trying to pursue their objectives, these collectivities tend to exaggerate their disadvantages and deprivations. Fifth, given the above scenario, nations and ethnies tend to believe that their material interests can be protected and cultural identity maintained only if they have a state or at least an administrative unit of their own. However, there is nothing inherent or natural in this tendency, but it is indicative of the eagerness to pursue equality and preserve identity simultaneously.

It will be clear by now that any effort to define the concepts of ethnicity, nationality and citizenship has to take into account a wide variety of situations if it is to come to grips with empirical reality. If we were to consider these concepts processually, the possibility of attaining clarity and establishing isomorphism between them and reality would be high. However, conceptualizations have been made that ignore the processual dimension, giving birth to what may be designated as the statist, the nationalist and the ethnicist perspectives (cf., Anthony Smith 1971). The statist views everything from the perspective of statecraft and state-building. But the legitimacy of the state is dependent not only on what it does, but also on who holds power and authority. To circumvent this difficulty state actions are simply labelled as actions taken in the interest of the nation. By this sleight of hand state and nation are treated as coterminous, yielding high pay-offs to the managers of the state; the state as an institution can be perceived as partisan, illegitimate and even oppressive, while a nation is naturally invested with legitimacy – indeed, it is often sacralized. This is so because the nation is taken to be the totality of the people, unlike the state which represents and upholds the inter-ests of a section of the people, be it class, gender, religion, race or language.

Because the statists tend to hijack the nation in the interest of a section of the people, the nationalists, particularly those from the discriminated and disadvantaged nations in a multi-national state, insist on the distinction between state and nation. The nationalist tends to demonize both the state (in so far as it is a captive of the dominant nation) and the cultural mainstream (if it displays hege-monic tendencies). The nationalist is convinced that each nation has its own genius and ought to have its own state, which is a prerequisite for the maintenance of its cultural identity. But historical experience and empirical facts contradict these assumptions. It is not true that all nations aspire to be exclusive states; several nations co-exist within the same state and realize their potentials. Conversely, there are sev-eral instances of one nation being divided into several states without necessarily blocking national creativity (e.g., Arabia). That is, the state–nation coterminality is neither an empirical fact nor an instant asset, but a distorted vision or an ideological preference. To view everything from a nationalist perspective is to resort to hegemony and produce chauvinism.

If the nationalist insists on the uniqueness of the nation, the ethnicist is committed to the preservation of the cultural purity of the ethnie. The ethnicist invariably forgets that all cultures have both assets and liabilities, and that it is therefore not always desirable to preserve all aspects of a culture. In addition, the notion of cultural purity is a myth, but, even if it were a fact, cultures cannot be preserved in their pristine purity in a fast-changing world. Further, in order to preserve cultures certain prerequisites need to be met, for instance, minimum population size, physical concentration and constant interaction. It should be remembered here that, in the name of cultural purity, ethnicists have – not infrequently – indulged in racism, slavery, un-touchability and female infanticide. Thus, there is not much to choose between state terrorism, nationalist facism and cultural relativism. The point I want to affirm is that all three perspectives – statist, nationalist and ethnicist – have substantial negative-value loads, viewed from the humanist perspective. And the patch-up is looked for by wishing away the state–nation, the state–ethnie or the nation–ethnie, and the consequent citizenship–nationality, citizenship–ethnicity and nationality–ethnicity ruptures. Indeed, it is necessary to recognize squarely both the specificities and linkages between them.

Let us now recapitulate some of the arguments presented so far. An ethnie is a collectivity, members of which share a common lifestyle, history and language, but whose identification with its ancestral homeland is weak or endangered. Ethnicity, then, is a product of attenuation between territory and culture. If an ethnie aspires to and is successful in establishing its moral claim over the territory to which it has migrated, and with which it identifies as its homeland, it becomes a nation. A nation, therefore, is a collectivity which has succeeded in establishing a moral claim over the territory it inhabits; it is the fusion of territory and culture that gives birth to nationhood. But, as I have indicated earlier, not all elements of culture are relevant or necessary. Language is a necessary ingredient, but religion and race are both irrelevant for constituting a nation (see chapters 4 and 9). This is not a matter of personal preference or faith, but of empirical necessity.

A nation may not always aspire to establish a legal claim over the territory on which it has a moral claim; if it does, and succeeds, it becomes a nation-state. What binds the people of a multi-national state together is common citizenship; it makes them a legal community, as opposed to the situation in a nation-state in which the legal and cultural community coincides. But to insist that a legal and cultural community should coincide in a polity is to jeopardize even the conceptual possibility of multi-national and poly-ethnic states.

The process conceived here is not unilinear. Just as an ethnie can be transformed into a nation and a state, the reverse process is plausible and often happens. State policies often lead to the ethnification of nations; people of persecuted nations migrate or are transported to far-off places, either within or across state boundaries. Whether or not they remain ethnies or become nations at their point of arrival would depend upon the particular conditions that await them or which they choose to be in. If the state can dismantle nations, it can also facilitate the transformation of ethnies into nations by enabling their empowerment and by settling migrants of the same cultural background into adjoining territories. Further, the possibility of an immigrant population becoming citizens (members of a polity) without becoming nationals (members of a cultural community), or being denied the possibility of becoming either citizens or nationals, are all empirically tenable. The point to be noted is the following: the moment one conceptualizes the citizenship–nationality–ethnicity linkage processually one succeeds in establishing substantial correspondence between empirical reality and conceptual tools, the first necessary step to constructing an authentic theory.

3

Avoiding Conflations and Subsumptions

In trying to keep the three notions of citizenship, nationality and ethnicity clear and concise, it is necessary to avoid both their conflation with and their subsumption under other concepts; it is also important to specify the critical minimum elements by which one can distinguish them from other concepts. I propose to undertake this task in this chapter. The twin concepts that are frequently conflated are those of state and nation (hence citizenship and nationality) and nation and ethnie (consequently nationality and ethnicity). Latterly, the tendency to subsume the concept of race under that of ethnicity has also become widespread. And just as ethnicity and nationality become conflated, so the subsumption of race under ethnicity seriously distorts the analysis of nation and nationality. In fact, it becomes a stepping stone to defining race as nation.

The conflation of state and nation

The tendency to conflate state and nation is so common that an effort to differentiate between them would appear to be a wild-goose chase. That the coterminality between citizenship and nationality has become a part of everyday life can be easily discerned from press statements such as, 'Indian national honoured in Germany'; 'British national found dead in San Francisco'; 'Five US nationals were trapped in the tragedy'. In all these cases the reference actually is to citizenship. Similarly, the word 'nation' in a 'five-nation initiative for nuclear disarmament', or the 'fifty-one-nation meet on European security', and so on, actually refers to states.

In most documents inter-state organizations and relations are referred to as international. Familiar examples are the League of Nations, the United Nations and the European Union. The term nationality is invariably invoked to refer to citizenship in UN documents. Similarly, in European Union documents such as the *Eurobarometer*, the term 'nationals' actually refers to citizens. I give these examples for two reasons. First, the application of the term 'nationality' becomes particularly problematic in all those cases where people of the same national origin belong to several states as citizens – and such cases are increasing. Second, the documents of the UN and similar organizations are formulated by 'experts' after an enormous amount of discussion and deliberation. If the tendency to conflate state and nation were confined only to the mass media and the civil servants of inter-state organizations, it could be allowed to pass. But unfortunately it is equally common among academics. Since state and nation are conflated so frequently, it is neither necessary nor possible to refer to most of the instances. Therefore, I shall confine myself to a small sample.

Karl Deutsch, a well-known expert on nationalism, maintains (1953: 3–5) that territory, language, history and social heritage pose problems in defining nation. In a later work he writes: 'The coming together of the state and people makes a modern nation. A nation is a people who have hold of a state or who have developed quasi-governmental capabilities for forming, supporting and enforcing a common will. And a nation-state is a state that has become largely identifiable with one people' (1969: 19). If one applies this definition to the existing states, it will turn out that most of them are not nations; and since several nations are still aspiring to have their own states, it seems that they are not yet nations. More important is the fact that some nations do not even aspire to, or have consciously renounced the aspiration to acquire statehood, as I pointed out in chapter 2. Thus, the wide gap between Deutsch's concepts of nation, state and the nation-state, and the reality on the ground, make them ill-suited for any meaningful analysis.

According to Anthony Smith, a prolific writer on the subject, three goals which inspire nationalist movements are citizen autonomy, territorial unity and historical identity: 'Together they go far towards defining the peculiar version of the "nation" and of nationhood as an ethnic fraternity that lies at the core of nationalist ideology' (1979: 48). Later in the same book (p. 172) he asserts:

> [T]he bureaucratic state fulfills for the nation its two primordial needs of stemming the uncontrollable march of time and enclosing a clearly

delimited space. To accomplish these and other tasks, the nation today, in a world of nationstates, requires the political might and scientific expertise of bureaucratic state. ... When a scientific state has taken 'root' and is regarded by its members as their true defense against external hostility and internal disintegration, which it becomes closely identified with the national history and territory, then it turns into a 'nation state' ...

Finally, in a later work Smith suggested that: 'A nation can be created in various ways and from a variety of bases and circumstances. The two commonest bases are a territorial state or political community and a community of culture ... nationalism binds together elites and masses in a single ethnic nation with a single legislative will' (1981: 18–19).

Smith first suggests that the nation cannot survive today without its own state. Here one may ask: how about Scotland, Wales, Catalonia, Brittany and several nations in the Indian Union or in the emerging European Union? Second, having laid down the teleological track for the nation, he suggests that in order to maintain the nation, the state should become bureaucratic and scientific. The fact that it is the bureaucratization of the state that triggers off the wrath of a wide variety of social activists in the affluent liberal democracies, and that it is the over-bureaucratization of the state that ignored the 'national' sentiments in the multi-national socialist states and which eventually resulted in their collapse, do not register with him. Third, there is no historical precedent to maintain that only the 'scientific state' can provide true defence to its citizens against external hostility and internal disintegration. Fourth, there is enormous evidence to show that in numerous cases state and nation have not fused into one to make nation-states (see Nielsson 1985: 27–56). Finally, it may be noted that the legislative will binds together not only the people of a single ethnic nation, but also of multi-national (e.g., India) and poly-ethnic (e.g., the USA) states.

Smith is right in maintaining that a nation can be created from a variety of bases and in various ways. But each of these bases – common territory, political community or culture – and the modes of establishing the nations would inevitably influence the end product, as is evident from the differing situations in Western Europe, Eastern Europe, North America, the Middle East, Latin America, South Asia and North Africa. History, traditions, the relationship with the colonial power, the modes of defining and recruiting citizens (descent, immigration), and the like, inevitably impinge on the internal milieux of the states in these regions. The coterminality between nation and state is absent in most cases. Therefore the conceptualization attempted by Smith (and several others like him) is not helpful.

The third and the last author I want to refer to among those who conflate state and nation is Giddens. He conceptualizes the nation-state, with special reference to Western Europe, as an entity that exists in a complex of nation-states, which 'is a set of institutional forms of governance maintaining an administrative monopoly over a territory with demarcated boundaries (borders), its rule being sanctioned by law and direct control of the means of internal and external violence' (Giddens 1981: 190). A few years later he writes: 'By a "nation" I refer to a collectivity existing within a clearly demarcated territory, which is subject to a unitary administration, reflexively monitored by the internal state apparatus and those of other states' (Giddens 1985: 116). The distinctive elements of the nation and the nation-state which Giddens lists are administrative monopoly over a territory; legal sanctions; direct control over violence; and the inextricable interlinkage between the modern nation and state. By and large Giddens's conceptualization is statist, and applies only to uni-national states. This is so because the attributes that he assigns to the nation and the nation-state are not easily transferable to multi- national and/or poly-ethnic states.

The administrative monopoly over a territory is not an attribute of a multi-national or a poly-ethnic state. In the case of the United States of America not only is there dual citizenship – federal and state – but also the federal and state governments have jurisdiction over different administrative matters; neither has an administrative monopoly in a specified territory. This is also true of Great Britain, Germany, Switzerland and, to a certain extent, Spain. Thus, it seems that administrative monopoly on particular territories is more a feature of mono-national unitary states, rather than multi-national 'federal' states. It could still be argued that the central, provincial and local governments together make the state, which would, indeed, be correct. But to the extent that a provincial government administers territories that are culturally different (that is, nations), as in Great Britain, neither the central nor the provincial government has a monopoly in administration. Even when the whole state territory is inhabited by the same nationality, a system of decentralization may exist. The Federal Republic of Germany, established in 1949, had eleven *Länder* (provinces); legislative powers were distributed between the federal and *Länder* governments. While the former had exclusive powers in foreign affairs, citizenship, currency and communications, the latter had considerable power in education, cultural affairs (radio and television) and police, and in some areas power was shared (Kolinsky 1981: 86–7).

I have already noted in chapter 2 that cultural pluralism begets legal pluralism. Thus, in a culturally plural state there would be different legal systems, the sanctions of which belong to different levels and contexts – federal and provincial, and state, religious or folk. In Great Britain, Scotland has legal institutions that are specific to it. Even in regard to control over violence there is a division of labour between the central and the provincial level in federal states. The defence forces, which are concerned with protecting the country from external aggression, are clearly the concern of the federal government. But in maintaining internal order the forces at the provincial level have an upper hand. The former is pressed into service only and solely if the latter is found wanting. Finally, while it is true that most nations are attached to some states, they do not all have their own states and some may not even want them. To conclude, I find that Giddens also uses the two concepts of state and nation interchangeably.

Some authors, however, claim to distinguish between states and nations. Prominent examples are Aron, Ernest Barker and Seton-Watson. Aron distinguishes between the two notions when he notes that even the French nation-state is not a 'community of culture' and is not entirely homogeneous, as the mother tongue of the Bretons, Alsations, Basques and Provençals is not French (1966: 750). However, he views the ideal type of nation as one in which the community of culture and political-military sovereignty coincide, and he identifies the nation as a political unit with three characteristics: 'the participation of all those governed in the state under the double form of conscription and universal suffrage, the coincidence of this political will and of a community of culture and the total independence of the national state with regard to the external world' (p. 295). Clearly, the ideal nation for Aron is a sovereign state, and nationals are those who vote and serve in the defence force, that is, they become its citizens. The lack of fit between the ideal and the actual is so great that the conceptualization is hardly useful.

Ernest Barker distinguished between the state and nation when he wrote: 'Historically the state precedes the nation. It is not nations which make states; it is states which make nations' (1948: 15). He acknowledges the disjunction between the state and the nation, citing the examples of Poland in the nineteenth century and the Austro-Hungarian state which was but a collection of nations. And yet he insists that in the light of the historical experiences of Europe since 1815, 'in some form a nation must be a state and a state a nation and a democratic state which is multi-national will fall asunder into as many democracies as there are nationalities . . . '. But confronted by contrary evidence in regard to Britain he concludes: 'State can be both multi-national and a single nation and can teach its citizens at one and the same time to glory both in the name of Scotsmen or Welshmen or Englishmen and in the name of Britons' (p. 17). Here, Barker is conflating state and nation and, as a result, citizenship and nationality. If he had remained coherent about his conceptions, as he insisted he would at the beginning of the book, he would have characterized Britain as a multi-national state, as the people share not only a common citizenship, but also have their specific national identities – English, Scottish, Welsh, Irish.

Seton-Watson is another author who intended to keep the distinction between state and nation, but did not quite succeed. He wrote (1977: 1): 'The distinction between states and nations is fundamental . . . states can exist without a nation, or with several nations, among their subjects, and a nation can be co-terminous with the population of one state or be included together with other nations within one state or be divided between several states.' This is an exceptionally clear statement on the relationship between state and nation. But after four pages he lists a strong disciplined army as an instrument for spreading 'national consciousness'. And of the three factors listed by him as important for the formation of national consciousness in Israel, state is one (p. 403). When the army is viewed as an instrument of the nation, and the state itself is considered as an important factor in the formation and spread of national consciousness, the distinction between state and nation is obliterated. Further, he refers to the Swiss nation and the Dutch nation, for instance, but he finds it difficult to accept the term British nation (p. 487).

Some authors, in the process of making a distinction between nation-states and state-nations (e.g., Glenn 1970: 347–66; Rejai and Enloe 1969: 139–54) have distinguished clearly between states and nations. Thus Rejai and Enole succintly observed: ' "state" . . . is primarily a political- legal concept, whereas "nation" is primarily psycho-cultural. Nation and state may exist independently of one another, a nation may exist without a state, a state may exist without a nation. When the two coincide, the result is a nation state' (1969: 143). Having said this, the authors argue that developing states are state-nations and suggest that a new nationhood can be established around the new states. However, they also suggest that it is not necessary for the ethnic groups to give up their identities and loyalties in order to be incorporated into the state-nation. This, in effect, amounts to saying that there are two 'national' identities, one proffered by the state and the other by the ethnic groups; state nationalism and ethnic nationalism appear to be two different types of nationalisms. This is confusing.

Socialists are not clear either, nor are they in agreement about keeping the distinction between state and nation. In 1971, at the Eighth Party Congress, General Secretary Honecker of the German Democratic Republic (GDR) claimed that 'a new type of nation, the socialist nation has come into being in East Germany' (cited in Connor 1984: 448). On the other hand, thirty years after the division of Korea, in 1975, the general secretary of the Korean Communist Party Kim Il Sung insisted that the two Koreas make one nation, although it was divided into two states (Connor p. 450). Paradoxically, the two Germanys have united, but the two Koreas have not yet.

It is necessary to recall here that in Article 1 of its 1968 Constitution the GDR was correctly described as 'a socialist state of German nationhood'; Article 8 expressed the hope that: 'The GDR and its citizens strive to overcome the partition of Germany imposed upon the German nation by imperialism, and support step by step rapprochement of the two German states until the time of their unification on the basis of democracy and socialism.' The same opinion was held by the Federal Republic of Germany: 'In the opinion of the Federal Government, a nation and therefore the German nation, cannot be created or abolished by mere act of law', and the situation was referred to as 'two German nations which preserve one nationality' (cited in Connor pp. 452, 475). The point of present interest is that it is wrong to label 'nations' as capitalist, socialist, secular or democratic. On the contrary, these adjectives can be legitimately invoked to refer to states. Having once arisen, the confusion persists because of the tendency to conflate state and nation.

Finally, anarchists, although they are anti-state and pro-nation and support national liberation movements as part of the wider struggle for freedom, do not make a clear distinction. At one time they were completely against the statist aspirations of the nationalists. And yet the most outstanding anarchist analyst of nationalism, Rudolf Rocker, wrote in 1937 in his *Nationalism and Culture*:

> The nation . . . is the artificial struggle for political power, just as nationalism has never been anything but the political religion of the modern state. Belonging to a nation is never determined as is belonging to a people, by profound natural causes . . . a nation as a rule, encompasses a whole array of different peoples and groups of peoples who have by more or less violent means been pressed into the frame of a common state. (cited in Ostegaard 1981: 187)

It is clear that Rocker is conflating state and nation. But he does distinguish between a 'people' and a 'nation', the former being the natural result of a social union and the latter being viewed as a state. In terms of the conceptualization that I am proposing, the people may make the nation, but to be a nation, a people should have its own territory. A people without a territory makes an ethnie.

The only author, as far as I know, who has made the conceptual distinction between the state and the nation and relentlessly stuck to it is Walker Connor. He has rightly castigated those who have used these terms interchangeably (1994).

The unstated assumption behind the conflation of the terms state and nation, or the unintended consequence of it, is that the population of a state ought to be homogeneous, and its citizens should be nationals. If non-national elements exist, either they should shed their cultural identity and assimilate themselves to its culture, or they should leave its territory. Nationalisms that define a nation as a people of common descent have, for instance, developed into Nazism and fascism, and have resorted to genocide. Therefore, the plea for avoiding the conflation of state and nation should not be dismissed as a fetish for conceptual purity; it has profound implications for human life.

The conflation of nationality and ethnicity

I have already noted that there is no consensus in the definition or evaluation of these concepts. To complicate matters they are also used interchangeably. For Weber, one of the earliest to define ethnic groups and nationality, the former could be identified by a collectively held belief in their common origin and heritage. This commonality could be anchored to a similar phenotype and/or culture as well as to historical memories of migration and colonization. But Weber preferred the term nationality (1968: 389). Bell (1975: 157) refers to ethnic groups as culturally defined communal groups. If the content of ethnicity is cultural, there is no need for the concept of nationality, as its content is also cultural. The attempts to define nation and nationality as political entities are not sustainable because they lead to another conceptual conflation, namely, between state and nation, as noted above; furthermore, they are not empirically admissible, as the maxim, attributed to Napoleon – 'To each nation a state, in each state one nation' – has not been realized even in Western Europe, the cradle of the modern nation-state.

Anthony Smith thinks that nationalism emerges from common bonds of religion, language, customs, shared history and common myths of origin: 'in a word, from common ethnicity and common culture' (1979: 43). In a later work he refers to the modern ethnic revival taking the form of nationalism, and defines ' "ethnie" or ethnic community as a social group whose members share a sense of common origin, claim a common and distinctive history and destiny, possess one or more distinctive characteristics and feel a sense of collective uniqueness and solidarity' (1981: 66). Is it that there is no distinction between nation and ethnie, and hence between nationality and ethnicity? Not quite; ethnie is a passive nation and nationality is active ethnicity because ethnic revival is 'the transformation of passive, often isolated and politically excluded communities into potential and actual nations, active, participant and self-conscious in their historic identities' (Smith 1981: 24). Thus, nations often grow out of and are constructed from ethnic materials. Notwithstanding important differences of both kind and degree between nationalism and ethnic sentiment, there is also considerable overlap between them, 'which is reflected in the lack of clarity surrounding the concepts themselves' (p. 85). My contention is that, in spite of overlaps between these concepts, there is a qualitative difference between them which can be located in the territorial dimension.

As Smith links nations and states, it is understandable, although not acceptable, that he considers ethnie as an isolated and politically excluded community. But Connor, who unambiguously distinguishes between state and nation, also considers ethnicity as passive nationalism, thereby leaving nation without any anchorage. He writes:

self differentiating ethnic groups are . . . nations, loyalty to the ethnic group, therefore should logically be called nationalism. We can describe the nation as a self differentiating ethnic group . . . It is therefore the self-view of one's group, rather than the 'tangible' characteristics that is the essence in determining the existence or non-existence of a nation. (Connor 1994: 40–3)

The failure to distinguish between nation and ethnie by Connor may be located in the manner in which nation and nationalism are defined. A nation is defined merely or mainly in psychological and emotional terms rather than in terms of any tangible characteristics. There are many others who have taken this line; a short sample follows. Seton-Watson feels that no 'scientific definition' of a nation is possible and all that one can say is: 'A nation exists when a significant number of people in a community consider themselves to form a nation or behave as if they formed one' (1977: 5). He recognizes that it is not possible to prescribe this number. However, what is relevant is that people should consider themselves and believe that they constitute a nation. Emerson's characterization is in the same vein: 'The nation is a community of people who feel that they belong together in the double sense that they share deeply significant elements of a common heritage and that they have a common destiny for the future' (1962: 95). And 'the simplest statement that can be made about a nation is that it is a body of people who feel that they are a nation' (p. 104). According to these authors, it is sufficient that a group of people feels that it constitutes a nation for there to be one. The difficulty is that a wide variety of groups – religious, linguistic, caste, racial, regional, tribal, and so on – may feel that they are nations. But the crucial element that provides for their feeling so as to make them a nation is left unspecified.

Eriksen rightly sees the distinction between nationals and ethnies as that between insiders and outsiders. But, as he attests the familiar position that a successful nation should have its own state, he is constrained to view unsuccessful nationalisms as ethnicities: 'Many of the ethnies condemned to such a fate eventually vanish through migration, extermination or cultural assimilation' (1991: 265). That is, ethnic groups can survive only if they succeed in establishing their own states. This is simply not true in the case of the New World, where a multiplicity of ethnic groups co-exist in one state. The ambiguity of Eriksen's conceptualization is evident from the cases he has presented to clinch his argument (pp. 268–75). The Sami (Lappish) minority, the First Nation of Northern Norway, becomes an ethnie just because it does not have a state of its own. So do the Trinidad-Indians, the immigrants from the Indian subcontinent. But there is a basic difference between the two peoples under reference: the Samis occupy their ancestral homeland; the Trinidad-Indians are in their adopted homeland. In the first case, in the Sami perspective an outsider has intruded the homeland; in the second case, the Trinidad-Indians constitute the outsider. Nobody contests the nativeness of the Samis, but the native Trinidadian's consider the Indians to be an ethnie. That different ethnies can nationalize themselves and co-exist as co-nationals without shedding their cultural identities is illustrated by the Mauritian case presented by Eriksen. The point here again is that it is not the state that is the crucial element in distinguishing nation and ethnie, but the nature of attachment to the territory and its legitimacy.

I would like to close the discussion on this theme by noting the implications of conflating nation and ethnie. This can be well illustrated with the help of a book entitled: *Ethnic Conflict in the Western World*, edited by Milton Esman (1977). The map on page 24 of this book identifies twenty-five 'selected ethnic homelands', all of which belong to people without their own sovereign states. Fifteen cases of homelands of those who have their own sovereign states and are majority communities are identified but they are not described as 'ethnic' presumably because they are 'national' homelands. I am making this plausible logical derivation because the ethnic homelands are referred to as minority areas. Therefore, one is entitled to argue that according to the authors of this book an ethnic group is a minority group with a homeland within a multi-national state. Conversely, a nation is a majority group with its own homeland and state.

It is also interesting to note the following from the map: (a) three of the states are without any national homelands – Yugoslavia, Switzerland and Belgium. They have only ethnic homelands; (b) four states – France, United Kingdom, Spain and Italy – have both national and ethnic homelands; (c) ten of the states have only national homelands; (d) no distinction is made between the homelands of those peoples that are divided between two or more states (Basques, Italians, Irish, Germans, French) and whose homelands are exclusively within one state (Scots, Welsh, Bretons, etc.); (e) several of the nations/ethnies are not mentioned, for example, Finland, Hungary and Rumania; and (f) Czechoslovakia is shown as one common block, presumably because there is only one homeland between the Czechs and Slovaks. This confusion, I suggest, is due to the inappropriate conceptualization of nation and ethnie, and hence nationality and ethnicity.

According to the conceptualization that I propose, a different perspective emerges. First, all homelands are national, be they ancestral or adopted. Second, there cannot be any ethnic homeland, as ethnicity is a product of dissociation and/or attenuation between territory and culture. Third, some states are mono-national, while others are bi- or multi-national. Fourth, the same national homeland could be divided between two or more states, as in the cases of the Basques, Germans and French. Fifth, most of the states have ethnies among their populations either because they do not identify the land of their current residence as their homeland, or because even when they do their claim is not accepted. That is, the process of transformation from an ethnie into a nation would occur only when two conditions are met: when a group adopts the land into which it has migrated as the homeland, and when the earlier inhabitants accept them as co-nationals (this is exemplified in the cases of those Indians who migrated to Fiji, Mauritius, Surinam etc). To conclude, if territory is the most crucial element of a nation, attenuation of peoples' association from that territory transforms them into another category, namely, ethnie. This is the rationale behind the distinction between nation/nationality and ethnie/ethnicity.

Among the numerous authors who have written on ethnic groups and nations, only a few distinguish between the two. Moynihan, for example, holds that:

... it is helpful to distinguish between ethnic group and nation, between ethnicity and nationality. It is a distinction of a degree. The nation is the 'highest' form of the ethnic group, denoting a subjective state of mind as regards ancestry, but also, almost always an objective claim to forms of territorial autonomy ranging from a regional assembly to fullblown independence. (Moynihan 1993: 4–5)

Moynihan's definition shares two features of the definitions of others. First, the distinction between nationality and ethnicity is one of degree and not kind. Second, nation and state are conflated, in that nation tends to form its own state. However, he provides a good starting point in terms of the conceptual proposal made in this book, as nation is viewed as a territorially anchored community.

The subsumption of race under ethnicity

The third item on the agenda of this chapter is to discuss the tendency to subsume race under ethnicity.[5] Once again this has become so common that it is neither necessary nor possible to refer to most of the authors who do so. Early instances of this tendency appear in Gordon (1978) and Montagu (1964); another oft-quoted example is Glazer and Moynihan (1975).

I shall refer to only two authors here, as they subsume not only race, but several other identities under ethnicity. Horowitz prefers an inclusive concept of ethnicity which encompasses differences based on colour, appearance, language, religion, common origin and their permutations and combinations (1985: 17–18). He writes: 'ethnicity easily embraces groups differentiated by colour, language, and religion; it covers "tribes", "races", "nationalities" and "castes" ' (p. 53). Horowitz defends at length the justification for including colour and race in his definition of ethnicity. Similarly, Bulmer writes: 'An ethnic group is a collectivity within a larger society having real or putative common ancestry, memories of a shared past and cultural focus on one or more symbolic elements which define the groups' identity, such as kinship, religion, language, shared territory, nationality or physical appearance' (1986: 54).

These authors absorb not only race but several other identities into ethnicity, thereby making the concept very ambiguous. They also conflate ethnicity and nationality, or treat nationality as a dimension of ethnicity, a theme that has already been discussed. To continue our discussion we need to ask and answer two questions: Which factors prompted the subsumption of race under ethnicity? Why should these notions be kept apart? But before I attempt to answer these questions

I would like to refer to one author who attempted to keep the distinction between them.

Van den Berghe (1978) notes the growing tendency in the American social sciences to treat race as a special case of ethnicity, and warns against this: 'Precisely because a racial phenotypical definition of group membership is far more stigmatizing than an ethnic definition and typically gives rise to far more rigid social hierarchies, it is important to keep the analytical distinction clear' (p. xv). Further, to abandon a stigmatizing label like race in favour of ethnicity will not do away with racism; it may in effect camouflage it to the advantage of the privileged group. Berghe's clarification is a useful first step. However, he characterizes both racial and ethnic groups in terms of common territory: 'such groups are concentrated in a substantial piece of contiguous territory which they see as their collective homeland' (p. xvii). Such a characterization creates problems in distinguishing between nation and ethnie. A racial group may acquire nationhood not because of its phenotypical features, but due to its claim to a common homeland. It follows that two or more races with a common homeland can make a nation. With these clarifications, let me turn to answering the two questions posed above.

Anthropological classification of the races is based on certain objective physical features such as cephalic index, texture of hair, blood group, among others. Thus the categorization of the three major human races – Caucasoid, Mongoloid, Negroid and their sub-types – is based on biological and genetic features, which by itself does not pose any problem. But when this fact comes to be associated with the idea that particular races – in fact peoples of differing colour – are believed to be superior, physically and intellectually, and hence have the right to dominate over other races, racism begins. Therefore, the point at issue is not whether the term race has any scientific justification or not. Even as it is based on a fallacious biological distinction linked to genotype and phenotype (Montagu 1964), to the extent that race and colour mould human attitudes and behaviour, it is a sociologically relevant variable. However, the clarification made by Jordan should be adhered to: 'Properly used, the term race is employed only with reference to physical traits, not to cultural characteristics such as language, religion or nationality' (1988: 75). Hence the need to keep the distinction between race and ethnie.

The belief regarding the superiority of races is buttressed and reinforced through certain historical events, in fact, historical accidents. Thus, the claim to the superiority of the white race is often sustained through the higher levels of economic development and scientific advancement achieved by the countries populated by them, but it ignores the fact that some of them did not achieve the assumed level of development (namely, the whites of Latin America), that tremendous advantages accrued to them through geographic dispersal towards the New World (e.g., North America, Australia), and that enormous wealth was accumulated through the economic exploitation of the colonies, most of which were populated by non-whites.

Races have a long history, but racism emerged only after different races came into contact, usually in a colonial context. Before the geographical explorations in the sixteenth century there was a rough coterminality between territory and race – black Africa, white Europe, yellow South-East Asia, brown South Asia. But with the emergence of the New World, and largely due to colonization and immigration, this pattern became disturbed and multi-racial societies emerged. In the beginning inter-racial interaction was limited and restrained, creating 'plural' societies in the colonies wherein different races lived in the same polity and exchanged goods and services in the market place, but neither legitimately transfused any blood nor transmuted their cultures (Furnivall 1948). In contrast, inter-cultural interactions have always existed within the same geographical region, as natives and migrants of the same phenotype, who professed different religious faiths and/or spoke different languages, intermingled.

If race is a biological fact, racism is an ideology and practice based on the assumed superiority of certain – traditionally only white, but latterly also yellow – races. The content of ethnicity is essentially cultural, and to be culturally different does not imply superiority or inferiority. And yet, it is not unusual for certain cultural collectivities to define themselves as superior and perceive the culture of others as inferior. The term ethnicism is proposed by some writers to refer to discrimination based on ethnicity (see Bacal 1991). In contrast, ethnicity is increasingly being viewed as positive, an identity marker, a search for roots. Thus the two terms ethnicity and ethnicism ought to be used to refer to the positive and negative aspects of ethnic groups.

The distinction between racism and ethnicism may be illustrated by an example. In the United States of America there were about seventy million Americans of Irish, Southern or Eastern European origin and of these some fifty million were Catholics. The white Anglo-Saxon Protestants (WASP) generally held the older generations of this group in 'collective contempt or at best in cold condescension'. But by the 1970s the descendants of this group were treated by the liberal establishment as 'reactionaries' or 'fascists' (Seton-Watson 1977: 218). The treatment meted out to blacks and Amerindians was vastly different and harsher. That is, a distinction between white ethnics and racial groups did exist. Inter-ethnic discrimination should be designated as ethnicism and oppression of the coloured as racism. When a collectivity is subjected to both ethnicism and racism the discrimination becomes cumulatively oppressive.

While racism is universally condemned as negative, to take pride in one's race is an affirmation of collective self-hood without necessarily disparaging other races, which could be viewed as positive. But we do not have a term to refer to the positive dimension of race. I have suggested the term 'racity' for this purpose (Oommen 1994a: 83–93). Racity refers to the tendency on the part of those belonging to a distinct physical type (race, colour) coming together and interacting so as to provide mutual support and succour to sustain themselves, particularly when confronted by an oppressive force. The mechanisms usually resorted to for this purpose would be formation of primary groups, voluntary associations and political parties to provide emotional support and to fight inequality. Thus, if racism is an instrument of oppression and stigmatization, racity could be an instrument to cope with the situation of domination and inequality and develop and nurture self-esteem. What I mean by racity is well illustrated by W.E.B. Du Bois:

> ... we are that people whose subtle sense of song has given America its only American music, its only American fairy tales, its only touch of pathos and humour amid its mad money getting plutocracy. As such, it is our duty to conserve our physical power, our intellectual endowments, our spiritual ideals; as a race we must strive by race organization, by race solidarity, by race unity to the realization of that broader humanity which freely recognizes differences in men, but sternly deprecates inequality in their opportunities of development. (cited in Essien-Udom 1962: 29)

With the near collapse of European colonialism and after the universal condemnation of Nazism and fascism, the belief in the superiority of races cannot be sustained any more. 'By contrast, ethnicity has become legitimate – people can openly claim some ethnic identity without lessened esteem, they can even show they are proud of it and in many cases actively seek redress from perceived inequalities in terms of such identities, without being officially banned' (Bjorklund 1987: 23). That is, ethnic identity is often the result of collective self-definitions and the search for roots, and is hence viewed as legitimate. But the tendency to subsume race under ethnicity has actually camouflaged the oppression that is specific to race. Therefore, if one wants to unfold the nature and practice of racism one should recognize the notion of everyday racism, which is inextricably intertwined with the very social fabric of multi-racial societies (Essed 1991). The moment one subsumes racism under ethnicism one denies empirically and conceptually the existence of everyday racism.

Everyday racism is practised mainly when interacting collectivities are physically distinct, and it manifests itself in the context of even impersonal and anonymous encounters occasioned by travelling, shopping, dining, and the like. But this type of racism also changes over time, as prejudices against particular races change. Thus, in former times all non-whites were subjected to racism in everyday encounters, although in differing degrees, but more recently the emergence of Japan and the Asian tigers as economic giants has changed the attitude towards the yellow race. In fact, it is now perceived as an economic threat (the new 'yellow' peril) by the white race, because today Japanese labour, goods, technology and management are evaluated positively. Everyday racism is no longer confined to the impersonal, anonymous contexts of interaction, but extends to the institutional realm too.

The difference between everyday racism and everyday ethnicism should be recalled here. Everyday ethnicism, in so far as ethnicity is rooted in culture and not in biology, surfaces only when one interacts with other ethnic groups. Thus, only, for instance, when one speaks to the shop assistant or to the flight attendant is one's linguistic background discovered or revealed. The manner in which the same language, say English, is spoken varies substantially, even among native white English speakers from the UK and the USA. The difference in spoken English is as pronounced between native English speakers on the one hand as it is between, say, the French and Germans on the other. Even as there is no racial difference between them, the 'ethnic' difference, as manifested in speech variations, is an identity marker. This is equally true of religious communities (Buddhist, Christian, Muslim) who may be drawn from different races. The common ethnic background may be revealed only in specific interactional situations (e.g., worship). Thus ethnicity may partly moderate discrimination based on race. That is, specific combinations of race and ethnicity conjointly determine the intensity of discrimination.

While the existence of racism at the interpersonal and institutional levels, that is, in the interactional and structural contexts, is recognized, these are usually viewed as two different domains – the private and the public. This mode of conceptualization cannot come to grips with the connectivity between the two. In contrast, everyday racism links the micro (experiential) and the macro (structural and ideological) levels and helps to cognize the continuity between the two. The mechanisms of everyday racism are: marginalization, which, in effect, perpetuates the dominant groups' values and norms, thereby indirectly putting an artificial ceiling to the aspirations of the dominated group; problematization, which controls the perception of reality by the dominated group either because it is 'incompetent' or because it is 'prejudiced'; and containment of the opposition by subjecting it to intimidation, patronization, the pressure to assimilate, cultural isolation and the denial of racism itself (Essed 1991: 289).

Having noted the danger involved when race is subsumed under ethnicity, the reasons which call for maintaining the distinction between them need to be listed. First, the traditional idea of the genetic inferiority of non-whites in general, and blacks in particular, has still not been abandoned (see Duster 1990). Further, black inferiority is increasingly reformulated as cultural deficiency, that is, culturalization of racism (Steinberg 1981). The racial stereotypes of the blacks (i.e., non-whites) as uncivilized, ugly, barbarian, dirty, aggressive and stupid are partly replaced by cultural beliefs portraying them as lazy and aggressive. The stereotypes about black labour being incompetent, black students being unintelligent, or blacks being prone to crime, to complaining too much, indulging in violence and being a nuisance, are obstinately persistent (Essed 1991). The most recent example of this is the racism that emerged in Western Europe thanks to black diaspora after World War II (see Barker 1981; Cheles et al. 1991; Von Beyme 1988). And ever since ethnicity has emerged as a powerful explanatory variable in sociology, especially in the USA, black cultural deficiency has been used widely as an argument to blame the blacks for their slow progress. Thus, racism has shifted from biological to cultural rationalizations and has simply been re-labelled ethnicity (Chesler 1976: 21–71).

Second, the ethnically different can be transformed over a period of time through a process of assimilation and enculturation, the mechanisms for which include religious conversion, replacing one's mother tongue by learning another language, or adopting a new lifestyle. But the racially different cannot thus become 'invisible', even when miscegenation is accepted and systematically pursued as an ideology and a value system. It can only lead to an elaboration of the physical types, as in Brazil (Ianni 1970: 256–78).

Third, ethnic groups, that is, cultural outsiders, may exist within the same physical type or race. Thus, those who belong to the same race may not all profess the same religion or speak the same language or have the same lifestyle. If one is to understand these intra-racial differences, one needs to recognize the conceptual distinction between race and ethnicity, the latter being reserved to refer to the distinctions based on culture. Racism and ethnicism, in other words, have different historicities and trajectories.

Fourth, unless we keep the distinction between race and ethnicity we cannot meaningfully retain the distinction between attributional ethnicity and interactional ethnicity (Oommen 1989: 303). It is necessary and useful to keep the distinction between these ethnicities, because in those situations where the differences in race and ethnicity co-exist, even if the crucial factor that regulates interaction is race, the cultural factor cannot be ignored. Thus, the social distance between a white Christian and a black Muslim is likely to be greater than that between, say, a white and a black Christian, other things being equal.

Fifth, in many countries and regions the focus is either on race or on ethnicity. This selective focusing seems to be largely dictated by reasons of statecraft and/or the convenience of the cultural and racial mainstream. The above tendency has given birth to what may be called aggregative racism. Thus, in Britain, 'black' incorporates African, Afro-Caribbean and Asian, in short, all the non-whites. This lumping together, although a convenient shorthand device from the perspective of the dominant whites, ignores the differences among non-whites and invites resentment from the 'superior races' among them. The yellow Southeast Asians, for instance, would consider themselves superior to the brown Southern Asians, who in turn consider themselves superior to the blacks. These distinctions are not sustainable on a scientific basis, but are important in the context of everyday life, as individuals and groups are distinguished and discriminated against on the basis of their colour. At any rate, the non-whites vary ethnically, as they are drawn from a wide variety of cultural backgrounds.

Sixth, subsumption of race under ethnicity is bound to conceal certain deep-rooted stereotypes and/or disadvantages anchored to race. One that persists claims that the blacks are hypersexual, thereby leading to sexual racism. In the history of the USA, black males have been objects of both hatred and fear, and have been lynched, jailed or murdered on the basis of allegations of sexual harassment of white women. Black women have been assaulted because they are seen as the sexual property of white men. These historical constructions of black sexuality persist even to this day (see Davis 1981). If race is not distinguished from ethnie, one cannot isolate certain dimensions of racism such as sexual racism.

Finally, some of the responses based on race will not be unfolded if we lump together race and ethnie. Generally speaking, whites only experience situations of decisive dominance. How do they react as a racial category when they are a disadvantaged or a demographic minority? Such questions can be meaningfully answered only if we disengage the concept of race from that of ethnicity. It seems that whites tend to develop negative feelings about racially mixed situations in which they are a demographic minority, although they retain their dominant status. This is revealed in a study of campus racism with special reference to the University of California (see Duster 1991). On the other hand, the non-white students often develop a suspicious mentality and a persecution mania, refusing to recognize their inadequacies and invariably interpreting their failures as discrimination by a racist faculty. Such disadvantages, it is widely believed by non-white students, are not shared by white students from a different ethnicity (say Germans or French) even when they do have genuine linguistic inadequacies (vis-à-vis English). Once again, what one notices is the distinctiveness of race as against ethnicity, in that whites and non-whites often tend to function as distinct blocks, ignoring their ethnic differences in multi-racial situations.

To conclude, not only should the conceptual distinction between state and nation be adhered to, but the distinction between nation and ethnie too is crucial. The nation is a territorially anchored cultural community in its ancestral or adopted homeland; ethnie is a nation or part of the nation dissociated from or marginalized in its homeland. Both are cultural communities. Race is a phenotypical category and may be distributed into several homelands and belong to different cultures; there are several nations for each of the races. A race may make a nation not because it shares common physical features, but because it shares a common homeland. Conversely, a race will become an ethnie if it is dislodged from or leaves its homeland. These distinctions help to distinguish between different kinds of solidarities based on citizenship, nationality, ethnicity and racity. These are qualitatively different solidarities.

4

Race and Religion: Untenable Factors in Nation Formation

I have suggested earlier that the process of an ethnie transforming itself into a nation is a long-drawn and tedious one. Of the several factors that influence and inhibit this process the two most important ones are race and religion. The first operates largely because of the positive and negative evaluations associated with colour, and the second does so due to the deep emotional identification that people develop with religion. As Crawford Young correctly asserts: 'Physical appearance is the most indelible attribute; where skin pigmentation serves to segment communities, only a handful of persons at the color margins may be permitted any choice of identity on racial lines' (1976: 43–4). As for religion, one cannot belong to two religions or be an atheist and a believer at the same time. In other words, both these identities are exclusionary in orientation. But people with phenotypical similarity or commonality of religion do not necessarily inhabit the same territory, identify with it as their homeland or speak the same language. Therefore, both race and religion are irrelevant factors in nation formation. They are, nevertheless, frequently invoked by leaders of all hues in mobilizing people in the name of nation and nationality.

As we have noted in chapter 3, race is a biological fact. But its being viewed as a non-biological 'reality' is at the root of many problems. Ernest Barker refers to three stages through which a scientific fact becomes a social construction in the case of linguistic groups. First, the philologist forms a conception based upon simple facts of a linguistic community. Second, the publicist misinterprets the idea of linguistic community into an unfounded idea of a community of blood or race. Third, the politician deftly adopts the misinterpretation and translates the imagined idea of the unity of blood into the actual unity of a great state (1948: 25). Hitler did precisely this with the notion of an Aryan race.

Race and nation

The notion of race has had a chequered career. It has been used in four different senses, creating enormous confusion: as a biological category (the anthropological sense); as a linguistic category (the philological sense); as a cultural category (the ethnological sense); and as a nation (the historical and political senses). This explains why we encounter Italian, French, German, Tamil, Bengali, Japanese or similar other 'races' in the utterances of nationalists and ideologues. The irrelevance of race for nation formation becomes clear if one keeps in mind that race is a biological category, which is the only correct sense in which the term should be used.

There is consensus on the proposition that a nation cannot be conceived without a homeland – ancestral or adopted (see chapter 9). From the dawn of history people of different races came to inhabit the same territory; they conjointly constituted nations. The idea of racial superiority propounded by the French writer Count Joseph Arthur de Gobineau (1816–82) is largely rejected now, and some (e.g. Ernest Barker) have even advocated racial blending within a nation, not only because he sees an inherent value in such endeavour, but also because it may produce positive results in producing superior pedigrees. However, the racial blending advocated was of proximate layers:

> There are, it is true, elements which it is better *not to mix* because they are so unlike that their offspring, with its ill-assorted mixture of *discrepant qualities*, will be ill-balanced and unharmonious. Miscegenation of East and West, or of white and black, has its perils. But inter-breeding of the different varieties of races of Europe, which unite a fund of similarity to all their differences, is an entirely different matter. (Barker 1948: 39; my italics)

It is important to remind ourselves here that although the first edition of Barker's *National Character* was published in 1927, the fourth and revised edition appeared in 1948, by which time one and a half centuries of race mixtures had been taking place between the white, red, and black races in the New World. In fact, in Latin America large-scale race mixtures had produced new physical types leading to the transformation of race from a biological to a cultural fact. In contrast, in North America, Australia and South Africa, where it happened on a limited scale and surreptitiously, inter-racial conflicts remained very intense as compared with Latin America. Therefore, blending races of 'discrepant qualities' may also have its positive pay-offs, contrary to what Barker may have thought.

At any rate, what is relevant for the present purpose is to remember that the coterminality between race and territory has been disturbed substantially with the geographical explorations of the sixteenth century and the colonialism that followed it. People of different colours – black, red, brown, yellow and white – co-exist in the New World, and most of them, irrespective of their colour, consider the countries of their present habitation to be their homeland. Further, there has been considerable miscegenation. In this changed scenario the idea of considering race (in its biological sense) as an important element of nation is conceptually untenable. The racial composition of the New World is such that to insist on race as an element of nation is to deny permanently the appellation 'nation' to these countries. Even in the case of the Old World, the race–territory coterminality is being increasingly disturbed due to migration. This is the rationale behind rejecting race as a factor in the conceptualization of nation and nationality. The conclusion that Deutsch reached after reviewing a large number of definitions of nation is therefore correct: 'Most serious writers have agreed that nationality is not biological and has little if anything to do with race' (1953: 13). But given the saliency of the race factor and its untenability to form nations based on race in the New World, I will pursue this analysis with special reference to the situation prevalent there.

Scientific conclusions and political ideology or expediency may often not fit well together. Even in the first 'new nation', the USA, the citadel of the most 'successful democracy', efforts were made either to exclude the 'wrong races' or to consider all physical types as if they belonged to a family or kin group, supposedly a prerequisite for a nation. In 1751 Dr Benjamin Franklin observed:

> The number of purely white people in the world is proportionately very small. *All Africa* is black or *tawny*. *Asia* chiefly *tawny*. *America* (exclusive of the new comers) wholly so. And in *Europe*, the *Spaniards, Italians, French, Russians* and *Swedes* are generally what we call a swarthy complexion, as are the *Germans* also, the *Saxons* only excepted who with the

English make the principal Body of White people in the Face of the Earth. I could wish their Numbers were increased. . . . Why should we in the sight of superior beings darken its people? [W]hy increase the sons of *Africa* by planting them in *America*, where we have so fair an opportunity, by excluding all Blacks and Tawneys, of increasing the lovely White and Red? But perhaps I am partial to the complexion of my country, for such kind of partiality is natural to Mankind. (as cited in Moynihan 1993: 93; italics in the original)

Franklin wanted the USA to be principally a country of 'lovely' white and red; the first because he belongs to that category, the second, perhaps, as a concession to the Amerindians because America is their ancestral homeland. He describes America as 'my country', a claim that the blacks, the browns or the yellows could have made with equal moral force, if not in 1750 then certainly by 1850.

However, the prejudice and contempt were not confined to racial categories alone, but enveloped the fellow immigrants from Europe. Drawing a distinction between the old and the new immigrants, Madison Grant wrote in 1916 (of course he referred to the old and new immigrants as 'races'):

The new immigration contained a large and increasing number of the weak, the broken, and the mentally crippled of all races drawn from the lowest stratum of the Mediterranean basin and the Balkans, together with the hordes of the wretched, submerged populations of the Polish Ghettos. Our jails, insane asylums and almshouses, are filled with this human flotsam and the whole tone of American life, social, moral and political has been lowered and vulgarised by them. (cited in Handlin 1957: 77)

Thus, not only the people of other races and colours but the inferior stocks of Eastern and Southern Europe too were viewed with disdain. But none of them – racial and ethnic groups – could have claimed the whole or parts of the USA (or other territories of the New World) as their exclusive ancestral or adopted homeland. It was the common adopted homeland for all of them.

Perhaps this is what prompted John Jay to write about the USA in the following terms, while completely ignoring the stupendous racial and ethnic diversity of his country:

With equal pleasure I have as often taken notice, that providence has been pleased to give this one connected country to one united people – *a people descended from the same ancestors speaking the same language, professing the same religion,* attached to the same principles of government, very similar in their manners and customs ... This country and this people seem to have been made for each other and *it appears as if it was the design of providence that an inheritance so proper and convenient for a band of bretheren, united to each other by the straight ties,* should never split into a number of unsocial, jealous, and alien sovereignties. (as cited in Connor 1994: 201)

Such an improbable characterization of the USA was made by John Jay precisely because of the wrong and widespread conception that originated and persisted in Western Europe, that a nation ought to be a people of common descent and culture. Thus, a wrong conception about an entity (here, nation) has led to an absolutely untenable conceptualization, leaving a great gap between concept and reality. On the other hand, if nation is conceptualized as a people who share a common homeland, ancestral or adopted, both the racist overtones of Benjamin Franklin's utterances and the unwarranted kindred orientation in John Jay's characterization of the USA become dispensable, indeed untenable.

Why race is irrelevant

Apart from de-territoralization of race there is yet another reason, in fact a more compelling one, why race cannot be the basis of nation formation. This is miscegenation. When two or more racial groups inter-breed in the territory that is their ancestral homeland (for the First Nations) or their adopted homeland (for the settlers), the prospects of their being separated territorially is almost absent. The early European settlers in Australia and South Africa were predominantly male, and they had sexual unions with the native women which led to to the creation of 'mixed bloods'. In the American antibellum South black slave families often lived at very close quarters to the master's family, and sexual relationships between the white male and black female were not uncommon. According to Robert P. Stuckert, '[o]ver 28 million white persons are descendants of persons of African origin', constituting 21 per cent of the Caucasian population in the USA in the 1960s (cited in Lincoln 1967: 540). Frazier reports that a twelfth of the slave population was of mixed blood, and that 37 per cent of the free Negroes in the US were categorized as 'mixed bloods' in 1850 (1957: 67). Pettigrew observes that due to miscegenation in the USA in the last three centuries a quarter of the gene pool of Negro Americans has become Caucasian in origin (1964: 71).

If race mixture in the Protestant Anglo-Saxon colonies was limited and surreptitious, in Latin America, which was colonized by Catholics, it was widespread, although there were substantial variations among the countries within the continent. There are different views about these variations. Some have argued that Protestant, Anglo-Saxon and Germanic people were less tolerant towards racial mixture than the Catholics who colonized Latin countries (e.g., Tannebaum 1947). There are others who hold the view that the miscegenation encouraged by the Spaniards and the Portuguese cannot be taken as an index of tolerance because it happened mainly through concubinage between white men and non-white women, which is more an indicator of sexual exploitation (Freyre 1946). These different views need not detain us here; indeed, it seems to be correct to think that 'irrespective of the colonial policy or racial attitudes of the various powers, European colonialism in the Americas has been characterized by rapid and extensive miscegenation and Westernization' (Van den Berghe 1970: 76).

What is relevant, however, for the present purpose is to take cognizance of the racial composition of Latin American countries brought about by miscegenation and immigration. To begin with, it may be noted that a distinction was made between European settlers, designated as Creoles, and recent arrivals called Peninsulares. But it was a continuous process; as Peninsulares became Creoles, new settlers arrived. Inter-marriages led to the existence of persons of mixed origins – the mestizos. All Latin American countries have multi-racial populations, although some draw their populations predominantly (that is, 60 per cent or more) from one race. Thus, Argentina, Brazil, Costa Rica, Cuba and Uruguay are all predominantly white, but Haiti is largely black and Bolivia is predominantly Amerindian. However, Chile, Columbia, the Dominican Republic, El Salvador, Honduras, Mexico, Nicaragua, Panama, Paraguay and Venezuela have predominantly mixed populations. Others have populations drawn more or less evenly from different racial categories. Ecuador's population was 50 per cent mixed and 30 per cent Amerindian in 1961; in 1959 Guatemala had 54 per cent Amerindian and 46 per cent mixed; and in 1961 Peru had 47 per cent Amerindian and 52 per cent mixed (see Crawford Young 1976: 430). In fact, the dominant tendency in Latin America is the emergence of a new physical type, variously designated as ladino, mestizo or cholo in different countries, which is becoming the 'mainstream'. The situation in the West Indies was similar. At the end of the eighteenth century the coloureds – products of miscegenation – comprised 5–20 per cent in the different islands, but at the time of emancipation in the mid-nineteenth century they outnumbered the whites. This was possible because sexual relationships between white men and coloured and black women in the West Indies were common and open (Lowenthal 1967: 588). This situation is completely different from the one that exists not only in the Old World, but also in the rest of the New World. The point is that race is a totally irrelevant basis of nation formation in the contemporary world, as all the racial categories have a conjoint claim on the territory they inhabit.

The case of South Africa is special in the sense that it is not a settler-majority country, but it was, at least until 1994, dominated by the European minority settlers, both formally and substantively. Further, the minority white settlers came to identify themselves so totally with their new homeland that they severed all connections with their ancestral homeland in Europe. The distinction made by Van den Berghe between micro-segregation (in the context of accessibility to public and private facilities in mixed residential areas), meso-segregation (the physical separation of races into residential clusters so as to have homogeneous settlements within multi-racial urban areas) and macro-segregation (that is, creating separate territorial, political and administrative units), is useful in understanding the severity of discrimination against and oppression towards the coloureds and blacks (1970: 210–11). All three types of segregations have existed in South Africa, none in Latin America and meso-segregation continues to exist in the USA. We are concerned here mainly with macro-segregation.

The policy of macro-segregation gave birth to the idea of separate homelands for the blacks and the Bantus – the only instances in recent history of 'nations' based on race. This policy was conceived by the third prime minister of the Union of South Africa, Dr H. F. Verwoerd, and it visualized the creation of autonomous units in a future 'South African Common Wealth' (Legum 1967: 483–95). The programme was to put together some eleven million (in the 1970s) Africans into seven rural Native Reserves, which constituted about 13 per cent of the territory of the country. There were three other elements to the policy: the Africans were to be further re-grouped on the basis of their culture and tribe; a programme of state-sponsored cultural revivalism was to be initiated; and some amount of local autonomy under the authority of government-approved tribal chiefs was to be provided. The Bantustans were not sovereign, but operated like local self-government units (Van den Berghe 1970: 214). Even the policy of apartheid could not create separate 'nations' based on races in South Africa, because the Bantustans could be established only in rural areas; because the urban and industrial areas were substantially mixed, as the Africans provided the bulk of the labour force; and because the coloureds (the mixed population) and the Indians could not easily be segregated. This meant that the possibility of creating viable, territorially anchored, cultural communities (nations) could not have been achieved, even in South Africa.

It may be noted here that miscegenation did occur, was tolerated and even welcomed when South Africa was first colonized, that is, from 1652 till the end of the eighteenth century. The opposition to it started only in the nineteenth century and became virulent by the twentieth, at which point laws were passed prohibiting sexual relations between the whites and the blacks (Van den Berghe 1970: 227–8). But the initial sexual unions had already given birth to a separate physical category – the coloureds. And all the racial categories – whites, Africans, coloureds and Indians – identified themselves with South Africa, which they saw as their common homeland. It is this changed situation that makes race an untenable basis of nation and nationality in South Africa.

Most scholars ignore the role of race in nationalism. Those who recognize it have a wrong perception of it: some castigate the dominant colonizer, the whites; others show sympathy towards the dominated colonized non-whites. Against this background it is interesting to note that Anthony Smith dwells at length on the 'positive' role of colour and race in developing a national identity in Africa and in the USA. But in terms of the conceptualization that I am proposing the 'racial nationalism' of Africa is a contradiction in terms because the people of Africa are already in their homeland. In waging the anti-colonial struggles, the Africans were only pursuing the aims of self-rule and equality. Colour differences have indeed been pressed into service by leaders of the national movements against the white colonizers, but it is not these that make them national movements. Struggles against people of the same colour, if they are perceived as outside intruders into the homeland, are national; otherwise the notion of internal colonialism makes no sense. That is, the critical point in nationalism is not the colour of the people, but their status vis-à-vis the national homeland (cf. Smith 1979: 105–10), whether they are insiders or outsiders. As for racial pride, self-respect and developing a positive evaluation vis-à-vis 'superior' races by oppressed races, I have suggested the term 'racity', as noted earlier in chapter 3. But colour nationalism is that effort to wrest an exclusive nation for a people of the same colour, be it black, white or brown. This possibility exists only when people of a particular colour can legitimately claim a given territory as their exclusive or predominant homeland. Before the American Civil War the theoretical possibility of two separate homelands for the whites and blacks did exist in the USA, not because they were two different races, but because each had a moral claim over its respective territory, in which it constituted the majority

population. Fighting against inequality is common to numerous categories – class, gender, age, religions and so on – and is not confined
to races. In so far as the struggles by these categories for equality is not
anchored to a territory, they are not 'national'. The first three categories, class, gender and age, cannot be anchored to territory. Religion and race can, but the 'nation-ness' of the struggle does not
emanate from these identities.

In the USA between 1760 and 1870 the Negro population increased
by 91 per cent in the fourteen southern cities, compared with an
increase of a mere 17 per cent of the white population. But gradually
the dispersal of the blacks started. The number of counties in the
'black belt' declined from 286 in 1900 to 180 by 1940, and the black
population decreased by about 50 per cent (Frazier 1957: 187–90). The
process of black migration from the South to the North gradually
accelerated, peaking in the 1940s when the number of Negroes living
outside the South jumped by almost 100 per cent. By the mid-1960s, 50
per cent of African-Americans lived outside the South, compared to a
mere one-tenth at the beginning of the twentieth century. In contrast,
in the industrial states of the North the Negro population increased
five to ten times faster than the whites between 1940 and 1950. In the
South during the same decade the white population increased thirty-
three times faster than the Negro population (Woodward 1966: 128).
It is against this background of demographic dispersal that the notion
of black nationalism in the USA ought to be viewed.

Black nationalism in the USA

There are several studies of black nationalism in the USA, but there is
no consensus about its content. For example, Bracey et al. (1970)
identify at least nine different orientations: racial solidarity; cultural
nationalism (Afro-American culture); religious nationalism; economic
nationalism with a thrust on bourgeois reformism; revolutionary nationalism geared to militant collective action; assimilationism and
integration; pan-Negroism or pan-Africanism; territorial separatism
aimed at establishing a separate homeland or for acquiring control
over the black community within the USA; and emigrationism, that is,
return to an ancestral homeland (pp. xxv–lx). The authors conclude
that 'the dominant thrust of black ideologies [i.e., national ideologies]
has been the desire for inclusion in the broader American society'
(p. liv).

Another study by Essien-Udom (1962) lists six dimensions of black
nationalism in the US: religious – creating a nation of Islam; race –
anti-white or Caucasian; economic development and social reform;

self government; identity based on common culture – language, music and dance; and the search for a common black homeland (1962: 17–62). It is clear that the search for identity (cultural and/or racial), the fight for equality, the struggle for material improvement, and the quest for solidarity are all designated as nationalism. But in terms of the conceptualization that I suggest, the search for establishing a common homeland is the first necessary step. Draper (1970) identifies three such basic orientations of black nationalism: emigrationism, self-determination and the Nation of Islam, all of which are informed by the territorial dimension. I will pursue this discussion with special reference to the efforts to establish a Negro homeland.

A common homeland is believed to be a basic criterion for the progress of the Negro, a belief that has been well articulated by Marcus Garvey, who initiated the movement for a separate Negro homeland in the 1920s:

> The Negro needs a nation and a country of his own, where he can best show evidence of his own ability in the art of human progress. Scattered as a mixed and unrecognized part of alien nations and civilizations is but to demonstrate his imbecility and point him out as an unworthy derelict, fit neither for society of Greek, Jew nor Gentile. (cited in Essien-Udom 1962: 17)

Drew Ali, the Black Muslim leader who founded the Moorish Science Temple in 1913, held a very similar view. He insisted: 'For a people to amount to anything, it is necessary to have a name (nation) and a land. Before a people can have a God they must have a nationality' (cited in Essien-Udom p. 34). That is, the genius of a nation can flower only on its own homeland. Without this the nation comes in for unfavourable comparison and treatment. Viewed against this orientation, it is not surprising that the idea of Negro emigration from the USA to a favourable site was initiated as early as 1815 by Paul Cuffee, a New England Negro sailor, following his voyage to Sierra Leone. This was followed by Martin Delany's exploratory voyages to the Niger in the 1850s. But Marcus Garvey's 'Back to Africa' movement in the 1920s was perhaps the most systematic effort. This idea was nurtured until 1951, when Senator Langer introduced a bill (which was not passed) in the US Senate advocating the establishment of a national home for American Negroes in Liberia. Although Langer continued his efforts until the 1960s through the Joint Council of Repatriation, which he had founded (Essien-Udom, pp. 19, 51), nothing concrete came out of it. American Negroes tried to make homelands in Canada (North America), Cyprus, Haiti (West Indies), Liberia (Africa) and in South

America in general. But they had no greater moral claim to any of these locations than they had in the USA.

In contrast to emigration was the idea of anchoring the Negro to America, but with an Afro-American orientation. Although an ardent advocate of pan-Africanism, W. E. B. Du Bois held:

> We are Americans, not only by birth and by citizenship but by our political ideals, our language, our religion. Farther than that our Americanism does not go. At that point, we are Negroes, members of a vast historic race that from the very dawn of creation has slept, but half awakening in the dark forests of its African Fatherland. (cited in Essien-Udom p. 28)

The Afro-American orientation has been growing steadily ever since and, in effect, means physical location in the USA while at the same time nurturing an African cultural heritage. The manifestation of this has been found in the demand for a separate homeland for the Negroes within the USA. Oscar C. Brown, a Negro lawyer and businessman, started the movement for the 'Establishment of the Forty-Ninth State' and sought political 'self-determination' for Negroes. But the American Senate did not approve of it. However, the idea of a black homeland within US territory continued to be pursued by the Black Muslim movement. Elijah Muhammad, the leader of the movement, said in his speech on 31 May 1959: 'separation of the so-called Negroes from their slave masters' children is a MUST. It is the only SOLUTION to our problem' (cited in Essien-Udom, p. 259). He reiterated the same point in his book published in 1965 entitled *Message to the Black Man*: 'We want our people in America whose parents or grandparents were descendants from slaves, to be allowed to establish a separate state or territory of their own – either in this continent or elsewhere' (cited in Bracey et al. 1970: 404). Drew Ali went a step further and claimed the whole of North America as the Negroland: 'it is only an extension of the African continent' (cited in Essien-Udom 1962: 34). Furthermore, he stated that 'the black man in the New World could make a greater contribution by remaining in America, rather than migrating' (cited in Essien-Udom, pp. 34, 61). It can be seen that there has never been a consensus on the question of a black homeland.

A major effort to establish a black homeland within US territory was the proposal made by Robert S. Browne at the Conference on Black Power which met in Newark, New Jersey, in July 1967. The proposal called for initiating 'a national dialogue on the desirability of partitioning the United States into two separate and independent nations, one to be a homeland for white and the other to be a homeland for black Americans' (cited in Draper 1970: 136). Another version of the same strand of thinking may be discerned in the proposals made by the Congress of Racial Equality (CORE). Roy Innis, a director of CORE in the late 1960s, proposed a three-phase plan. During the first phase it was visualized that a community self-determination bill would be introduced to enable blacks to assume control of the economy of their own communities. In the second phase they were to take over the management and control of their institutions – schools, hospitals, police, government. The third phase would see the promulgation of a new US constitution giving birth to a two-nation set-up, 'when America's blacks cease to relate to the larger nation as a dependent colonized people and begin to assert power through the control of their community institutions and capital instruments, the black "colony" will then in fact be a "nation within nation" ' (cited in Draper p. 140). There were other proposals of a modest nature, such as the one made by W. H. Ferry in 1968 to establish a system of black colonies which would confer de jure status to the de facto entities; a black colony was defined as a community with a 75 per cent black population. The idea of black city-states has also been put on the agenda by some (see Draper pp. 168–73).

It is instructive to look at the practical feasibility of these proposals. I have drawn attention to the substantial population dispersal of blacks from the South to the North and of the whites from North to South. The proposed black homeland, designated as the Republic of New Africa, was to consist of five states: Mississippi, South Carolina, Louisiana, Alabama and Georgia, consisting of a population of a little over 10 million in the 1960s. The percentage ratio of whites to blacks in the proposed republic was 67.4 to 32.6 at that time. To make it a black majority state (say around 75 per cent), it would be necessary either to re-locate about two-thirds of the resident white population, or to move in two to three times as many blacks (Draper p. 142). Similarly, the idea of blacks assuming control over local communities is of limited value. In the 1960s, of the 418 counties in the proposed Republic of New Africa the whites were in a majority in as many as 319 (Draper p. 143). Finally, although the prospect of establishing black city-states may appear to be attractive given the ongoing process of the 'blackening' of the US cities, the fact that the inner cities are predominantly populated by the black underclass makes such units economically unviable. The demand that these city-states should be financially supported by the federal or provincial states is unlikely to find political support given the racial distribution of the population of the USA.

There is yet another contradiction in the black self-determination movement. While the Black Muslims think that Christianity is the greatest enemy of the black nation, and hence advocate conversion to Islam, the non-Muslims resist it. One of the informants of Essien-Udom declared: 'I am a Baptist born, and a Baptist bred and when I die I'll be a Baptist dead.' Another said: 'This is a white man's country. It is a Christian country. . . . I think it is dangerous for the Negro to add to his problems the fact of being a religious minority. I am an American' (cited in Essien-Udom 1962: 322).

Finally, the orientation to the African homeland itself is splintered. While Black Muslims relate to Egypt or Morocco as their ideal, Black Christians look to Ethiopia or Liberia. Thus, black Africa is largely left in the lurch, as it were, thereby diminishing the importance of the colour black as a symbol and of Africa as a spiritual homeland. And the fact is that the American Negro came primarily from Ibibo, Ibo, Yoruba and Bambora, that is, contemporary states such as Calabar, Oyo, Dahomey and Mali (Crawford Young 1976: 29–30).

The ambivalence in regard to identifying a common homeland, the ambiguity regarding the 'appropriate' religion for Negroes, and the untenability of staking a moral claim on any part of the US territory as the homeland point towards the artificiality of black nationalism. To complicate matters, 'even Muslim masses do not support Black nationalism and therefore its goal – a Negro Zion – is unrealistic', according to Essien-Udom (1962: 324). The Negroes' tendency to relate themselves to Africa as a spiritual homeland, and to respect and absorb the African heritage is natural, but it only indicates that they are not yet full-fledged nationals in their adopted homeland. However, they share this predicament with their fellow Americans – white, yellow and brown.

In the light of this analysis, I suggest that race cannot be the basis of nation formation in the contemporary world, for the following reasons. First, the de-territorialization of races – white, black, yellow or brown – has led to their dispersal into almost all continents; second, races do not profess a common religion; third, no race belongs to an exclusive speech community; fourth, races have never been 'pure', but today there is a considerably greater race mixture, particularly in some parts of the world (e.g., Latin America); fifth, peoples of the same race do not necessarily share a common history or a common set of institutions; sixth, there is no evidence to suggest that the inhabitants of the ancestral homelands will readily accept one or another of the races that emigrated from there centuries ago; finally, there are enormous intra-racial conflicts among the different racial groups. It therefore seems clear that whichever criterion is adopted race cannot be a basis of nation formation.

In other words, there are different nations among each of the races, as they have different homelands and constitute different speech

communities. While in some of these nations one or other race constitutes the majority, there are always some people who belong to
other races. If these minorities do not identify with the country into
which they have migrated, they remain ethnies. Thus, those black
Americans who aspire to a separate homeland of their own have not
yet become full-fledged nationals; and this is also true of some other
racial groups in the USA.

The religious factor

I propose to argue that religion as the basis of nation formation is
untenable for two main reasons: de-territorialization and proselytization, both of which unsettle the identification of a religious community with a given territory. I shall empirically explicate the
argument with special reference to South Asia (India, in particular),
this being the most religiously plural region in the world. But before I
attempt this, it is useful to consider the thesis in general terms.

As in other contexts, scholarly opinions are diametrically opposed
in this case also. Hans Kohn propounded what he called the 'universal
sociological law', namely, 'religious groupings lose power when confronted with the consciousness of a common nationality and speech'
(1932: 229). In the same vein Deutsch (1969) suggested that religion
could not destroy nationalism any more than Catholicism, Protestant-
ism, Buddhism and Islam could consolidate peoples of different nationalities. On the other hand, W. C. Smith holds: 'The driving force of
nationalism has become more and more religious, the more the movement has penetrated the masses' (1957: 75), and Anthony Smith lists
religion as a defining feature of nation (1981: 64). The problem partly
arises from the ambiguous characterization of religion, leading to
coinages such as secular religion, civic religion, political religion and
the like, which actually refer to an intense identification with nation
and nationalism, earlier believed to be an exclusive preserve of religion. To avoid the unwarranted mixing of religion and nationalism, it
is necessary to define nationalism as a secular ideology, as suggested
by Anthony Smith (1973: 26).

In pressing my argument that religion cannot be the basis of nation
formation, I shall discuss two authors, both of whom consider it to be
an important ingredient of nation. Ernest Barker, having conceded
that the secular trend was fast becoming visible, remarked: 'nations
long dreamt for their national unity in some common fund of religious ideas' (1948: 14). But this caution disappears when he writes:
'the connection between religion and national life is obviously close. In
some cases we may even say that religion is the nation and the nation

is what it is in virtue of its religion' (p. 151). Barker points out that the Greek nation survived largely because of the Greek Orthodox Church, that Scotch national unity is sustained due to the Scottish Church, and he elaborates the role that the Anglican Church played in consolidating the English nation. Other examples cited are Holland and Switzerland, where Calvinism played a prominent role. In all these cases the idea of a national church came to be deeply institutionalized following the Reformation in the sixteenth century.

However, the idea of a national church is patently antagonistic to the notion of a universal church profferred by Catholicism, as well as to the concept of *umma*, the universal community nurtured by Islam. In those nations where two or more Christian denominations (as in Germany) or two or more religious communities (as in Lebanon or India) co-exist, nationality becomes a nonsense if one takes this view to its logical end. Even in the case of uni-denominational nations, those who refused to belong to the official church, or rationalists, secularists, atheists and agnostics – in one word 'the deviants' – will have to face serious negative consequences. In fact, this is precisely what happened in England. The non-conformists established their own congregations which ignored the Established Church, but had to pay a heavy price: 'They could not hold office, muncipal or national and by various statutes they were deprived even of the social right of maintaining schools and giving instruction' (Barker 1948: 171). This means that the idea of fusing citizenship and churchmanship as a goal is not a viable one even in uni-denominational nations, as the first is common to all and the second applies only to a section. In the contemporary world most nations (I am not referring to states) are multi-religious and multi-denominational, and hence religion cannot be the basis of nation formation.

The disastrous consequences of invoking religion to define nation is obvious in Bosnia, Israel or India, among other places. The mother tongue of the Muslims of Bosnia-Herzegovina is Serbo-Croat. In the 1953 census they were Yugoslavs, while most of the other two nationalities were identified as, or identified themselves as, Serbians or Croats. By the 1960s the category of Muslim was introduced. As a result they declared that they were Muslims, although some retained the previous identifications. In the 1971 census the Muslims became the largest identity group in the Republic, counting nearly 1.5 million and challenging the dominant position of the Serbs, who understandably did not like the shift. Both the Serbs and the Croats hoped that the Muslims would join them (Schopflin 1993: 174). The crucial issue here is the wrong labelling of a national category (Bosnians) as a religious category (Muslims). In fact, the three religious collectivities

– Catholics, Muslims, Orthodox – and the two linguistic groups –
Croats and Serbs – are all nationals of Bosnia, in that Bosnia is their
common homeland. The moment the national identity becomes the
monopoly of one or another collectivity in a common homeland, other
nationals are ethnified; they are instantly perceived as outsiders.
Herein lies the crucial significance of appropriate conceptualization
and its careful application.

In a very persuasive article Steven Grosby convincingly argues that
ancient Israel was a nation (1991: 229–65), a common homeland of the
twelve tribes with clear territorial boundaries, thereby contesting the
popular idea that nationality is an exclusively modern phenomenon.
He shows that the trans-tribal national sentiment of Israel was that of
a broader kinship which characterizes even modern nations. However, the difficulty arises when he attempts to identify the specificity
of the nation – and hence Israel – as one consisting of the putative
descendants of Abraham, Isaac and Jacob, who worshipped a common God:

> The ancient Israelites at some point during their history became a
> nation when they believed that the territory of Israel in its entirety
> belonged to them . . . and only to them because Yahweh their God and
> the only God to be worshipped in the land (and thus, whose law was
> the only law to be obeyed in that land) had promised it to them. (Grosby
> 1991: 242)

As a general characterization of ancient Israel this is probably admissible, but the problem arises when it is used as a frame of reference
to describe and define other nations (which Grosby often does),
and/or contemporary Israel. To start with, it may be noted that the
concepts of nation and state are conflated, in that Grosby refers to
citizenship, constitution and kingship of 'nations'. But I shall let it
pass, as the theme has already been discussed in chapter 3, and focus
on other problems. First, there are several nations both ancient and
contemporary whose entire territory did not belong to any particular
people. Second, to the extent that the peoples of a territory have
different religions they have different gods. Third, if there are different gods they may have different legal systems. Fourth, if each of
these gods promises the entirety of the land to his people and orders
them to obey only his laws, human life is bound to become nasty,
brutish and short – indeed, the nation will be dismantled quickly.

There are some other difficulties too with Grosby's position. Israel
itself eventually gave birth to other religions and both Christians and
Muslims also claim that they are the descendants of Abraham; that

Yahweh, the God of Abraham, is their God too; that the land of Israel is their ancestral homeland and that their ancestors were Israelites; and that their gods have promulgated laws to be obeyed by them. Grosby's analysis cannot cope with the problems arising out of these claims and contentions. And these are not the only problems. Gods migrate to conquer or colonize new lands, sometimes in near and sometime in far-off territories. In fact, Grosby acknowledges the former, when he refers to the unification of northern Israel and southern Judaea and to Yahweh becoming the god of northern Israel for the first time under David and Solomon (p. 258), and to 'the expanding boundaries of the Assyrian empire and hence of the expanding territory of the Assyrian god, "Assur" ' (p. 252). He points to the contrasting orientations of the two gods, Assur and Yahweh, the first expansive and the other delimiting. Further, '[the] deities of Christianity and Islam are universal, transnational deities', as Grosby recognizes (p. 254). If we follow the logic of what Yahweh did to Israel and her people, the whole world will have to be promised by the gods of Islam and Christianity to their respective followers.

What is the way out of this impasse? Grosby provides a clue, perhaps unwittingly: 'An empire encompasses within its territory many different peoples with their respective deities' (p. 251). This is also true of city-states. If we disapprove of empires and city-states because of their undemocratic structures and inadequate participative possibilities, it does not mean that we should reject these structures lock, stock and barrel. Selective retention and selective rejection are not only possible, but are often needed. The religious pluralism of empires needs to be revived and incorporated into contemporary nations. We need to conceptualize nation as a homeland of all those people who identify themselves with it, irrespective of their religious faiths. We must orient our gods to co-exist in harmony with other gods.

It is necessary to conclude the discussion on Israel with a brief reference to the formation of the state of Israel. The 1917 Balfour Declaration promised a Jewish homeland, and not the state of Israel. The King–Crane Commission sent by President Wilson in 1919 found that 90 per cent of the population in the territory identified for the Jewish homeland was non-Jewish (that is, Arab); after the establishment of Israel the Arab population was reduced to 10 per cent. Both Jews and Arabs had a legitimate moral claim to the territory of Israel, which was their common homeland. But the moment religion was invoked to define nation, and the project to build a state based on a single religious community was initiated, the processes of genocide and culturocide were unleashed. As Emerson rightly concludes:

The conception of creating a Jewish national home in Palestine could not possibly be squared with the principle of self-determination . . . on the basis of any generally accepted criteria. . . . Palestine has been the ancient Jewish homeland many centuries ago; but to accept the legitimacy of claims to self-determination whose basis is possession broken off two thousand five hundred years earlier would be to stir up such a host of conflicting and unrealizable demands as totally to discredit the principle. (1962: 313)

Religion and nation in India

Most state populations in the world today are culturally heterogeneous, and an important dimension of this is religious diversity. There is no polity in the contemporary world with such a staggering religious heterogeneity as India. Presently, I will examine the implications of employing religion to define nation and nationality by adverting to the claims made by Hindus, Muslims and Sikhs in India. I propose to do this based on two processes invoked by religious nationalists: territorialization and homogenization.[6]

By territorialization I mean a tendency on the part of a religious collectivity to claim that a specific territory is its exclusive homeland. To start with, it may be noted that such a claim is logically untenable in the case of proselytizing religions such as Buddhism, Christianity and Islam. (This is not to deny that these religions have sacred sites and cities, even city-states.) These religious collectivities have been dispersed across vast territories far beyond the lands of their origin, through conquest and colonialism. The project of Christianizing the world and the notion of a universal Islam both rebel against territorialization. In fact, the main anchorages of proselytizing religions are in alien lands. For example, while there are several Buddhist majority 'nations' in the world, those who profess Buddhism constitute a mere 0.7 per cent of the population in India, where Buddhism originated. The biggest two enclaves of Islam are South Asia (India, Pakistan and Bangladesh) and Indonesia. Christianity was appropriated first by Europe, and then it spread to Latin American, Africa and Asia.

However, the coterminality between territory and religion is logically sustainable in the case of non-proselytizing religions such as Judaism and Hinduism. In fact, ancient Israel was a nation in that it was a people with its own homeland (Speiser 1960: 157–63). Hinduism is also a non-proselytizing religion and the notion of 'Hindu Rashtra' (nation) is very much in vogue today. But a moment's reflection makes it amply clear that the project for a Hindu nation is not sustainable. This is evident from the differing boundary demarcations of Hinduism. That is, there is a series of Hindu identities and not just one ideal type. Let me list the three most prominent ones: first Hindus are simply the original and obvious inhabitants of Hindustan, that is, India; second, India is the common homeland of Hindus, that is, all those who profess religions that originated in India; and third, Hindus are those who belong to the clean castes and who occupy the Indo-Gangetic belt and speak Indo-Aryan languages.

The Hindu is thus defined in at least three different ways and by invoking different variables: territory, religion and caste or language, all of which pose problems in defining Hindus as a nation and/or nationality. I shall list these presently. It is true that 83 per cent of the Indian population is classified as Hindu in the census.[7] To begin with it may be noted that the claim that India is the Hindu homeland was made with reference to undivided India, in which the proportion of Hindus was much smaller than it is in divided India. On the other hand, undivided India had the largest Muslim population in the world. Even after partition, India remains the second biggest Muslim country. Similarly, 80 per cent of the world's Zoroastrians live in India. Hindu nationalists counter this point by suggesting that these people are outsiders (Oommen 1990b: 43–66), which in turn brings in the question as to the time-span required for the nativization of a people in a country. The Zoroastrians have been in India since the eighth century; the Muslims came to the Kerala coast as early as the seventh century; the Syrian Christians of Kerala claim to have been converts since AD 52. An overwhelming majority of Muslims and Christians are converts from Scheduled Castes and Scheduled Tribes, who were among the original inhabitants of India. Therefore, if one takes the criterion of nativeness seriously, a majority of both the Muslims and the Christians have a better claim to be Indian nationals, because the Aryan Hindus, who claim to be the original inhabitants, came to India only some 3,500 years ago.

Hinduism, although not proselytizing, is migratory. At least twelve million Hindus live outside the Indian subcontinent (Jain 1989: 299–304), which is the traditional sacred land of Hinduism. In some countries (e.g. Fiji, Surinam, Mauritius) they constitute majorities. Would it be correct to say that those Hindus who have settled down outside the Indian subcontinent cease to be Hindus because they do not live in their ancestral homeland? The absurdity of the question is patent, but it emanates from the assumptions made by Hindu nationalists. And where does one put the agnostics, rationalists and secularists in the scheme of Hindu Rashtra, or for that matter in any nation constructed on the basis of religion? Finally, the Hindu nationalists' claim implies the annexation of Nepal, the Hindu majority neighbour, as part of the scheme for consolidating the Hindu nation.

It is not true that only Islam and Christianity have colonized new territories and in that process either annihilated or marginalized the native populations. The dominant religions of Sri Lanka are Buddhism and Hinduism (both of Indian origin) and the original inhabitants of the country, the Veddas, constitute just one per cent of the Sri Lankan population today. In the process of Aryanizing India, the country's native populations were subjected to culturocide. Buddhism has been vigorously proselytist and Hinduism acutely assimilative. Therefore, religion–territory coterminality is not axiomatic even in the case of religions of Indian origin. The Hindus belong to a multiplicity of speech communities, that is, there are several Hindu nations. To grapple with this problem, Hindu nationalists project Sanskrit as the common ancient language of all Hindus, and Hindi, written in the Devanagari script, as the national language of India. But they encounter several difficulties and severe resistance in this context. First, although Sanskrit is a rich and ancient language, it is not a living language and is spoken only by a handful of people today. Second, Tamil has an equally legitimate if not better claim, as it is not only an ancient and rich language, but also a vibrant living language spoken by some 50 million people in India. Third, Hindi, defined expansively to include numerous dialects, is spoken only by 38 per cent of India's population. Finally, there are a dozen languages in India each of which is equally developed and spoken by 10 million or more people (Oommen 1990b: 43–66).

The fallacious claim about religion–territory coterminality is also implied in the claims advanced by Muslims and Sikhs that they constitute nations. The alien immigrant element in the Muslim population of South Asia is negligible; the overwhelming majority of Muslims are converts from local castes and tribes. Therefore their claims that particular areas of the Indian subcontinent are their homeland is legitimate and authentic not because they are Muslims, but because they have a moral right to these territories. If the Muslims were not natives but immigrants eager to return to their homeland (as the Jews did in the wake of the Zionist movement), they would not have succeeded in staking their claim. There are nevertheless several difficulties in advancing the claim that Muslims qua Muslims constitute a nation in India.

First, none of the areas claimed by the Muslims as their homeland (as in the case of other religious groups) was populated exclusively by them, despite substantial transfers of Hindu and Sikh populations from these areas. Therefore, the claim that they were and are Muslim homelands is not tenable not because Islam is an 'alien' religion, but because nativeness and nationhood cannot be defined in terms of religious faiths and affiliations. The so-called Muslim homeland is as much the homeland of the non-Muslims of that region.

Second, even if a section of the Muslims are immigrants to India, to the extent that the migration occurred several centuries ago, and since they identify with the territory presently inhabited by them as their homeland, the claim ought to be accepted as legitimate. This is no concession to the alien elements in the Muslim population because there are several alien elements among Hindus – Kashmiri Pandits, Magi Brahmins, Rajputs, to mention but a few – whose nativeness is not questioned by Hindu nationalists.

Third, Pakistan, which emerged in 1947, although populated predominantly by Muslims, could not be sustained as one nation for long because of the absence of geographical contiguity and linguistic uniformity. In fact, Islam became an irrelevant variable in maintaining the unity of Muslim Pakistan. Its split was the outcome of demands that were mainly based on territory and language.

Fourth, the Hindi-speaking Muslims, popularly referred to as Bihari Muslims, instantly became alien elements in Bangladesh, the state of the Bengali-speaking Muslims. Even the Hindi/Urdu-speaking Muslims, who had migrated to Pakistan from India, are not accepted as natives and remain Mohajirs, the stigmatized outsiders, even to this day. Thus the Muslim nationalists deny native status even to immigrant co-religionists. This clearly points to the superficiality of religious nationalism.

Fifth, the predominantly Muslim but multi-lingual Pakistan continues to have serious tensions and conflicts between its different linguistic groups – Punjabis, Sindhis, Baluchis – that is, the nations that constitute the state of Pakistan. Each of these collectivities defines its respective linguistic regions as its homeland. Thus it is clear that homeland can only be anchored to speech communities and not to faith communities.

Once India was partitioned, no territory could be claimed as a Muslim homeland, except for the Kashmir valley. However, this claim is ambivalent for two reasons. First, Kashmir itself is partitioned and apportioned between India and Pakistan for geopolitical reasons. Second, there are others in Kashmir (e.g. Kashmiri Pandits) who lay claim to the territory as their homeland with equal intensity and authenticity. In such a situation the only route available to those who falsely claim that the Kashmir valley is an exclusive Muslim homeland is to intimidate, terrorize and flush out those who make counter –claims. In the current exodus of Kashmiri Pandits from Kashmir, what one witnesses is the inevitable consequence of the perverse notion that there exists coterminality between territory and religion, that is, the territorialization of religion. It can be seen that the territorialization of religion leads to the ethnification of minority and weak nations.

After partition the Muslims of India did not have a decisive majority in any part of the country except in the Kashmir valley, the Laccadive and the Minicoy Islands. But Muslims constituted about 12 per cent of India's population, counting around 70 million in the 1950s. Though their absolute number was substantial, they were thinly dispersed all over the country. This made them susceptible to assimilation into the linguistic regions (nations) that they inhabited, which in turn necessitated the invention and maintenance of new symbols to preserve their socio-religious identity. The Urdu language, written in Persian-Arabic script, is the most important symbol invoked by the Muslims to highlight their cultural specificity and nationality within India. But the project remains ineffective in investing nationhood on Muslims on an all-India basis because of the pattern of their demographic distribution.

The language of the majority of Muslims in India is not Urdu; it is only in two provinces – Uttar Pradesh and Bihar – that one finds Muslims who are also Urdu speakers. These two states account for only one-third of the Muslim population and one-half of the Urdu speakers in India. In Jammu and Kashmir, although the official language is Urdu, the Urdu speakers constitute a meagre 0.27 per cent of the Muslim population. On the other hand, most of the Urdu speakers are from states where the proportion of Muslims is very low. This disjuncture between Urdu and Islam has further muted the possibility of Urdu nationalism emerging as an authentic force in independent India (cf. Brass 1974).

The Sikh claim to nationhood also assumes religion–territory coterminality. But before India's partition (in 1921), the Punjab, now claimed to be the Sikh homeland, had a Muslim majority of 51 per cent. By 1961, although the Muslim population was reduced to a mere 2 per cent (both because of re-allocation of territory and migration), the Sikhs constituted only 33 per cent and the Hindus were in the majority with 64 per cent. As religion was not accepted as the basis of constituting politico-administrative units in independent India, the only hope was to carve out a Sikh majority province by employing language as the criterion. The Sikh leadership therefore staked its claim for a separate province based on the Punjabi language, which was formed in 1966. However, even in the new province the Sikhs had only a thin majority of 53 per cent. Thus, in spite of two successive partitions in 1947 and 1966, the Punjab cannot be viewed as the exclusive homeland of the Sikhs; they do not constitute a decisive demographic majority. The remaining 47 per cent of the non-Sikh population also considers Punjab to be its homeland. But a fatal error by Punjabi Hindus in disclaiming their real mother tongue provided a thin veneer of legitimacy to the crystallization of the idea that the Punjab is the Sikh homeland (see Nayyar 1966).

There is another reason why the Sikh claim to Punjab as their homeland is untenable. Although 78 per cent of Indian Sikhs live there, the remaining 22 per cent are dispersed all over India. This demographic dispersal may be traced to two factors. First, in the wake of partition a substantial proportion of the Sikhs who had migrated to India settled outside the Punjab. Second, the Sikhs are an enterprising migratory community in search of economic opportunities. The logical corollary of their insistence that Punjab is their exclusive homeland is to render instantly the Sikhs outside Punjab and the non-Sikhs inside Punjab as aliens, outsiders and refugees.

The point I want to make is this. A people's claims to nationhood are based on their moral claim on a specific territory as their homeland. Such a claim cannot be sustained by a religious collectivity because of the disjuncture between religion and territory. It follows that the claim to nationhood by Hindus, Muslims and Sikhs based on the assumption and the argument that the whole of India or specific parts of India constitute their exclusive homeland is untenable.

The claim to nationhood or nationality by a religious collectivity necessarily implies the process of cultural homogenization, that is the creation and imposition of a common lifestyle. In independent India this has been articulated in different contexts and forms. I will pursue the present discussion with special reference to Hindus and Sikhs, and this for two reasons. First, the claim to nationhood by these religious collectivities has not yet been realized, unlike in the case of the Muslims in the Indian subcontinent. Second, the Hindus and Sikhs were, and to a certain extent today still are, sharing a common lifestyle, although every effort is made to over-emphasize their specificities, while ignoring the commonalities.

The Hindu advocacy of homogenization has been articulated in different ways. If in the 1960s and the 1970s the preferred phrase was 'Indianization', now it is 'Hindutva'. Hindu nationalists insist that the advocacy is disassociated from and devoid of any narrow religious context and content, but refers to a lifestyle common to the people of India as a whole, and hence a Hindu is one who follows this lifestyle. If lifestyle includes matters of dress, food, worship, art forms, marriages and family patterns, there is very little common even to the

Hindus of different regional-lingustic areas, quite apart from the different religious communities of India. This, however, is not to deny that there exists a civilizational unity encompassing the multiplicity of collectivities inhabiting India, but this envelops the people of South Asia as a whole and is not confined to the population of the Indian state.

There is another context in which the advocacy of homogenization surfaces in India, namely, that of a common civil code. It should be noted here that a common civil code for Indian citizens is a constitutional promise, and liberals, secularists, rationalists, feminists and atheists also support its implementation. But when a uniform civil code is advocated by Hindu nationalists the conservative elements among the religious minorities perceive in it a threat to the preservation of their cultural identity. It is useful to recall here that the Hindu conservatives resisted tooth and nail the introduction and implementation of the Hindu Code Bill because they feared that it would erode the specific cultural identity of the Hindu community (Donald Smith 1963). On the other hand, the very fact that such a commonly applicable bill had to be formulated points to the very diversity of Hinduism, as it existed in different regions and among various communities of India.

To those religious communities whose members are distributed across different states and who have a common religious authority, the idea of terminal loyalty to the state, particularly when the state is not governed by their co-religionists according to the injunctions of the religious texts, would be an anathema. Herein lies the source of rupture in the Hindu nationalists' advocacy of a uniform civil code and its resistance by conservative elements, particularly among Muslims and Christians. It may be recalled here that the state in independent India has not yet mustered sufficient courage to introduce the constitutionally promised uniform civil code, but it did implement the Hindu Code Bill in spite of resistance from conservative Hindu elements.

The Sikh project of cultural homogenization has been more successful because the Sikhs are a minority, because they are uni-lingual, and because Sikhism is more egalitarian in its value orientation. And yet the attempt at homogenization faces, and is likely to face, several obstacles. First, the dominant agent of Sikh nationalism is the Jat peasantry concentrated in rural areas. In the event of Sikh religious nationalism succeeding in wresting a state for itself, the 'protection' now available, particularly to the Mazhabi (Scheduled Caste) and the Nirankari (a sect not recognized by the Sikh ecclesiastical authority) Sikhs from the Indian state as well as from the all-India political parties, will disappear. Understandably, the Sikh segments that are likely to perceive the emergence of a Sikh state as a sure invitation to Jat domination are almost certain to put obstacles in the process of homogenization.

Second, the Sikh project of homogenization would inevitably mean that the current freedom available to *sahajdharis* (shaven ones) will diminish. Not only will the insistence on being *keshdharis* (unshorn ones) intensify, but in all probability brute force may be used to transform the 'deviants' into conformists. In fact, available evidence suggests that even *keshdharis* will be forced to follow a more rigorous and puritan lifestyle (e.g., by giving up smoking). Inevitably, organized resistance to such codes of conduct will eventually crystallize when the insistence on homogenization becomes more intense and authoritarian.

Third, the urban, secular middle-class professionals, bureaucrats and intellectuals (both *keshdharis* and *sahajdharis*) are likely to be indifferent, if not hostile, to the efforts to introduce a more uniform lifestyle. Pushed to the wall, they may even articulate their opposition. These spokes in the wheel of homogenization may abort the fruition of Sikh religious nationalism.

The ideology of homogenization, then, is not only geared to the standardization of values, norms and practices. It also implies the revival of obsolescent traditional values, norms and practices which are not relevant to the present, and the imposition of those values on others, both 'deviant' co-religionists and religious minorities. This is so because the reference point of homogenization advocated by religious nationalists invariably relates to the original vision and practices of their founding fathers, but ignores the context of the latters' advocacy. That is, religious nationalisms carry with them the inevitable tendency of revivalism. Further, religious nationalists endeavour to create a societal ethos buttressed by the values of the dominant religion within the polity. Neither Hindu nor Sikh nationalism is an exception to this inherent tendency.

To conclude, I have argued in this chapter that two objective factors – de-territorialization and miscegenation – make it impossible to invoke race as a basis of nation formation. More importantly, to form nations on the basis of race is to accept racism as an ideology – an unacceptable proposition. Similarly, de-territorialization and proselytization objectively render it impossible to conceive of nations based on religion. Further, to consider religion as the basis of nation formation is to endorse religious nationalism, which would eventually degenerate into religious fundamentalism.

Part II
The Empirical Process

The Trajectory of Ethnification

5

Colonialism and European Expansion

I have suggested in chapter 4 that neither race nor religion are relevant factors in nation formation in the contemporary world because both are de-territorialized in the context of colonialism. However, de-territorialization of religion is a phenomenon that started much earlier, with the spread of Buddhism (particularly at the time of Emperor Asoka in the third century BC) from India to other Asian countries. But there is a crucial distinction between de-territorialization of religion in pre-colonial and colonial times; in the former it was the religion that migrated, in the latter it is the people. This led to the creation of the predominantly Christian New World, and to the conversion of a substantial population to Christianity in the non-European Old World – Asia and Africa. The latter fact holds true for Islam too, which also vigorously indulged in conversion. This proves that while the religious conversion of a people as such need not ethnify them, their dislocation from their homelands does. But if the religion into which conversion occurs is viewed as 'alien' by the cultural mainstream, the converted may feel ethnified.

Colonialism ethnified three distinct categories of people: the original inhabitants of the New World, that is, the First Nations; those who were brought to the New World as slaves, that is, the Africans; and those who were exported to the colonies as indentured labourers, that is, the Asians.[8] The nature and processes of ethnification varied in each case and I will discuss them sequentially. But before that a few general remarks will be in order.

The Hobbesian advocacy of the right of the people living without adequate means of survival in densely populated regions of the world to migrate to sparsely populated regions provided European colonialism with the required legitimacy. But the Hobbesian warning that such migrants were not to exterminate the local people or snatch from them their possessions was seldom heeded in the New World. The legitimation for colonizing the Old Worlds of Asia and Africa, which were densely populated, was found in the civilizing mission of colonialism. Even Karl Marx, who categorically denounced colonialism, thought that the emancipation of India from her age-old morass was the unconscious tool of history in the hands of Britain. Luthy is more categorical in his positive assessment of European colonialism: '*Europe's colonization of the world was neither a chain of crimes nor a chain of beneficence; it was the birth of the modern world itself*; not one of the former colonial peoples remember it with gratitude; for it was alien rule, but none wishes to turn the clock back, and that is colonialism's historical justification' (1957: 7; italics in original).

The 'nationalists' from the colonies clearly rejected this view. Jawaharlal Nehru, for example, contended that the ideology of British rule in India was that of 'the *herrenvolk* and the master race' (1952: 68–9). Abdulgani was more explicit: 'In our experience colonialism is the child of capitalism. In its inevitable wake colonialism brought us national disunity and poverty of a degree which has probably never been known in the West. . . . The development, physical and mental, of our peoples has been stunted by colonialism . . .' (1955: 44). However, there is a crucial difference between what colonialism did in Africa and Asia, and what it did in the New World. In the latter, colonialism subjected the original inhabitants to a process of utter marginalization in their own homeland. This has become a deep-seated psychic fear in the case of all people who are threatened with extinction, marginalization and minoritization, irrespective of the sources from which they are facing the threat.

The following sample of quotations is taken from Horowitz (1985: 176–9) who reports from different authors: 'The Fijian National Party was to prevent Fijians from succumbing to competition as the North American Indians, Hawaiians, and Maoris had done'; the Sindhis (from Pakistan) 'do not want to be turned into red Indians'; political leaders of the Malay Party in Malaysia warn that the Malays might become 'like Red Indians in America'; the tribals of Bihar (India) fear that if they are dispossessed of their land, 'they will become extinct like the American Indians'; Karens in Burma 'believe that a Burmese-dominated nation . . . will mean their gradual extinction'; the Muslims of the Philippines are fearful of eventual extinction. These examples are not exhaustive but indicative, and point to the fact that the ultimate result of ethnification is not only culturocide but also genocide. And it is true and widely believed that the First Nations were subjected to these processes. In what follows I will briefly describe the process of ethnification which the First Nations were subjected to in Australia, Canada and the United States of America.

The First Nations

In order to appreciate the damage done to the First Nations one must note that these three countries – Australia, Canada and the USA – have 18 per cent of the earth's land surface, but only 6 per cent of its population. Of their total populations, barely 1 per cent consists of the original inhabitants and about 90 per cent is of European origin. To get a clearer picture of the process of ethnification I will provide a brief demographic profile of the First Nations, starting with the United States of America.

The earliest settlers, the Red Indians, subsequently referred to as American Indians and more recently labelled as Native Americans, have been gradually displaced from most of their ancestral territory. Currently, they constitute less than 1 per cent of the total US population. Of these, nearly 50 per cent live in reservations created specifically for them, the remaining being either 'integrated' with others living in mixed localities, or persisting as 'cultural islands' in agency towns. The 260 reservations, with a mere 750,000 persons, are self-governed entities, outside the jurisdiction of the US Constitution. The isolationist policy of the American state, coupled with the 'retreatist' mentality persisting among a minority of the natives, has resulted in their being left behind. Today, they have the lowest average income in the USA. As Jarvenpa observes (1985: 29): 'Reservations and reserves [have] perpetuated racial segregation, administrative paternalism and a lower class status for Indian people.' And in the ethnic stratification of the United States, the Native Americans constitute the last but one layer, just above the Afro-Americans.

Estimates of the number of Native Americans at the time of contact with the Europeans vary between 2 and 5 million (see Snipp 1987). In the four centuries following this contact, and by the early twentieth century, their population had dwindled to about 250,000. The factors contributing to this dramatic decline were disease, war, forced migration and slavery (Nagel and Snipp 1987: 1–41). The fact that their numbers dropped substantially soon after the emergence of the 'first of the new nations' as a state is particularly important. From 1920 onwards, however, the population of Native Americans started increasing, and by 1980 they numbered 1,423,000. The leading factors contributing to this stupendous increase include a federal policy that helps to stabilize their land base and which provides specific services to reservations; the urbanization of Native Americans; and a change in the Census Bureau's definition of 'Indian' which began to accept the respondents' own self-definition of race (Nagel and Snipp 1987).

The nature and content of self-definition by a collectivity is crucial in determining its identity. Invoking two perspectives on ethnic identity – fixed and fluid – Nagel and Snipp (1987: 7) conclude: 'Some portion of the 1.4 million American Indians no doubt conforms to the fixed identity model – continuously, biographically and culturally American Indians. Another portion of the 1.4 million American Indians conforms to the fluid identity model – discontinuously, situationally and volitionally American Indians.' As for the content of self-definition, there are two possible referents in the present case: specific tribes or the broad category of Native Americans. The 1980 census data reveals that Native Americans tend to be affiliated to tribes that are federally recognized, because 'federal recognition endows tribes with legal, material and cultural resources that greatly enhance their survival' (Nagel and Snipp 1987: 18).

In terms of my conceptualization, the Native Americans who live in reservations and agency towns are national groups: they are in their own homeland and are able to maintain their own distinct style of life. Only those Native Americans who are dislocated from their original habitats, and not fully assimilated, constitute an ethnic group. But, because they ignore the distinction between nation and ethnie, most analysts put all Native Americans into the same category. On the other hand, given the US federal policy of according official recognition to specific tribes, the Native Americans tend to underplay their 'pan-Indian' national identity. 'Pan-Indianism is still a segmented, decentralized political movement, and some tribes have remained relatively autonomous ethnic enclaves removed from the mainstream of pan-Indian political ideology' (Jarvenpa 1985: 43).

Van den Berghe (1983: 238–52) identifies three elements common to the policy pursued by the colonizers in Australia, Canada and the USA. First, the use of military operations aimed at the deportation or extermination of the native population; second, de-tribalization through a process of inter-breeding by means of extra-marital relations between native women and white men, creating a stigmatized segment of population unacceptable to the dominant society; third, by conferring a special legal status and creation of machinery of internal colonialism to administer groups on a collective basis, giving birth to 'reservations'. The reservations had a twin function: releasing land for the white immigrants, and ensuring the isolation of a population cognizable as 'alien', which in effect meant territorial apartheid. In so far as the First Nations were transformed into ethnies, the rationale of applying a different set of norms and values became justifiable in their case. Thus, limited autonomy was conceded to reservations, though it has often been wrongly referred to as pluralism, the equivalent principle of 'separate but equal' that was applied to the blacks.

It is useful to recall here the four broad processes identified by Blauner (1972) in the case of reservations in the USA, and which are equally applicable to Australia and Canada. First, involuntary incorporations on reservations, and group segregations which provided a framework for keeping the natives apart from the general population; second, the provision of special legislations and specific administrative arrangements, which thereby maintained a façade of autonomy, while undermining political self-determination through state controls; third, the introduction of a set of debilitating economic restrictions which not only curtailed the self-sufficiency of the group, but blocked the mobility of the individual; fourth, the substitution of the cultural ethos of the community by the replacement of the native religion and language with those of the colonizer. It is thus clear that in the process of colonization the First Nations were reduced to small and scattered minorities dominated by a majority with a different cultural, religious and linguistic background. A few broad features of this process may be listed here.

First, the dominant group or the state lumped together a large number of distinct nations, which differed in terms of territory, language, dialect, modes of earning a livelihood, and the like, into one category, by resorting to shorthand labels such as 'Indians', and 'aborigines'. This strategy of 'encompassing ethnicity' distorted the identity of the First Nations. Second, the nationals were displaced from their original habitats (that is, their 'nations' were dismantled), which subjected them to a process of ethnification by depriving them of their moral claim over their ancestral homeland. A third feature was the dispersal of the nation into new and unfamiliar territories where they were treated as outsiders, aliens and refugees. A fourth was the creation of enclaves (that is, reservations) into which these nations were consigned and to which only very limited autonomy was conceded. But given their small size and dispersed locations most of the enclaves were neither economically nor politically viable, so that the effective power and control had to be retained by the colonizing state. Fifth, the assimilation of those nationals who choose to live in urban areas, usually as an under class, generally led to their pauperization and immiseration. Sixth, 'civilizing' and 'Christianizing' these nations eventually culminated in de-culturation, as they not only lost their own culture but failed to internalize a new one. In short, the 'gifts' of colonization in the end meant robbing the nationals of their land and their cultural integrity, and their being consigned to the bottom of the stratification system. This happened both in Australia and North America, in spite of the subtle variations in the different colonial systems (Bienvenue 1983: 30–42).

There is enormous documented evidence to show that on all indices – income, health, education – the First Nations rated dismally lower than the white colonizers. But what is not adequately known or documented is that the development of identity among them is inextricably intertwined with the demands for land rights and compensation for dispossession and loss of land rights. This point is well made by Roosens, who discusses at length the land rights of the original inhabitants of Canada. The 1763 royal proclamation recognized the rights of Indian and Inuit people over parcels of territory that were under the control of the federal government of Canada. In 1912 the province of Quebec accepted this obligation with regard to the aborigines in its territory:

> To this day, vast areas of land have never been militarily conquered or even inhabited by the French, English or later Canadians. Nor has that land been formally relinquished by the native peoples. This allows the Indians and Inuit to say that, under norms of Western law the appropriation of the land of their forefathers is largely a legal fiction, a one sided declaration put on paper by the colonizers without the agreement of the owners. (Roosens 1989: 21)

This position is actually vindicated by the James Bay Convention signed in 1975 between the Canadian federal government, the province of Quebec and private companies on the one hand, and groups of Cree Indians and Inuit people on the other. The convention was ratified in 1978, and consequently the Crees and Inuits surrendered 250,000 square miles of land, but retained exclusive or special rights to still larger chunks of ancestral land. They were also given a collective compensation of 225 million Canadian dollars, to be paid over a period of twenty years (Roosens p. 21). The point is that the claim of the First Nations over their ancestral land is not legal fiction, but is accepted even by the Canadian and Quebec governments. In fact, the representatives of the First Nations who negotiated with the Canadian government in 1969 demanded 85 per cent of the territory of Quebec.

Tribes inhabiting specific reservations had a sense of strong identity with them. The territory of the village had symbolic value, as their

ancestors had lived there for centuries and were buried there. Articulating the perspective of the Hurons, one of the tribes living in the
reservations, Roosens writes: 'who ever lived there with full rights, as
a co-owner was a Huron and not a Canadian'. Therefore, the Cana-
dians – that is, the non-native immigrants described thus by the First
Nations – should 'not be permitted to live there' (p. 97), according to
one of Roosens's informants. In spite of the tremendous symbolic
value the reservation had for the First Nations, the 1969 White Paper
of the Canadian government advocated the dismantling of all reservations as specifically Indian spaces (p. 97). This clearly points to the
acceleration of the process of ethnification at work.

Countering the process of ethnification unleashed by the dominant
group, the First Nations are insisting on their right to define themselves. This was well articulated by the Australian aboriginal historians at the time of the bicentenary celebrations in 1988:

> Despite institutionalization, enforced 'assimilation' and domination by
> the white presence, aboriginal people have remained since the British
> invasion a separate people. In the last fifteen years, with the removal of
> most restrictions on our freedoms, we have been moving rapidly to-
> wards a sense of ourselves as a separate nation. . . . It must be clear that
> Aboriginal contributions to Australian history have fundamental cultu-
> ral and political purposes. We are reclaiming our right to identify and
> define ourselves. (Working Party 1988: 21, 25)

This quest for a collective identity in their own ancestral homeland by
the aboriginal people – in other words, an assertion of their nationhood – is qualitatively different from the assertion of ethnic identity
of the territorially dislocated Afro-Americans.

As I have noted earlier there is only one case of a persistent claim for
a separate homeland in the New World by the settlers: that of the
French in Quebec. It is instructive to recall here that the political elite,
the bureaucracy and even social scientists reinforce this claim, but
ignore the more morally forceful claim of the First Nations. The political elite of Quebec do not have a uniform perception about the
position of their province in Canada; there are at least three clear
articulations. First, statist-oriented federal liberalism sees Canada in
terms of the equality of the French and English peoples. This view
recognizes the linguistic and cultural duality of Canada. Second, cul-
tural-nationalist liberalism insists that the 'cultural sovereignty' of
Quebec be recognized in the primacy of the French language in government and in private business in Quebec. In this view Quebec
should continue as a part of federal Canada. Third, the national-statist

perspective of the Parti Québécois (PQ), formed in 1967, wants to secede from Canada and establish Quebec as a sovereign state (Smiley 1977: 186–7). But none of these discourses provides any space for the recognition of the First Nations; in fact they are totally ignored. This is important from the perspective of our analysis because PQ defines the British–French relations in colonial terms, not recognizing the fact that the French too have colonized the First Nations.

Parti Québécois defines itself and is described by analysts as a national movement. This is a correct description because what the party aims at is to establish Quebec as the national homeland of the French speech community. But it commits a fatal error in denying the same right to the original inhabitants of the territory of Quebec – the First Nations. PQ insists that Quebec is different from the other provinces of Canada in that it is 'a homeland of a people with its own culture, its own history, its own language, and its own future. More-over its people are one of the two co-founders of Canada' (Roosens 1989: 79). Further, what the party demands is de-colonization by the English who, it is argued, have no right to colonize the territory of Quebec. The British have annexed the 'New France' without consult-ing or obtaining the consent of her people. What British colonialism aims at is the marginalization of the French language and the liquida-tion of the identity of the French people. Therefore, the party wants the French people to be 'masters in our own home'.

There is no space in the discourse of PQ for the First Nations. When it refers to them, it is done, paradoxically, to reinforce the French claim over the territory of Quebec. Thus, the fact that the James Bay Commission recognized the right of the provincial government of Quebec to sign the treaty with the First Nations is cited as evidence that Quebec is lord and master of its territory. In fact, the forefathers of the French Québécois are portrayed as pioneers in penetrating and domesticating the harsh land of Canada. 'They were the first to ex-plore America and certainly the first to occupy Canada. The PQ never mentions colonization of the Amerindians. The French community is not presented as a colonial authority but as a colonized people . . . ' (Roosens 1989: 81–2).

The 'Dorin Commission', named after the chairman of the com-mission appointed to assess the response of the Amerindians of Can-ada to the White Paper of the minister of Indian Affairs, presented its report in 1971. The report recognized that the province of Quebec did not fulfil its obligations to the Amerindians as stipulated in the 1912 agreement with the British Crown. It also referred to the paternalistic attitude adopted towards the First Nations by the Canadian and Quebec governments. It concluded that Indian rights were sustainable even in terms of Euro-Canadian legal norms. But as Roosens (1989: 78) notes:

> The Dorin Report is cleverly written to support Euro-Canadian inter-
> ests and takes no account of historical interpretations put forward by
> the Indians and the Inuit. . . . The argumentation in the report is based
> on the supposition . . . that it is inconceivable, almost ridiculous, and
> certainly anachronistic to challenge the integrity of the territory of the
> present province of Quebec. This integrity is accepted as an acquired
> right, a historical fact that has been consecrated by the passage of time.

Paradoxically, the time involved from the point of view of the French in Quebec is only two centuries, but the time perspective, spanning numerous centuries, of the First Nations in pressing their claim over the territory of Quebec is thrown to the wind. This orientation also pervades the several judicial pronouncements made by the courts in French Canada.

It is understandable that leaders of political parties, movements and even the bureaucracy, including the judiciary, should take a partisan view in matters such as the claims made by weak and minority peoples. But when social scientists ignore the force of both facts and reasoning, it is difficult to understand it. Most analysts of 'ethnic' conflicts in Canada focus only on those between the English and the French (see, for example, Smiley 1977: 197–203; Brazean and Cloutier 1977: 204–27). It is instructive to note here that the French constituted an absolute majority only in Quebec (81 per cent) and had a substantial presence in New Brunswick (34 per cent) in 1971. Speakers of 'other mother tongues', that is, other than English and French, constituted a majority (50 per cent) in north-east territories and a substantial presence in six other territories (ranging from 14 to 27 per cent) (Smiley p. 180). The 'other mother tongues' are spoken mainly by the First Nations. But as their mother tongues are not conferred any official status by the state of Canada, the people themselves slip out of the analysis of the social scientists.

While arguing forcefully the case of Quebec, Brazean and Cloutier rightly remark that Canada was not formed in 1867, the year when the present federal political arrangement came into being. They push back the creation of Canada to 1774, when the French language and the Catholic religion were given official status (1977: 210). But the authors completely forget that for the First Nations, Canada was formed several centuries before 1774. Thus it is clear that the process of ethnification of the First Nations, which started with the onset of European colonialism, continues unabated. Further, it is abetted and perpetuated not only by politicians and bureaucrats, but also by social scientists.

Africans in the New World

Africans were brought mainly as slaves to the Americas in the course of five centuries, from the fifteenth to the nineteenth. Curtin estimates (1967: 268) that some 400,000 African slaves were brought to the USA; by the 1970s their descendants formed the black population, which amounted to 23 million. In contrast, 1.6 million Africans were taken to Spanish America and 3.6 million to Brazil. But, due to a different pattern of incorporation through miscegenation, the white–black dichotomy has disappeared in Latin America, and a colour continuum has emerged. North America and Latin America represent two different patterns in this context, and I will discuss the cases of Brazil and the USA at some length as illustrations.

The case of Brazil provides a contrast to that of the USA, and is interesting for two reasons. First, most of the 'exported' Africans were taken to Brazil, which now has the largest number of people of African descent of any state in the world, save Nigeria. Second, Brazil is often referred to as a 'racial paradise', and both the state and the white elite have persuaded themselves and others to believe that no racial problem exists there. Two routes are identified for the elimination of stratification anchored to race, and the discrimination that is based on it. The propagandists of racial democracy and racial paradise argue that the problem can be and is being solved through miscegenation in Brazil. The earlier goal had been the stamping out of the black population, through the process of 'whitening'. Latterly, the white population too is said to be disappearing, and the whole population is believed to be 'browning'. The most vocal advocate of this approach was Freyre 1946; 1959; 1963: 1–6). Modernization brought about by industrialization is the second route identified for the transformation of race relations. According to this view, with increasing industrialization, ascriptive socio-racial and primordial relations will disappear in favour of achievement-oriented and class-based social relations more appropriate to modern society. The most visible representative of this approach is Fernandes (1969).

Both these approaches have been criticized, but we are here concerned only with the first. It has been pointed out that miscegenation has not led to the disappearance of race or discrimination based on race, but has only created a veritable continuum of physical types. Discrimination continues subtly. Be that as it may, it is clear that racial riots and black social movements are relatively few in Brazil, and the crass discrimination based on race or colour in everyday life is not experienced as in the USA (see Hasenbalg n.d.), although the race–class conjunction unfolds the familiar pattern. Thus, even after a century following the abolition of slavery, the residential segregation of blacks and mulattoes is evident in urban Brazil based on their class position. The mulattoes and pardos occupy an intermediate position between the blacks and whites. A disproportionate number of non-whites live in rural Brazil where there are far fewer opportunities for upward social mobility. The whites are concentrated in the industrially prosperous south-east. In 1980, while 64 per cent of the whites lived in the south-east, only 25 per cent of the non-whites lived there. In 1980 74 per cent of the whites and 60 per cent of the non-whites were urban residents.

Accessibility to education too varied based on race. Although free public education is available up to the eighth grade in Brazil, the average years of education in 1976 were 4.5 for whites, but only 2.9 for non-whites. According to the 1980 census, 48 per cent of non-whites had had less than one year of school education, while the figure for the whites was 25 per cent. The inequality increases as the level of education goes up. In 1980, 9 per cent of the whites and 4 per cent of the non-whites between the ages of 9 and 11 had received schooling. In contrast, 5 per cent of the whites had 12 or more years of education but only 0.8 per cent of non-whites had the same level of education.

This inequality necessarily persists in the occupational context. In 1980, 25 per cent of the whites and 10 per cent of the non-whites were in the non-manual occupational groups. The unskilled and underpaid workers were mainly non-whites. Similarly, in agriculture and domestic service, non-whites were represented disproportionately. Understandably, the income inequalities between the whites and non-whites were substantial, given the disparities in education and occupation. Thus, in spite of racial democracy, the inequality between the whites and non-whites persists (Hasenbalg n.d.), although a small, visible, urban middle class has emerged among the non-whites.

However, it is of great importance to note that although the ideology of Afro-Brazilianism is not altogether absent among Brazilian blacks, there is no effort on the part of the Brazilian population of African descent to migrate to other destinations, including Africa, and/or to establish a new homeland. This is in sharp contrast to the situation in the USA. Generally speaking, the people of African descent view Latin America as their homeland as much as people of other racial backgrounds. This is a testimony to their transformation from an ethnie to a nation. In contrast, the collective alienation of the US

Negro is telling in that it is articulated through a variety of social protests and movements.

Brought to the USA as slaves, the Negroes have had a chequered history of struggle, protest and gradual emancipation (Franklin 1967; Meier and Rudwick 1975) and yet they still largely make up the lowest societal layer. American Negroes have latterly been labelled as Black Americans, the semantic change being indicative of the increasing dignity with which others perceive them, and they define themselves. The most recent label preferred by them is Afro-Americans, suggestive of their attachment to their ancient ancestral homeland. They now constitute about 12 per cent of the American population. The policy of affirmative action initiated by the state facilitated the upward mobility of a large number of blacks. The vast majority of them, however, are still concentrated in the lower income groups, and income disparity between them and the whites still persists (Farley 1984). Concentrated in specific urban settlements, the Afro-Americans could capture political power in several city governments, leading to the phenomenon of the 'blackening of urban America', a phrase with a racist motif, but one that captures their spatial distribution pattern. This, in turn, however, has reinforced the segregationist syndrome in the US metropolitan schools, which cater mainly for black children (Farley 1985: 18–20).

While the American dilemma, represented by the gap between constitutionally guaranteed rights and privileges and their translation into practice, to which Myrdal (1944) called attention five decades ago, still persists, it had certainly been reduced by the 1980s. There is no consensus in this regard, however, and there exist at least three distinct views. First, there is the optimistic view, which holds that the practice of racial discrimination has declined considerably, if not disappeared entirely, and that a person's skin colour has little to do with his or her achievements in education and occupation. Second, there is the pessimistic perspective, which portrays the changes that have occurred as superficial and minimal. Third, there is the cautionary opinion, which holds that mobility among the blacks has led to sharp differentiation among them, between a successful elite group and an impoverished underclass.

After a careful examination of the available data, Farley (1985: 4–28) suggests that none of these views can be sustained. While in sectors such as education, occupation and earnings of employed workers there is considerable reduction of disparity between the whites and blacks, there is no improvement in regard to employment. Further, 'there is a great deal of convincing evidence showing that blacks and whites seldom share the same urban neighbourhoods . . . and that

economic factors account for little of the observed residential segregation of blacks from whites' (Farley 1985: 17). This racial segregation is
not a consequence of the desire of the Negroes to live in all-black
areas; in fact many prefer to live in racially mixed areas (Pettigrew
1973: 21–84). In regard to schooling, the picture is mixed in that in
most rural areas of the South, in small and medium-sized cities in all
regions and in southern metropolises where schools are organized on
a countywide basis, black and white children attend the same schools.
Similarly, the majority of black college students now do not go to
traditionally black colleges, but attend predominantly white colleges
and universities. Thus, the dual educational system is disappearing at
a rapid speed (Bullock and Lamb 1984). On the other hand, the changing demographic profile of the largest metropolises of the USA results
in their educational institutions being predominantly black. It is clear
that race and colour continue to be critical in transforming the Afro-
Americans into a distinct collectivity.

It is instructive to examine briefly at this juncture the career of the
concept of equality in the USA with special reference to the blacks, to
understand the present situation. Alexis de Tocqueville (1956) was
probably one of the earliest to recognize and eulogize the near universal existence of equality as a value and practice in the USA. He
attributed this to the novel idea of individualism, which took deep
root in the first 'New Nation' as against the persisting feudal values
and practices of the Old World. And yet, Tocqueville seems to be
referring only to the clauses and content of the US Constitution and
not to the values and attitudes that prevailed in American society at
that time (the mid-nineteenth century). If indeed he based his observations on the empirical scene of the day, it was at best confined to the
white intra-racial scenario and not the inter-racial situation that en-
compassed the white masters and their Negro slaves. Stephen A.
Douglas, an articulate representative of the Republicans, declared on
21 August 1858: 'I believe this government was made on the white
bases. I believe it was made by white men, for the benefit of whites
and their prosperity for ever, and I am in favour of confining citizenship to white men, men of European birth and descent, instead of
conferring it upon negroes, Indians and other inferior races' (from
Angle 1958: 111). Even Abraham Lincoln, the incurable democrat who
had argued that there was no reason why the Negro should not be
entitled to all the natural rights listed in the Declaration of Independence, conceded that the physical difference between the whites
and the Negroes 'will probably forever forbid their living together
upon a footing of perfect equality', and agreed with Douglas that the
white and the Negro were not equals in colour, 'perhaps not in moral

and intellectual attainment', but insisted that, 'in the right to eat the bread . . . which his own hand earns, he is my equal and . . . the equal of every living man' (Angle 1958: 117). The ambivalence in Lincoln's position was loud and clear, as he held the view that equality, as enumerated in the Declaration of Independence, could be guaranteed to the Negro without conferring the rights associated with full-fledged citizenship.

Anthropological research concludes that 'There is no fundamental difference in the ways of thinking between primitive and civilized men', and 'A close connection between race and personality has not been established' (Boas 1963: 8). Yet, Americanization, that is, total assimilation with the dominant Anglo-American mainstream, or the idea of a melting-pot, did not find favour with many because both would eventually have led to the destruction of the previous identity. Consequently, the 'pluralist' alternative was advocated as the only viable solution. This arose out of the belief that each race and religion had a distinctiveness that ought to be preserved, and every attempt at assimilation would be degenerative in terms of inheritance and undesirable in view of the social consequences. This version of pluralism, which is precariously proximate to relativism, gradually became articulated in a modified version: 'separate but equal'. It seems, in retrospect, that this doctrine facilitated the proliferation and subsequent fusion of several proximate layers, although the basic differences across racial groups persisted. However, President Harry Truman's report on the Commission on Civil Rights, published in 1947 holds the view that separatism was incompatible with equality.

These developments gradually led to the launching of the policy of affirmative action as a remedial measure to facilitate the mobility of the disadvantaged. It is of signal importance to note here that the principle of special opportunity for some openly recognizes inequality based on group membership. On the other hand, the belief in equal opportunities for all on the basis of citizenship was based on the individual as the unit of society. These two principles have often been in conflict, and are perceived differently by the traditionally privileged and those who benefited through the policy. If affirmative action is viewed by the underprivileged as an essential prerequisite for their well-being, it is recognized as a definite obstacle by the privileged, as it endangers the principle of 'merit', and blocks achievement. This is so because the privileged believe that affirmative action is anchored not to equality of opportunity, but to distributive justice.

It is necessary to situate the policy of affirmative action in the USA in its historical context. First, the policy became necessary because the much-heralded value of equality of opportunity never left the drawing-board as far as the blacks were concerned, although it had been theoretically 'in practice' for two centuries in the USA. It is well known that the blacks were deliberately excluded from the process of industrialization, and when whites and blacks began to compete in the industrial marketplace the result was friction. Had a black proletariat emerged in the normal course of events, it would in turn have resulted in the existence of a black bourgeoisie through inter- generational occupational mobility. In the absence of such an occupational base, and in the context of heightened social and material deprivation wrought by status incongruence, perhaps the only plausible political response in a democratic polity was to take recourse to the policy of affirmative action.

Second, not only did a black industrial proletariat not emerge, but the pauperization and marginalization of the Negroes took place. This was in spite of the fact that the material condition of the slaves in the USA had been much better compared not only with blacks elsewhere, but even with the white peasantry. To quote Sowell: 'The average life span of nineteenth century American slaves was slightly below that of Whites in the United States, but the same as the life span in Holland and France and greater than in Italy and Austria. Slaves in the US lived an average of thirty six years, peasants in Ireland nineteen years' (1981: 187). And yet, the take-off in terms of mobility did not occur in the case of the US blacks. A third point is that the artificial situation created by affirmative action led to an internal polarization among the blacks. As Marable pointed out:

> The highest 20 per cent of all black wage earners held almost 45 per cent of the aggregate income received by all black families; the highest 5 per cent share of aggregate black income was 15.9 per cent. . . . The point here is that economic difference between the growing black elite and the majority of black wage earners is even greater than it is between white workers and the white petty bourgeoisie. (1980: 95–6)

Fourth, this income disparity is an indirect measure of the collapse of the institution of the family among the majority of Afro-Americans. Sowell, a virulent critic of the policy of affirmative action, admits that there has been a steep increase in the incidence of female-headed households among blacks in recent decades. And the 'proportion of black population that is working has been declining both absolutely and relatively to whites. . . . Black teenager unemployment in 1978 was more than five times what it had been thirty years earlier' (Sowell 1981: 222). The latest trend is even more frightening. By the mid-eighties more than half of the black children were born to single women;

births to single black women increased from 38 per cent in 1970 to 57 per cent in 1982 (Norton 1985: 93). Further, 'the average black child can expect to spend more than five years of his childhood in poverty: the average white child, ten months' (Norton p. 79).

Clearly, inequality between blacks and whites has persisted, in spite of the acceptance of individual-based equality and its 'practice' for two centuries. On the other hand, a small but artificial black middle class has emerged in a short span of two decades, thanks to the policy of affirmative action.

It is clear that racial inequality persists both in Brazil and in the USA. But there are two crucial differences. First, while in Brazil the colour line is a continuum, in the USA it is largely a dichotomy between the whites and the blacks. Second, the collective alienation of the people of African descent is pronounced in the USA but is relatively absent in Brazil: in the former they remain largely an ethnie (outsiders); in the latter they have become nationals (insiders). The single most import-ant factor accounting for this transformation seems to be miscegena-tion in Brazil, and its absence in the USA.

Ethnified Asians

The third category ethnified by colonialism that I propose to discuss in this chapter is of Asian background. Primarily of Indian and Chinese descent, these people were taken to British colonies to work as contract labourers. The export of indentured labour created 'a new system of slavery', to recall the evocative phrase of Hugh Tinker. Although the departure years coincided with poor harvests and/or famine, the coolies (that is, wage workers) were frequently tricked into the process of migration and were subjected to the most inhuman treatment not only during the voyages, but also at their points of arrival and in the work place (see Tinker 1974: 126–235). From the numerous cases, I shall discuss the situation only in two countries – Fiji and Malaysia – as they have specificities of their own and both reinforce my argument.

Fiji consists of 844 islands in the South Pacific. These islands became a British colony on 10 October 1874, when Chief Cakoban ceded them to Britain. Three elements of British policy are of relevance here. First, land was not taken away from the Fijians, that is, the original inhabit-ants, as a result of which it was not available for commercial exploit-ation, and 90 per cent of it remained with the native Fijians during the colonial period. Second, non-Fijian labour was imported to work in the plantations of the Europeans. Thus, from 1879 to 1916 some 60,537 Indians were brought to Fiji. About 50 per cent of these workers returned to India, and those who remained became legal residents of Fiji for whom equal privileges, as other British subjects of the colony, were promised. By 1945 the Indians outgrew the native Fijians in number (Premdas 1993: 251–74). This policy had three implications: the Fijians were spared from working in modern plantations, which allowed them to continue their conventional lifestyle; the law implied that the British did not aspire to settle in Fiji, but to remain as guests; and even as the Indians were allowed to settle down and promised equality, they could not own any land. This is paradoxical, because the Indians were engaged mainly in agriculture, that is, as workers in sugar plantations. Thus ownership and cultivation of land was clearly disengaged. The third relevant element of British policy led to the creation of a separate Fijian administration, which recognized the traditional hierarchical political structure. This facilitated indirect British rule without coming into direct conflict with the native Fijians (Premdas pp. 252–3).

By 1990, 40 per cent of Fiji-Fijians (the original inhabitants) still depended on land and communally owned 83 per cent of the land in the name of some 7,000 patri-clans. As the law prohibits private individuals from selling land to non-Fijians, the Indians lease land from the Fijians; about 62 per cent of leased land is held by them. But a Fiji-Fijian urban middle class emerged thanks to the government's employment policy in the civil service, the military and the professions. On the other hand, their penetration in the business sector remained weak (Watters 1969).

Fiji-Fijians have interpreted the Deed of Cession of 1874, through which Fiji became a British colony, as a legal instrument conferring paramountcy, that is, the right to govern Fiji (Hagen 1978: 2–18). When popular representation began in 1904, although the 2,440 Europeans were represented through two nominated members, the 22,000 Indians were unrepresented. However, by 1916, one Indian was nominated to the House of Representatives. Fiji-Indians demanded adult franchise (it was advantageous to them, given the demographic distribution), but the Fiji-Fijians insisted on the communal roll system which favoured them. By 1966, a party system had emerged (Premdas 1993: 258–9). To start with Fiji had two parties. The Alliance Party (AP) combines three racial associations – one, the dominant partner, led by the Fijian chiefs; an association of general electors (Europeans, Chinese and others); and an Indian association, which is the weakest of the three. The second party is the National Federation Party (NFP), the bulwark of Fiji-Indians. Therefore, while the Indian votes were split, the Fijians voted as a block, ensuring the continuation of AP in power till 1977. In the general elections of that year the dominance of

AP and of the Fijian chiefs was challenged by the Fijian association within the Alliance, and a new party, the Fiji National Party (FNP) emerged. As a result, the Fijian vote was now split also. The AP was reduced to a minority party in the House of Representatives (24 out of 50), giving a thin majority (25 out of 50) to the Fiji-Indian NFP, which included an independent who supported the party. The sole representative of FNP was opposed to both AP and NFP (Murray 1980: 43–7).

The Governor-General, however, appointed the leader of AP as prime minister. This created not only a constitutional crisis, but also popular resentment among the Fiji-Indian community. It led to a constitutional crisis because the Governor-General acted arbitrarily, ignoring conventions and reinterpreting the powers of his office. This prompted the Fiji-Indians to demand constitutional reforms. The immediate cause for resentment was due to the fact that the claims of the NFP to form the government had been ignored, although it had a majority in the House of Representatives. From the perspective of the Fiji-Fijians, it is their natural right to rule in their ancestral homeland. For the Fiji-Indians, Fiji is their adopted homeland and they too have every right to rule the country. While both are citizens (although the Fiji-Indians would rightly bemoan their 'second-class' citizenship), the Fiji-Indians are not yet accepted as co-nationals by the Fiji-Fijians. The Fiji-Indians remain an ethnie, a community of outsiders in Fiji.

The ethnification of the Fiji-Indians is also evident from the fact that they are excluded from certain crucial sectors of the state. The public service is the largest single source of employment in Fiji. In 1968, out of 645 graduates with university degrees 464 were Indians, 77 Fijians, 63 Chinese, and 31 others, but this was not reflected in the employment pattern (Vasil 1984). The representation of Indians in the armed forces is extremely lopsided. In the 1970s, in a regular force of 395, 372 were Fiji-Fijians, 5 were Fiji-Indians and 18 others; of the 563 in the territorial force, 502 were Fiji-Fijians, 29 Fiji-Indians and 32 were others; in the naval squadron with a strength of 71, as many as 59 were Fiji-Fijians, 2 Fiji-Indians and 10 others (Premdas 1993: 267–9). Viewed against the fact that the population of Fiji-Indians constituted 51 per cent and that of Fiji-Fijians 44 per cent in 1975 (Murray 1980: 42) and that the demographic situation has not changed substantially since then, the under-representation of the former is blatantly clear. This fact is particularly pertinent for our analysis because, generally speaking, the tendency of every state is to recruit into the defence forces those persons whom one can trust. Those who are not full-fledged nationals have only a slim chance of being entrusted with the responsibility of defending the state borders.

The process of ethnification which was at work for several decades culminated in 1987 when the slogan 'Fiji for Fijians' was invoked, and the democratically elected government was overthrown by the military. According to the new constitution, only a 'native' Fijian can be a president or prime minister of Fiji. The Fiji-Fijians, with 46 per cent of the population, were allocated 54 per cent of the seats in the House of Representatives and 50 per cent of the positions in public services. Even in taxation, the Fiji-Fijians are favoured.

I would like to conclude the discussion on Fiji by listing factors which led to the ethnification of Fiji-Indians. First, they were uprooted from their ancestral homeland and were incorporated into the British colonial plantation system with an inferior status – as contract labour. Second, although the mainstay of Fiji-Indians was and continues to be agriculture (sugar-cane farming), they are not allowed to own the land they cultivate. This is particularly pertinent because sugar accounts for more than 50 per cent of Fiji's foreign exchange and 80 per cent of Fiji-Indians are cane farmers. Third, although the Fiji-Indians constitute a demographic majority, or nearabouts (around 49.5 to 51 per cent), they are not viewed as legitimate partners in the governance of their adopted homeland. Fourth, in spite of the fact that the educational advancement and achievements of Fiji-Indians is substantial, their representation in the public employment system is limited. Fifth, the mistrust with which they are viewed is amply evident in their gross under-representation in the defence forces. Finally, the popular slogan 'Fiji for Fijians' and the governmental measures to 'facilitate' Indian emigration from Fiji clearly reinforce the ethnic (outsider) status of Indians in Fiji.

The case of Malaysia is similar in several respects, but different in some aspects. If the major contenders in the theatre of power and politics in Fiji are Fiji-Fijians and Fiji-Indians, those in Malaysia are the Malays and the Chinese, with the Indians constituting the third group. Chinese migration to Malaya was accelerated in the first decades of the twentieth century. In 1911 only 8 per cent of the Chinese living there were born in Malaya; by 1923, 29 per cent of the Chinese in Malaya were Malay-born. Thus, the migrants became settlers within a relatively short span of time. In 1931 Chinese constituted 39 per cent of the population and the Malays 45 per cent, the rest being mainly Indians (Roff 1967: 110, 128). When the Chinese and Indians started demanding access to public employment and political representation, the Malays, already a demographic minority in their homeland, felt threatened.

The Malays were almost exclusively Muslims, and they dominated rural Malaya. The main occupational base of Indians, predominantly

Tamil-speaking Hindus, were the modern plantations started by the European colonizers. In contrast, the Chinese, largely Christians, dominated the urban scene with trade and commerce. This was reflected in the political situation too. While the Malay parties were initially led by the traditional aristocrats, gradually the civil servants and school teachers took over. In contrast, the Chinese parties were led by the business elite and the university-educated professionals (Horowitz 1985: 565).

The non-Malays, Chinese and Indians, were brought mainly by the British. But the non-Malays could not own land in Malaysia and the interests of Malays were protected by granting special rights to them. In 1957, when Malaysia got independence, the non-Malays constituted 50 per cent of the population, 37 per cent were Chinese, 11 per cent were Indians and 2 per cent others. The Malays were designated as the sons of the soil – Bumiputra – consisting of the Malays, the natives of Sabah and Sarawak. The cultural division of labour was fairly neat and clear. The Bumiputra were mainly rural, engaged in farming and fishing. The Indians gradually diversified occupationally, combining plantation work with urban retail trade and professions, thus joining the Chinese in the occupational structure. The control of the government was under the Bumiputra, who also ran the military and civil services (Mauzy 1993: 106–127).

The Bumiputra population gradually increased after independence, and by the early 1990s it came close to 60 per cent. The policy of special assistance started by the British is continued by the 'national' government and is expected to do so till economic parity comes about. The parity issue is relevant only in private sector non-agricultural occupations, as the Malays have the monopoly in land ownership and in government jobs. Parity in those areas where there exists disparity between the Malays and the non-Malays would mean cumulative domination by the former and further marginalization of the latter.

However, to allay this fear the government has promised to consider the demand of non-Malays for access to land and public employment. One of the policy documents of the government states: 'The non-Bumiputra expectation of greater access to public sector employment, educational opportunities and participation in land schemes will be considered together with the progress made by the Bumiputra in the private sector' (cited in Mauzy 1993: 120–1). The private sector under reference here means the small and medium-sized business enterprises in which the Chinese and the Indians dominate at present. In the meantime, the focus has gradually shifted with the liberalization of the economy, as exemplified by the following statement showing a policy slant: 'There will be more emphasis on the capabilities of the

Bumiputra to manage, operate and own business rather than on achieving specific numerical targets of equality of ownership' (cited in Mauzy p. 121). To bring about parity in business enterprises or to inject efficiency in management, government intervention is not likely to be an effective instrument. Therefore, disparity in the private sector between the Malays and non-Malays will persist. This being so, the present disparity in public sector employment between the Malays and non-Malays will also continue.

The ethnification of the non-Malays – the Chinese and the Indians – is brought about through three specific measures. The first is by officially designating the Malays as Bumiputras, ignoring the fact that most Chinese and Indians were also born and grew up in Malaysia. While they are citizens (second-class citizens at that), they are not nationals, as they are considered outsiders. Second, by denying equality of opportunity to non-Malays in public employment a sense of collective alienation is created among them. Third, the cultural policy of the state fosters Islam as the national religion, and Bahasa Malaysia as the national language, both of which are alien to the cultural heritage of the Chinese and the Indians. The recent demand by a section of Muslims to replace civil law by Islamic law and to use the Arabic script for Bahasa Malaysia is an indication of the aggravating process of ethnification of non-Malays.

The two Asian cases that we have dealt with clearly point to the process of ethnification to which the settler populations are subjected. In both cases immigration was occasioned by colonialism. And yet, the situation obtaining in these countries with regard to immigrants is radically different from that of the white immigrants in the New World. An immigrant collectivity's claim to legitimacy at the point of destination is conditioned by three factors operating in unison: the time of arrival – the earlier the arrival, the greater the legitimacy; the mode of incorporation; and the striking power of the groups involved – nationals or ethnies. That is, prior occupancy of the territory in itself is not likely to provide much legitimacy to a group's claim, as exemplified by the case of First Nations in the New World. But if the earlier occupants have the potential to reverse or balance the power relations, they may gradually gain legitimacy. Two important elements here are the size of the national community and their striking power. The case of the South African blacks fits this description.

However, even when the size of the group is substantial it may not acquire the requisite striking power for quite some time if it has been incorporated into the system with a stigmatizing status (e.g., the African slave in the Americas). But the stigma may erode gradually if the source of the stigma is done away with through state or official action (abolition of slavery), and/or if a proper ideology (e.g., racial paradise) is adopted, and an appropriate mechanism (e.g., miscegenation) is introduced. This explains the difference in the social standing between the blacks in North America and in Latin America, although both share a common predicament with regard to class inequality.

National groups that are economically backward, as in Fiji or Malaysia, would stake their claims to legitimacy based on their being the sons of the soil, and hence their entitlements to special previleges from the state. The collectivities whose internality to the system is questioned (the ethnies), on the other hand, will stake their claims to legitimacy based on their sacrifice for the development of the country and/or on the basis of the principle of merit. But these latter claims are not likely to be accepted by the insiders, the nationals. Thus it seems that the decisive element in establishing 'legitimacy' is the striking power of the collectivity, be it nationals (Fiji-Fijians) or ethnies (whites in the New World).

6

Proletarian Internationalism and the Socialist State

European colonialism was initially prompted by the search for riches, although the flag invariably followed trade, and the economic and political motivations became intertwined. However, the 'legitimacy' of colonialism was expected to be established through the process of rationalization provided by the civilizing mission, although this was rejected by its victims, as we have noted in chapter 5. Proletarian internationalism of the socialist states was also rejected by its victims, but its trajectory was entirely different. If colonialism had to invent its ideology gradually, proletarian internationalism started with an ideology, however ambiguous it might have been. Both ideological ambiguity and praxiological aberrations conjointly contributed to the ethnification of the victims of proletarian internationalism. And the assumed relationship between nationalism and socialism in the Marxist discourse remains 'a permanent, unresolved, theoretical difficulty of Marxism and a practical difficulty of socialist movements' (Kolakowski 1978: 88).

In spite of this pronouncement by Kolakowski, Marxist intellectuals hold that nationalism should be avoided at all costs and that it would finally disappear and socialism would triumph. Deutscher, for example, exhorted that:

> Socialists must be internationalists even if their working classes are not. Socialists must also understand the nationalism of the masses, but only in the way in which a doctor understands the weakness or the illness of

The Empirical Process

his patient. Socialists should be aware of that nationalism, but like nurses, they should wash their hands twenty times over whenever they approach an area of labour movement infected by it. (1971: 110–11)

To Deutscher, nationalism is pathological; socialists should be constantly chary of it and scrupulously avoid it. But to Hobsbawm nationalism was already on its deathbed, although he was writing in 1990, a time around which nationalist upsurges were sprouting again in several parts of the world:

> After all, the very fact that historians are at least beginning to make some progress in the study and analysis of nations and nationalism suggests that as often happens the phenomenon is past its peak. The Owl of Minerva which brings down wisdom, said Hegel, flies out at dusk. It is a good sign that it is now circling round nations and nationalism. (Hobsbawm 1990: 183)

But all indications are such that the Owl of Minerva is not yet circling nations and nationalism, as they are both live contemporary phenomena. And historians seem to have changed their conventional agenda; they are more and more given to study the present (designated as contemporary by them) rather than the past. However, the deeper problem in Hobsbawm's observation lies in his conflating state and nation, because he avers that in practice only three criteria be allowed for a people to be labelled as a nation. These are historic association with a state; the existence of a long-established cultural elite possessing a written national and administrative vernacular; and proven capacity for conquest (pp. 37–8). That is, the owl that Hobsbawm is referring to is circling not nations, but nation-states. I am prone to think that even though nation-states as politico-administrative entities are dying, nations will survive as cultural entities.

Ambiguity and ambivalence

The sources of ambiguity about nations and nationalism in Marxism are mainly of two kinds. First, the belief staunchly held in the *Communist Manifesto* that, owing to the development of the bourgeoisie and the world market, freedom of commerce and uniformity in the mode of production, national differences and antagonisms between people will gradually disappear (Marx 1932: 340). Second, the ambivalence regarding the principle of 'self-determination of nation', a phrase which was invoked by Marx himself in 1865 in the context of supporting the right of Poland for self-determination. If national antagonisms are to disappear with the onward march of capitalism, the relevance of national self-determination should also disappear.

Apart from this, there are two difficulties about the principle of self-determination itself. First, there was a strand in proletarian internationalism which viewed the principle as untenable both in theoretical and practical terms. In theory, the principle of national self-determination could not be reconciled with the basic tenets of Marxism. In practice, it was feared that the principle would give rise to unending demands, resulting in the proliferation of new states: 'Nations and mini-nations are cropping up on all sides announcing their right to form states. Putrefied corpses are climbing out of age old graves filled with the sap of a new spring, and peoples without a history who never yet formed an independent state, feel a powerful urge to do so', wrote Rosa Luxemburg with utter contempt after the October Revolution about the demand of smaller nations for self-determination (cited in Kerning 1973: 82). Even those who endorsed the principle of national self-determination gave precedence to socialism when it came to its application. Thus Lenin wrote in 1918: 'the interests of socialism are above the interests of the right of nations to self-determination'. This is so because 'Marxism is incompatible with nationalism, even the most "just", "pure", refined and civilized nationalism', asserted Lenin (cited in Carr 1966: 432).

However, even when the right to self-determination was conceded in particular cases, it was a privilege only of the proletariat. Thus, Lenin maintained that the Social Democratic Party, as the party of the proletariat, should consider as its 'positive and principal task to advance the self-determination of the working class, within each nationality rather than the self-determination of the peoples and nationalities' (1934, vol. II: 322). Stalin was of the same view. The principle 'ought to be understood as the right of self-determination not of the bourgeoisie but of the toiling masses of a given nation' (cited in Deutscher 1949: 185). Trotsky also concurred:

> ... we give full support to the principle of self-determination, whenever it is directed against feudal, capitalist and imperialist states. But whenever the fiction of self-determination in the hands of the bourgeoisie becomes a weapon directed against the proletarian revolution, we have no occasion to treat this fiction differently from the other "principles" of democracy perverted by capitalism. (1922: 86)

Admittedly, conceding self-determination to a section of the population within a nation is not a practical proposition, because the right refers to the governance of one's homeland; there is no homeland exclusive to the proletariat or to the bourgeoisie. But if we assume for a moment that the proletariat can be given the right to self-determination, then we have to reconcile this idea with the statement that the proletariat has no fatherland.

It may, however, be noted that the statement that 'the workers have no fatherland' is amenable to at least three interpretations, as Davis maintains. First, the underdog position of the proletarians makes them incapable of absorbing any national culture. Second, workers as non-owners of property have no stake in the country of their birth. Third, the class-consciousness of the workers renders them capable of transcending their national feelings (1967: 11–13). Be that as it may, the last of these interpretations is more plausible because nationalism is often viewed as a narrow bourgeois sentiment and the participants in nationalist demonstrations were said to be drawn from the middle class, as Davis (pp. 74–5) himself notes. But the fact is that in the German Democratic Republic in June 1953 it was the workers who rebelled against the Soviet Union; in Hungary in October 1956 it was the industrial workers who fought against the Soviet army and defended their factories against Soviet invasion; in Poland, again in October 1956, it was the Warsaw workers who fought against Soviet counter-revolution; and in Czechoslovakia it was the workers who fought for a communism with a human face, that is, without Soviet intervention. The point here is that in all these cases the workers fought as nationals and not as members of a class, not as the proletarians (Seton-Watson 1977: 439). Thus, the Marxist doctrine of proletarian internationalism bristles with both theoretical and practical difficulties in the context of national self-determination. The issue is further complicated because of an unwarranted distinction made between nations.

Engels had accepted the Hegelian distinction between 'historic' and 'non-historic' nations; the latter were counter-revolutionary and hence to be de-nationalized or exterminated. But after 1848 both Marx and Engels gave primacy to nations in place of class. The forces of enlightenment were represented by nations such as Germans, Italians, Magyars and Poles, and by the proletariat. Russian and Slavic nations represented the dark forces, such as feudal aristocracy and the bourgeosie. The Mexicans were 'lazy', the Slavic people were referred to as 'barbarians', 'petty bull-headed nations', and it was hoped that 'The next World War will cause not only reactionary classes and dynasties but also entire reactionary peoples to disappear from the earth. And that too would be progress' (Blackstock and Hoselitz 1952: 56–84). The two most 'scoundrelly nations on earth' were the Chinese and the Yankees, the former 'patriarchal swindlers', the latter 'civilized swindlers' (Marx and Engels 1964: 174).

Marx and Engels referred to the less developed nations as 'people without history', 'remains of nations', 'ruins of people', and so on, whose hope of salvation lay in their becoming attached to more progressive nations, which were 'large', 'well defined', 'historical', 'great' and which possessed 'undoubted vitality'. The support to national movements was to be selective, depending upon who led the movement, and what stage the society in which the movement was taking place had reached. The national movement led by progressive nations in the pre-capitalist stage was to be supported. Marx's support for the national struggle of Poland, the first major nation in Europe divided between three states – Russia, Prussia and Austria – between 1795 and 1919, was intended to administer a blow to Russia, 'the citadel of reactionary force' in Europe those days. Similarly, the rationale for support for the Irish national struggle was that 'the English working class will never accomplish anything before it has got rid of Ireland' (cited in Wright 1981: 152).

Lenin operationalized the idea into a strategy which had three elements. The first was the promise (before the assumption of power) of the right of self-determination to all nations and nationalities, including the right to secession, and national equality to those who wanted to remain within a multi-national state. Second, after the assumption of power, the right to secession was to be suspended and the process of assimilation through territorial autonomy would be initiated, for all compact national groups. Third, the party was to remain centralized and free of all nationalist inclinations (Connor 1984: 38).

Stalin's summary of the Bolshevik policy in 1917 sounds very close to Lenin's view: '(a) the recognition of the right of peoples to secession; (b) regional autonomy for peoples which remain within the given state; (c) specific laws for guaranteeing freedom for national minorities; (d) a single indivisible proletarian collective body, a single party, for the proletarians of all the nationalities in the given state' (1935: 73). But, in reality some of the nations and nationalities were clearly dominating the power structure. Thus the 1917 list of the Council of the Peoples' Commission consisted of fifteen persons of which fourteen were Slavs (one of whom was a Jew) and one was a Georgian – Joseph Stalin (Moynihan 1993: 116–7).

Even the Internationals were not out of the national grip. The First International was convened, paradoxically enough, to express support for the Polish national movement. The Second International was dominated by one national party – the German Social Democratic Party. The Third International, convened by Lenin, was almost completely dominated by a single national party – the Bolsheviks. And, the Fourth International, dominated by Trotsky, was never able to attach itself firmly to a national movement or a party although it sought to do so (Wright 1981: 159). The point is that even the proponents of the doctrine of proletarian internationalism could not practice it. In fact, in Stalin's hand it led to the decimation and destruction of numerous nations in the multi-national Soviet Union.

The hope ingrained in Marxism-Leninism was that nations would melt away under the impact of socialism, but the reverse actually took place; that is, the 'nationalization of socialism', to recall the persuasive phrase of E.H. Carr. But this happened not at the hands of national chauvinists drawing their daggers against proletarian internationalists, but at the insistence of socialists themselves. I have already referred to the ambivalence displayed by Marx, Engels, Lenin and others in the context of their efforts to keep the balance between proletarian internationalism and nationalism. Others were no exception.

Sun Yat-sen was a great proponent of assimilation of national minorities. In 1921 he said that the non-Han people of China were destined 'to be melted in the same furnace, to be assimilated within the Han nationality' (cited in Connor 1984: 67). And yet, after two years he pleaded for 'the right of all racial groups of China to self-determination; the right of course was not equated with the right of secession. In 1924, Sun referred to the right of self-determination of all nationalities in China' (Connor pp. 67, 83). The Chinese Constitution of 7 November 1931 had stated: 'The Soviet Government of China recognize the right of self-determination of national minorities in China, their right to complete separation from China, and to the formation of an independent state for each national minority' (cited in Brandt et al. 1952: 220).

In 1936, Mao Tse-tung pronounced that 'the Moslems must establish their independent and autonomous political power' and handle all their political, religious and cultural matters (Connor 1984: 81). And in 1945 he insisted that the Kuomintang (Nationalist Party) should grant the right to self-determination for all racial minorities in China. It may be noted here that three terms, national, racial and religious, are invoked to refer to 'national' minorities. However, since the issue referred to is self-determination, the collectivities are clearly 'nations', cultural groups with a territorial base, and therefore one may ignore the confusion created by the reference to 'racial' minorities and Muslims (religious groups). But even the term 'national minorities' is not apt, in that the reference is to territorially compact groups, all of which are majorities (unless the demographic balance of the area is disturbed by state-sponsored colonization, as in the case of Tibet) in their respective homelands.

In China, apart from the Hans, all are 'minorities', even when their numbers are substantial, simply because they are in the territory of the Chinese state. The point is, China is 'homogeneous' only when viewed from the perspective of the dominant nation, constituting over 93 per cent of the total population. Therefore, the only sane policy would have been to recognize the right of non-Han nations to maintain their cultural identity, and concede them a certain level of political autonomy. And yet, the nationality policy of China was geared towards liquidating the cultural identity of all the non-Han peoples and fusing them with the Great Han nation. National dress, language, dance, music and other cultural identity markers of non-Han nations were discouraged. Multi-national communes were created, inter-marriages with Han people were encouraged and the Hans were transplanted into the non-Han regions. Even the study of minority national cultures and histories were discouraged. All these led to the ethnification of non-Han minorities.

Tito had chided the ruling clique of Yugoslavia in 1948 for exclusively focusing on the Serbs, Croats and Slovenes, while ignoring the interests and identities of Albanians, Macedonians, Montenegrins and Muslims. He held the view that national liberation would be meaningful only if it really brought freedom, equality and brotherhood to all the nations consisting of the Yugoslav people (see Connor 1984: 128–71). In 1972 Brezhnev, the General Secretary of the Communist Party of the Soviet Union, contended that 'a Soviet Socialist culture' had emerged in the USSR, but conceded that it manifested itself in diverse national forms although it was 'internationalist in its spirit and character' (see Connor, p. 207). Similarly, the socialist leadership of Czechoslovakia asserted that the Czechs and the Slovaks were one nation. Tito, Brezhnev and the leaders of Czechoslovakia were all torn between internationalism on the one hand and the nationalisms of their states on the other.

Of the sixteen Marxist-Leninist states, of which some still exist, only one, namely Cuba, is in the New World, and has a settler-majority population which is categorized on the basis of race and colour and not on nations and nationalities. Of the remaining fifteen states, five were substantially homogeneous, with a dominant nation accounting for 95 (or more) per cent of their population in the 1980s. These were Albania (97 per cent), German Democratic Republic (97 per cent), Hungary (96 per cent), Democratic People's Republic of Korea (99 per cent) and Poland (98 per cent). The states that had one dominant nation making up 75–94 per cent of the population were: Bulgaria (85.8 per cent), Cambodia (90 per cent), Mongolia (89 per cent), the People's Republic of China (93 per cent), Rumania (88 per cent) and

UWE, BRISTOL LIBRARY SERVICES

Vietnam (86 per cent). And four were substantially heterogeneous in that the dominant nations accounted for less than 70 per cent of the state population: Czechoslovakia (65 per cent), Laos (67 per cent), USSR (52 per cent) and Yugoslavia (36 per cent) (see Connor 1984: 209–11).

While it cannot be asserted that the greater the heterogeneity the greater the intra-state conflicts based on inter-nation tensions, it is interesting to note the following. First, of the five near-homogeneous states, one (GDR) has been dismantled but through a process of fusion, and the others remain intact. Second, conflicts between nations are mainly concentrated in states which are multi-national, with staggering diversities, and which were dismantled through a process of fission. Third, in some of the states, irrespective of their scale or heterogeneity, inter-nation problems persist. Examples of this are afforded by the problems of Turks in Bulgaria, of Tibetans in China, of Hungarians in Rumania and the Mon-Khmers in Laos. In what follows I will discuss the case of the Soviet Union at length to illustrate the implications of the nationality policy of Marxist- Leninist states.

The practice: the Soviet case

Stalin had already started the campaign in the 1920s against the non-Russian nations, including Ukraine, which was the second largest in the Soviet Union. The Ukrainians, usually referred to as 'Little Russians', could not be described as backward. Ukraine is an ancient nation, with its own territory, language and culture. The problem was that although they were under Communist control, the Ukrainians did not become reconciled to the system. In the 1920s a number of people belonging to non-Russian nations had been executed or imprisoned because they had complained about Russian political and/or cultural hegemony (Connor 1984: 394). But the 'punishment' administered to the different nationalities had varied and had continued for decades, as is revealed through Khrushchev's 1956 speech. All the Karachai people were deported from their homeland in 1943. In the same year the autonomous Kalmyk Republic was liquidated. In March 1944 the autonomous Chechen-Ingush Republic was liquidated and its people were deported. In April 1944, the autonomous Kabardino-Balkar Republic was renamed the Kabardian Republic and all the Balkans were deported to far-away places (see Chalk and Jonassohn 1990: 304).

The count of people who were subjected to genocide and ethnification in the Soviet Union stood at 2,753,356 on 1 January 1953. The break-up is as follows: Germans, 1.2 million; Chechens, 316,000;

Ingush, 84,000; Crimean Tatars, 165,000; Lithuanians, 100,000; Estonians, 20,000; Latvians, 40,000; Meskhetian Turks, 50,000; Greeks, 52,000; Moldavians, 45,000; Karachai, 63,000; and the remaining number consisting of nearly a dozen other peoples (Tishkov 1991: 607). It is clear from the list of nations that the punishment was not confined to 'non-historic', 'backward' or less developed nations, whatever the manner in which one defines these terms. Clearly, it was based on the actual or assumed opposition to the political establishment of the Soviet Union of the day.

Apart from executions, imprisonments, and deportations, other milder forms of punishment were administered to keep the possible belligerency of the people in control and/or to facilitate their rapid 'progress' by attaching them to more developed nations. The major mechanisms invoked in this context were the re-drawing of the boundaries of national territories so as to create artificial administrative and political units, and state-sponsored or facilitated colonization, particularly by the Russians of the non-Russian national territories.

The Soviet policy of meddling with territories of nations within the state varied according to the level of crystallization of national consciousness. Thus, in Central Asia, where national consciousness was inchoate, the political-administrative borders were redrawn so that the Kazakhs, Kirghiz, Tadzhiks, Turkmen, and Uzbeks could develop separate national identities, as against Bukharan, Turkic or Muslim identities which were viewed negatively. In contrast, the Armenians and the Georgians, possessing a high level of national consciousness, were grouped along with the Azerbaijanis to create a consolidated Transcaucasian Federal Republic. This arrangement continued till 1936, and when it was dismantled the three successor union republics were not formed on the basis of national identities (Connor 1984: 302–3).

It seems that the Soviet policy was deliberately geared to creating heterogeneous politico-administrative units through the manipulation of natural national borders, as may be inferred from the following data. First, within the fourteen non-Russian union republics the proportion of the relevant titular population varied from 49 to 89 per cent. Second, of the fifteen Autonomous Soviet Socialist Republics (ASSR) of the Russian Soviet Federative Socialist Republic (RSFSR) only in three did the Russians constitute a majority in the 1970s, while in seven no national group was in a majority. Third, a large proportion of people were left out of the union republic that bore their name. In the extreme case (Armenians) the majority lived outside the republic, but on an average the excluded people accounted for 15 per cent of the total (Connor, pp. 302–4).

On the other hand, migration, particularly of the Russians to the non-Russian union republics, had substantially decreased the homogenity of the population of the latter. Thus, by 1959 Russian presence had increased in thirteen of the fourteen non-Russian republics, the increase being from 7.5 to 16.7 per cent, averaging at 9.2 per cent. These figures ought to be seen against the fact that the natural increase in the populations of the non-Russian republics, particularly the Asian ones, was substantially higher compared with that of the Russians. Conversely, the Russians within Russian national territory decreased from 86 per cent in 1917 to 77 per cent in 1970 (Connor, pp. 306–8).

The demographic composition of the fourteen non-Russian union republics between 1959 and 1979, worked out on the basis of the data provided in Connor (pp. 305, 307), unfolds an interesting picture. In only five was the titular population 75 per cent or more. In seven republics it varied between 51 and 75 per cent. And in two of the republics the titular nations contributed below 50 per cent of their populations. These were Kazakh SSR with 32 per cent, and Kirghiz SSR with 44 per cent. If in most cases the Russians were prompted to migrate, they preferred to do so to areas such as the Baltic republics. Thus, in Latvia in the 1970s only half of the population was Latvian, the majority of the rest being Russians. In terms of the conceptualization I propose, a substantial proportion of the populations in the Soviet Union during this period were ethnies, as they were living outside their ancestral homelands and as they had not yet adopted the territory of their residence as their homeland.

Viewed the other way round, of the fourteen non-Russian republics, one (Kazakh SSR) had 43 per cent of its population during 1959–79 drawn from the Russians. In such a situation the immigrants were despised by the host society, despite their power. Conversely, it also marginalized the nationals, thereby subjecting them to a process of ethnification. At the other end of the continuum, three of the republics had less than 10 per cent of their populations drawn from the Russians. The minority immigrant populations in such situations are compelled to live in an alien cultural milieu, often resulting in the erosion of their identity and leading to their ethnification. The ten republics that fell between these two extremes had 10–39 per cent of their populations drawn from the Russians. This type of situation is the most prone to conflict, because nationals are not likely to accommodate the ethnies. When the ethnies mobilize, the nationals will resist, as the latter's striking power is substantial. The situation became further complicated because the immigrant group, in the present case the Russians, were perceived as watchdogs of the 'imperial government' in Moscow, on whose behest they had migrated or were 'planted'. The fact that the immigrant Russians occupied all the important positions even at the local level further aggravated the situation (see Yamskov 1991: 603–60).

When we look at the dispersal of the non-Russian nations another interesting scenario unfolds. In the extreme case (the Armenians) as many as 38 per cent lived outside their accredited republic during 1959–70, but registered a slight decrease to 34 per cent during 1970–9. In two cases, those of the Kazakh SSR and the Tadzhik SSR, 21.5 and 23.7 per cent respectively of their nationals lived outside the republics during 1959–70, but registered a slight decrease to 19.3 and 22.8 per cent respectively in the 1970s. Generally speaking, the trend was the same in most cases in that the percentage of nationals living outside their homeland decreased slightly during the period under reference to around 1 per cent or less, except that of Russians. During 1959–70, 16.5 per cent of the Russians lived outside the SFSR. The figure for 1970–9 was 17.4, registering a 1 per cent increase. However, it is important to recall here that the absolute number of Russians living outside their homeland was substantial, because they constituted around 53 per cent of the USSR's total population during the period under reference. That is, some 40–5 million Russians lived outside their ancestral homeland.

The non-Russian population of the Soviet Union was around 47 per cent during the period of our analysis. Of the fourteen non-Russian nationalities, in ten cases the number of those living outside their own nations was below the Russian average, and in four cases it was above. It is fairly safe to assume that in spite of the variations in the size of nationalities, around 30 million non-Russians lived outside their titular nations. This means that around 70–5 million Soviet citizens were living outside their ancestral homelands during the 1959–79 period. It is of particular importance to recall here that these people were not voluntary migrants in search of better economic prospects in new lands, but persons located outside their homelands by the state as party bureaucrats, civil servants, professionals or industrial workers. This forced migration of a massive population was justified or was justifiable only in the name of socialism, which ignored their national identity and upheld proletarian internationalism.

On the other hand, the Russian population was gradually declining (51 per cent in 1989), leading to the possibility of the Russian nationality becoming a minority in the 1990s. This was due to the differing demographic dynamics between the European and Asian populations, and also to emigration. Between 1979 and 1989 the Russian population increased by 5.6 per cent. The figures for Ukrainians and

Belorussians were 4.2 and 6 per cent respectively. In contrast, it was 34 per cent for Uzbeks, 32 per cent for Kirghizians, 45 per cent for Tadzhiks, 34 per cent for Turkmenis and 25 per cent for the Azerbaijanis. The cultural homogeneity of several Asian republics also increased during the 1980s, as the Russians departed from most of them. On the other hand, the Russians continued to migrate to Ukraine, Belorussia, Latvia, Estonia and Kazakhstan, thereby increasing the heterogeneity of these republics during this period. Further, the emigration of several ethnies – Germans, Jews and Greeks – from the Soviet Union (the combined figure for 1989 being 235,600) contributed to the increasing homogeneity of the national populations of the USSR (see Tishkov 1991: 609).

The demographic composition of particular republics posed or avoided threats to the Soviet state, depending upon the level of national consciousness and the inclination to secede. The cases of the Baltic republics provide interesting contrasts. The demographic situation in Lithuania provided an apt moment for secession, with 80 per cent of Lithuanians and all others constituting numerically insignificant minorities (Russians, 9 per cent; Poles, 7 per cent; and Belorussians, 2 per cent) as secession required only a two-thirds majority in favour. In contrast, the situation in the Latvian republic was much less threatening from the perspective of secession, with only 52 per cent being Latvians and 34 per cent Russians; other minorities constituted the rest. The Estonian situation was only a shade better than that of Latvia, with 61.5 per cent Estonians and 30 per cent Russians. But it is probable that the ethnies may gradually adopt the republics of their residence as homelands, as exemplified by the case of the Russians in Lithuania. In a public opinion poll conducted on 6 April 1990, 50 per cent of the Russians living in Vilnius, the Lithuanian capital, supported the declaration of the Supreme Soviet of Lithuania in favour of secession (Tishkov 1991: 610–11).

The Armenian–Azeri conflict

In concluding the discussion on the theme of ethnification provoked by the attenuation between territory and culture in the erstwhile Soviet Union, it is helpful to refer to the Armenian–Azeri conflicts which were triggered off in 1987. The conflicts started in Nagorno-Karabakh, an Armenian enclave in Azerbaijan, and Nakhichevan, an Azerbaijani enclave in Armenia. While a variety of factors were at work – history, cultural differences, economic deprivation, to mention a few – the most important cause of 'conflict is the threatened loss of numerical advantage that has undergirded the position of one ethnic

group in a given territory' (Yamskov 1991: 635). The conflict in Nagorno-Karabakh was based on the mutually irreconcilable conceptions of
national territory entertained by the contenders – Armenians and
Azerbaijanis – leading to armed conflicts between the two groups and
resulting in the expulsion of all Azeris from Armenia, and most Armenians from Azerbaijan. The situation became so bad in early 1990 that
the remaining Armenians had to be vacated from even the large cities
of Azerbaijan (Yamskov 1991: 639).

The Armenians were distributed into three republics: the Armenian
SSR, the Nagorno-Karabakh region in Azerbaijan, and southern Georgia. The substantial decline of the Armenian population and the un-
precedented multiplication of Azerbaijanis threatened the former
with the possibility of becoming a minority in their accredited homeland. The demand to unite the Armenian inhabited territory into a
single homeland gradually crystallized. On the other hand, Azeris of
the Nagorno-Karabakh view this patch of territory as their homeland
too, and with equal force, as, despite demographic realities, the region
is an integral part of the Baku hinterland by virtue of its topography.
The fact that the Armenians are predominantly Christian and the
Azeris are almost exclusively Muslim is very frequently invoked to
'explain' this conflict which, in reality, is simply about contending
claims for the same homeland. That the Kurdish Muslims continue to
live almost undisturbed in Armenia even after the violent expulsion
of the Azeri Muslims, points to the irrelevance of religion qua religion
in this context. In fact, 'the bloodiest conflicts, to date, have occurred
in Central Asia between groups that share the same religion' (Tishkov
1991: 615).

One comes across two diametrically opposed views in the context of
the conflict, one supporting and the other opposing the Armenian
claim over Nagorno-Karabakh. While both take recourse to history to
support their argument, the cut-off point in history on which they fall
back varies markedly. Huttenbach, drawing mainly upon recent, that
is, twentieth-century history, argues the case for Nagorno-Karabakh
being integrated with the Armenian SSR (1990: 5–14). The main points
he makes are the following. First, Nagorno-Karabakh is predominantly an Armenian enclave; in the 1970s, 80 per cent of its population was
constituted by Armenians. He supports the Armenian argument that
topography is less important in modern times, given the developed
state of technology. Second, there is a massive popular movement in
favour of unification of the territory with that of the Armenian SSR.
The movement is supported by all sections and shades of opinions of
Armenian people both inside and outside Nagorno-Karabakh, including those who are members of the Communist Party. Third, the

movement for unification lay dormant during the authoritarian phases of the Soviet Union, particularly during the Stalinist and the Brezhnev regimes, which were unsympathetic to the Armenian case. But during the relatively liberal political climate, the Armenians articulated their position clearly, in a limited way in the 1950s during Khrushchev's time, and more openly and vividly after perestroika was introduced by Gorbachev.

In contrast, Yamskov, (1991: 631–60) also drawing upon history, but pre-twentieth-century history, seems to make the case in favour of the Azeris. His arguments are the following. First, in 1845 the population of historic Karabakh included 30,000 Armenians and 62,000 Azeris. Second, the Armenians of eastern Armenia and northern Azerbaijan, which include Nagorno-Karabakh, are nineteenth-century immigrants from Turkey and Persia, who have added substantially to the Armenian population. Third, the Armenians are mainly a settled people, but the Azeris are largely nomads, a pastoral community. Fourth, the Azeri pastoralists spend the summer months in Karabakh which they consider to be their land. Fifth, the census was usually taken when the nomads and semi-nomads were in the winter pastures, leading to undercounting of the Azeris. That is, Azeris have every right to claim the contested territory as their homeland, whether viewed as ancestral or adopted.

Ignoring these facts, and often surreptitiously using religion as the basis of nation and nationality, the people of a common homeland were grouped into different politico-administrative units. This bred estrangement and conflicts, which resulted in the uprooting of sections of both Armenians and Azeris from their homeland, leading to their ethnification. It happened on a large scale in the USSR as a whole following its breakup, and was not confined to Armenians or Azeris. On 14 May 1992 Mikhail Gorbachev, while speaking to the US Congress, said: 'One problem which is assuming an acute and at times dramatic character in Russia is that of ethnic enclaves which thanks to the break up of the formerly unified state organism, are being violently separated from their accustomed motherland and now find themselves on the other side of a national boundary' (cited in Moynihan 1993: 5).

The demographic dispersal in the Soviet Union gave birth to a series of tensions and conflicts linked to the specificity of situations, of which the following may be noted. First was the expectation on the part of nationals that ethnies, particularly those who did not have an accredited homeland in the Soviet Union and/or were territorially dispersed, should leave their present territory. This was exemplified in the cases of the Poles in Lithuania; the Gagauzi in Moldova, the

Germans and Koreans in Kazakhstan, Tadzhiks and Meskhetian Turks in Uzbekistan, the Kurds, Lesghians, Talyshi and Armenians in Azerbaijan, to list a few. The conflicts between these groups were essentially between nationals and ethnies, insiders and outsiders.

Second was the possibility of a series of conflicts between different nationalities and nations with acknowledged rights to belong to the state territory of USSR, but which were situated outside their national homelands. During 1988, 1989 and the first nine months of 1990 such clashes resulted in 10,049 deaths, 8,951 casualties and rendered 583,200 persons refugees. More than 330,000 people fled Azerbaijan, 173,000 fled Armenia and 64,000 fled Uzbekistan during the same period, according to the USSR Ministry of Internal Affairs (see Tishkov 1991: 618–9).

Third, ethnification made the principle of self-determination sometimes meaningless and often difficult to put into practice. The latest Soviet Constitution provided for the 'freedom of nation-state formations to choose their own ways of life, institutions and symbols of statehood'. But given the combinations of national and ethnic populations of the union republics, it is difficult to choose ways of life, institutions or symbols specific to a collectivity. In fact, it is precisely the exercising of this freedom that often led to conflicts between insiders and outsiders. The real issue is who constitutes the nation or people: particular nations, or those who reside in specific republics? If the former makes the nation, the latter is denationalized or ethnified. If the latter makes the nation, in several cases the nationals become ethnified as they are marginalized and/or minoritized.

Fourth, the sense of historical retribution has been crystallizing in several cases. The deported people want to come back to their ancestral homelands, those who were artificially brought together want their specificities to be recognized. Thus the Chechen–Ingush ASSR wants to be separated into two republics; the Crimean Tatars and Volga Germans are demanding the return of their lands and restoration of the autonomous status they lost in the 1940s; and the Gagauzi are unhappy with their subservient status within Moldova (Tishkov 1991: 625).

Ethnification through culturocide

The language policy followed in the Soviet Union was an important instrument of ethnification. The policy had a three-tier structure: eradication of the ninety or so languages of those peoples without union republic status; provision for the continuation of the languages of those nationalities with their own republics; and the compulsory use of Russian as the sole teaching language everywhere. But the ultimate goal was one of assimilation, including the Russian language, in the utopian vision of Stalin (see Connor 1984: 254–77). There was however no consistency in the application of the proclaimed policy. Five of the fourteen peoples who had been assigned union republics – Armenia, Estonia, Georgia, Latvia and Lithuania – had high levels of national consciousness and their own long and proud literary traditions. In these cases the pressure of imposing the Russian language was moderate. In all other cases it was considerable. Even the second biggest nation in the USSR, Ukraine, which had a well-formed and long national tradition was not exempt, as Russian and Ukrainian were believed to be similar (Connor pp. 259–60). However, this evaluation was not shared by the Ukrainians, as may be discerned from a petition addressed to an official of the Ukraine SSR, which reads as follows: 'As a result of Lenin's instructions, higher and secondary specialized education in Ukraine was Ukrainized during the twenties and thirties. Teaching in the institutions of higher learning was conducted in Ukrainian. . . . During the period of the Stalin personality cult, this Leninist principle of higher education in Ukraine was forgotten (cited in Nogee 1972: 518–9). The language law of 1958–9 clearly pointed towards mono-linguism. The party programme approvingly noted in 1961 that 'the Russian language has in effect become the common medium of intercourse and co-operation between all the peoples of the USSR' (cited in Connor 1984: 262).

The significance of this denial of freedom to use one's language should be seen in the context of Stalin's 1913 definition of nation, which rightly gave great importance to language. He averred in 1950: 'without a language understood by a society and common to all its members, that society must cease to produce, must disintegrate and cease to exist as a society' (Stalin n.d.: 76). Therefore, to deny a nation the right to use its language was, in effect, to destroy that nation.

The discriminatory treatment of smaller nations, particularly when they were dispersed into several republics, was almost automatic. For example, the Armenians in Nagorno-Karabakh and the Armenians, Azeris and Ossetians in Georgia complained that the authorities of the relevant union republics denied the required facilities to teach their language. When this denial is seen in conjunction with the substantial territorial dispersal of nationalities that we have noted above the problem is self-evident. The situation was still worse in the case of those peoples – Greeks, Talysh, Tats and Lesghians and Kurds – who were not attached to any territory, that is the ethnies in the Soviet Union (see Yamskov 1991: 643). Only Russian was elevated as the universal language of the USSR.

The possibility of sustaining one's cultural heritage was substantially endangered when a part of a nation was allocated or belonged to a union republic other than its own. This is well illustrated by the Armenian case. The Armenian teachers of Nagorno-Karabakh were trained either at Stepanakert or in Baku and were not allowed to study in the capital of neighbouring Armenia, called Yerevan. While a course in 'The history of the Armenian people' was taught in the schools of Armenia, the Nagorno-Karabakh schools taught 'The history of Azerbaijan', even in the Armenian schools. Understandably, the orientation and emphasis of the two histories varied. 'In these courses the same historical events receive diametrically opposite interpretations' (Yamskov p. 643). Consequently, the Armenians living in the Azerbaijani territory were gradually 'de-historicized'.

The government-owned and managed television network aggravated the situation by controlling the content, quantity and source of transmission. To illustrate, the Armenian-language television station in Nagorno-Karabakh was controlled from Baku by Azeri bureaucrats. The Armenian request for transmission from the neighbouring Armenia was not acceded to initially and when it was done, the proportion of Armenian–Azeri broadcasts was unfavourable to the latter (Yamskov p. 643). Such measures de-culturalize minorities living outside their accredited republics.

If in matters of culture control is exerted directly, in matters of state security it is done in an indirect and subtle manner. For example, both the Latvians and Ukrainians had complaints in this context, although their perceptions varied. One Ukrainian described the situation thus: 'Millions of young Ukrainian men came home after several years service nationally disoriented and linguistically demoralized and became in their turn a force exerting an influence for Russification on other young people and on the population at large' (cited in Dzyuba 1968: 137). In contrast, the Latvians complained:

> During World War II, two Latvian divisions and a special aviation battalion heroically fought as part of the Red Army. Today, however, there is no separate Latvian military unit; Latvian youths in the military are purposely not assigned to the Russian units stationed in Latvia, but are scattered throughout the Soviet Union as far from Latvia as possible. (Cited in Saunders 1974: 436)

If the Ukrainians felt de-nationalized through an unwarranted Russification, the Latvians thought that they were perceived as a potential danger to the security of the Soviet state. Both led to collective political alienation. In several Soviet successor states, in spite of laws on the equality of citizenship, the ethnies feel discriminated. For example, in Kazakhstan the citizens of the erstwhile USSR automatically became citizens, and yet there have been instances of Russian emigration due to discrimination. But in some of the successor states even formal equality is not provided for. In Estonia, non-Estonians who were born in the state have to pay a higher price for acquiring property (e.g., housing). Generally speaking, in all Soviet successor states there exists a distinction between nationals and ethnies.

The Case of Post-Soviet Latvia

The consequences of the nationality policy pursued by the Soviet Union may be illustrated through a brief discussion of the situation in post-Soviet Latvia, probably an extreme case (Muiznieks 1995: 1–23). Latvia's population was 77 per cent Latvian and 8.8 per cent Russian in 1935. By 1989 the Latvians were reduced to 52 per cent and the Russians totalled 34 per cent. Although the composition of the population started changing in favour of the Latvians after 1989, by 1994 they still only constituted 54 per cent of the population, while the Russians accounted for 33 per cent. During the Soviet period the Latvians were compelled to learn Russian which became the language of public life, relegating the Latvian language to the realm of private communication. In 1989, 68 per cent of the Latvians claimed a command of Russian. On the other hand, of the total resident population in Latvia only 62 per cent claimed any knowledge of Latvian, while 82 per cent had common knowledge of Russian (Muiznieks, pp. 2–3).

While it was not possible to articulate opposition to state policy during most of the Soviet period, the enunciation of glasnost started the process. By 1987 sections of Latvian nationals started demanding a stop to immigration into Latvia and the upgradation of the Latvian language for its use in public contexts, and they expressed a desire to be 'masters of their own land'. On the other hand, the demand for independence was largely opposed by the non-Latvian immigrants of the state. This was evident from a March 1991 survey, according to which 90–5 per cent of all Latvians supported the demand for independence, but only 38–45 per cent of non-Latvians did so (see Muiznieks p. 4). The Latvians came to cognize the non-Latvian segment of the population as an enemy to be flushed out. Such a perception was reinforced by the presence and activities of a pro-Russian group drawn from non-Latvian sections, predominantly of Russian background.

To counter the menace from the internal enemy the Latvian nationalist elements have insisted on a special status for themselves. This was articulated by the Popular Front in 1988 thus: 'the Latvian people have the status of the indigeneous nation in the Republic because Latvia is the historic territory of Latvians, the only place in the world where the Latvian nation, the Latvian language and culture can be preserved' (cited in Muiznieks p. 8). This claim is clinched by pointing out that, according to the 1989 census, 97 per cent of all Latvians were born in Latvia, while the figure for non-Latvians was only 49 per cent. Understandably, some Latvian political groups characterize the non-Latvian residents as 'occupiers', 'colonists', 'illegal migrants' etc., and demand their repatriation to their homelands. Thus the polarization between nationals and ethnies is loud and clear.

The distinction between nationals and the ethnie is reflected in the granting of citizenship and the distribution of political power. Thus, while Latvian nationals constituted only 56 per cent of the population of Latvia in early 1995, they accounted for 79 per cent of all Latvian citizens, 89 per cent of deputies in the Parliament and 100 per cent of ministers (Muiznieks p. 9). The situation is not likely to improve in the near future, as knowledge of the Latvian language is made compulsory not only for government jobs, but also to acquire citizenship. A complicating factor is the emerging 'cultural division of labour', to recall Hechter's (1975) term. While the Latvian nationals have a near monopoly in the political and bureaucratic structures of the government, the Jews and Russians dominate the emerging capitalist economy. This is ready ammunition in the hands of nationals to attack and expel ethnies.

To conclude, the legacy of the Soviet nationality policy will continue to have its negative impact in most Soviet successor states for several decades to come. The only way out is to grant citizenship to ethnies who, in turn, should adopt the territory of their residence as their homeland: in other words they should become nationals. But to become nationals should not mean assimilation by renouncing their identity, but the co-existence of different nations in the same territory as equal citizens.

It is evident from the foregoing analysis that, in spite of the doctrine of proletarian internationalism purported to be in practice in the Soviet Union, its polity remained utterly multi-national in that the people anchored themselves strongly to national identity. Further, all efforts to relegate national identities to the background so as to create a 'socialist man' utterly failed. In addition, 'Great Nation' chauvinism and inter-nation bickerings continued to persist, leading to the ethnification of millions of Soviet citizens. The more important measures that contributed to ethnification are the following, as is evident from the discussion in this chapter. First, the creation of artificial politico-administrative units ignoring national boundaries. Second, de-territorialization of nations and their dispersal into several distant spatial locations. Third, state-sponsored colonization of the territory of smaller and weaker nations, particularly by the dominant nation. Fourth, preventing the use of national languages of smaller and weaker nations for education (particularly at higher levels) and in the mass media. Fifth, the distorted teaching of history, ignoring the specificities of the histories of weak and small nations. Sixth, denial of entry into and effective participation of non-Russian nationalities in the critical sectors of the economy and polity. The conjoint impact of these measures was the collective alienation of a massive population ready to strike at the one-party state and its managers when the opportune moment arrived.

7

The Nation-State and Project Homogenization

The old nations of Europe formed before 1789 were products of conquest and did not possess the 'national consciousness' that is invariably attributed to the post-1789 nations. The new concept of nation in Europe was a creation of the French Revolution, which made cultural (and not racial) homogeneity a necessary prerequisite of nation-states. It was assumed that for effective governance a state must be a homogeneous nation. As Wallas puts it, European statesmen thought:

> . . . no citizen can imagine his state or make it the object of his political affection unless he believes in the existence of a national type to which the individual inhabitants of the state are assimilated; and he cannot continue to believe in the existence of such a type unless in fact his fellow citizens are like each other and like himself in certain important respects. (1921: 287)

Although the fusion between citizenship and nationality was not realized even in Western Europe (as we shall see soon), the idea of homogenization caught the imagination of intellectuals and politicians everywhere, ineluctably leading to the ethnification of a large number of weak and minority nations all over the world. In this chapter I will discuss the trajectory of ethnification in the Old World – Europe, Asia and Africa.

The obsession with the nation-state in Western Europe was so incredibly pervasive that, irrespective of ideological persuasions, there

existed a certain amount of consensus on the desirability of constituting them. Barker predicted that a world system would emerge 'in
which each nation is also a state and each state is also a nation' (1948:
126), although this was not true even in Britain, the first nation in the
world, which had been in existence for over two centuries when he
was writing. Hitler maintained: 'We as Aryans are . . . able to imagine
a state only to be the living organism of a nationality which not only
safeguards the preservation of that nationality but which, by further
training of its spiritual and ideal abilities, leads to its highest freedom'
(1939: 595). Given this ideological consensus, European state-making
moved in the direction of homogeneity through deliberate attempts
'to homogenize the culture of subject population through linguistic,
religious and . . . educational standardization' (Tilly 1975: 78). And,
the result was, according to Hobsbawm, that state, nation and society
converged 'in the process of an effort to represent an entire society or
people' (1983: 265).

On the other hand, racially and/or culturally heterogeneous societies and nationalism, it was believed, could not co-exist. Thus, for
Furnivall, 'Nationalism within a plural society is itself a disruptive
force, tending to shatter and not to consolidate the social order' (1939:
468). The belief that Western states were nations and hence stable
political entities fit for participative democracy and that the 'new
nations' of the Third World were ill-suited for democratic governance
because of the absence of coterminality between state and nation,
gradually crystallized and became consecrated as an axiom. However, this complacency about the West was shattered in the latter half
of the twentieth century, a fact that some, at least, began to acknowledge (e.g., Connor 1994; Esman 1977).

In this chapter I propose to argue that the nation-state was only an
aspiration, in fact an unfortunate aspiration, which was never realized
even in Western Europe, and that, in pursuing this aspiration, numerous nations (usually smaller and weaker ones) within multi-national
states have been subjected to ethnification. In its consequences the
ideology of homogenization pursued by the nation-state is not altogether different from that of proletarian internationalism, although
they both varied drastically in the strategies adopted. Further, what
was common to both ideologies was the fear that the doctrine of
national self-determination would result in a proliferation of states
that would be unsustainable in economic and political terms. It seems
that Carnot had anticipated Rosa Luxemburg, and had written almost
in the same vein as early as 1793, against the backdrop of the French
Revolution: 'If any community whatever had the right to proclaim its
will and separate from the main body under the influence of rebels,

etc., every country, every town, every village, every farmstead might declare itself independent' (cited in Emerson 1962: 297). Proletarian internationalism attempted to establish multi-national states, but it was infested by Great Nation chauvinism, whether of the Russians, the Hans or the Serbians, and this gradually led to their break-up and delegitimation. In contrast, the homogenization project of the nation-state eventually absorbed the smaller and weaker nations as ethnified entities. I will illustrate this point with reference to a few selected cases drawn from different regions of the Old World.

Western Europe

From Western Europe I will discuss the first nation-state of Europe (Great Britain), the nationstate that was a product of revolution (France), and a state wherein the coterminality between state and nation is claimed to have been achieved (Germany).

Great Britain

The first nation-state of Europe, namely Great Britain, is a veritable multi-national state, although almost all writers, at least until recently, referred to it as a nation. Wales was joined with England in 1536, Scotland in 1707 and Ireland in 1800, through different Acts of Union. And yet, the three non-English nations maintain their distinct identities through the following devices. First, they all have their own separate national flags. Second, Scottish identity is strongly expressed through the Church of Scotland (Presbyterian, as distinct from the Anglican Church of England), educational institutions and the legal system. Third, Wales maintains its identity by keeping Welsh as one of the official languages (along with English) and by continuing its distinct religious tradition of non-conformism expressed through the Methodist revival, the dissent of the Baptists and the Independents, so much so that Gladstone asserted in 1891 that 'the non-conformists of Wales are the people of Wales' (see Morgan 1971: 156). Fourth, in spite of the union between Ireland and Great Britain, intermittent civil war persisted between the two, finally leading to the division of Ireland in 1921. Most of Ireland became the Irish Republic, an independent sovereign state. But the six counties of Northern Ireland, largely Protestant, continue as a part of Great Britain, and were bristling with persistent problems at the time of writing. Given these facts, it is impossible to describe Great Britain as a nation-state, that is, an entity in which nation and state are coterminous.

Apart from this, the process of ethnification was and is still at work in the three non-English nations in different ways. Wales is often described as the 'Celtic fringe' and 'just a geographical expression'. The people of Wales are accused of 'obstinately adhering to its antique language'; nobody recognized the existence of the 'Welsh question', and the economic aspects of Welsh nationalism were 'killed by kindness'. According to the 1961 census only a fifth of the adult population could speak the native language and in the industrial centres of Wales and along the English–Welsh border it has practically died out. However, during the process of rapid industrialization and consequent urbanization the Labour party secured a substantial base in Wales which prompted it to take a quasi-nationalist position. One important measure was the creation of the position of a Welsh Secretary of State in 1964. The University of Wales is viewed as an institution of great national importance by the Welsh, and an effort to defederate it in the 1960s was stoutly opposed. A significant indicator of Welsh nationalism may be discerned in the formation of Plaid Cymru, the Welsh Nationalist Party, in 1925. Although till the 1960s the party did not register any visibility in the elections, in the 1970 general elections the thirty-six Plaid Cymru candidates secured 12.4 per cent of the votes polled in Wales (Morgan 1971: 153–71), but did not win any seats. The percentage of votes polled by Plaid Cymru in general elections gradually declined from 11.7 per cent in 1974 to 8.3 percent in 1987. However, during the same period they won two or three seats in all the elections (Lutz 1990: 249–66). It may also be noted here that Welsh nationalism has taken a different turn in recent times. As late as 1974, Plaid Cymru boasted of its opposition to the UK's entry into the European Community. But latterly the emphasis has been on 'freedom' for all 'nations of Britain' within the framework of the EC. A 1990 poll revealed strong support for Welsh devolution, with 56 per cent favouring a Welsh assembly (Keating and Jones 1991: 311–24).

As noted above, the Scottish case is somewhat different in that the British state explicitly protected the major institutions of the Scottish nation, and the union appeared to be in good health until the first quarter of the twentieth century. The Scottish elite perceived the union not as 'an annexation but as an association'. Furthermore, they were adequately compensated for abjuring political power through economic advancement. In the bargain, however, they lost their language. Gaelic was spoken in 1707 by 30 per cent of Scottish families; in the 1970s by barely 1.5 per cent (Esman 1977: 252–3). In spite of this apparent 'integration', or perhaps because of it, two perceptions gradually crystallized. The first was that most Scots believed that they were still a nation voluntarily associated with Great Britain. But, and this is the second perception, for the British elites, Britain was the nation and Scotland simply 'North Britain', an economic region. These two perceptions, Scotland as a nation and Scotland as a mere economic region did not become politically salient until recently (Esman p. 255). To complicate matters the English seemed to hold the Scots in great contempt. Billy Wolfe, chairman of the Scottish National Party (SNP) during 1969–79, wrote in his autobiography that when he was in the British Army he was often told that the Anglicized Scot is not only civilized but is the best kind of person in the world. When the SNP leader Jim Sillars made his first speech in the House of Commons after his election in 1988 the English Tory MPs taunted him by shouting 'Speak English', obviously a disparaging reference to his accent (Kellas 1991: 69–70).

The discovery of oil in the North Sea off Scotland in the early 1970s changed the career of Scottish nationalism. The discovery made Scotland economically very valuable for Great Britain and increased the country's possibility of becoming a viable independent state. The British saw the oil as the common property of the entire 'nation', but the Scottish nationalists saw it as their own exclusive national asset. The advantage of oil, according to SNP, cannot be enjoyed if Scotland remains a mere economic region within Great Britain. The oil could redeem Scotland only if the Scots are exclusively in charge in their territory. Rich Scots or poor Britons is the option according to SNP (Esman pp. 267–70). The SNP did make an impressive show in the 1974 elections, compared with its earlier record. But only 33 per cent of the Scottish electorate supported the plan of setting up a semi-independent parliament in Edinburgh and 14 per cent supported Scottish Home Rule in the 1979 referendum. However, in the 1985 referendum 35 per cent favoured independence (Keating and Jones 1991: 321). Further, the SNP, which opposed the UK's integration with the EC earlier, have, since 1988, favoured 'Independence in Europe', that is, greater autonomy within the framework of the EC, although the Conservatives continue to seek further integration between Scotland and England (Kellas 1990: 428).

Northern Ireland is a more complicated case. But we need to note only the following points for the present discussion. English is the sole official language of Northern Ireland, and the use of Gaelic is not encouraged; a majority of the people living in Northern Ireland are of Scottish or English ancestry and are usually referred to as Scotch-Irish; and the conflict in Northern Ireland is not essentially a conflict between Protestants and Catholics, but between insiders and outsiders, nationals and ethnies, as may be discerned from the following letter to the editor, which appeared on 12 July 1970 in the *New York Times*:

> The overwhelming majority of the Irish people, North and South, are united in their desire that the British get out of Ireland. The only exception to this view comes from a British ethnic group which constitutes a local majority, not in the entire six occupied counties, but in a small enclave within a thirty mile radius of Belfast. (cited in Connor 1994: 63)

It seems to be fairly clear that the Irish people, except for the Protestants in Northern Ireland, think that the British state has treated their homeland as a colony and sponsored colonization of the island by non-Irish British citizens. It is acknowledged that the teaching of national history has been positively Anglocentric in England and is often distinctively different from that in Ireland. Admittedly, the perception of Great Britain as a 'nation' differed across her nations (see Samuel 1989). Consequently, two types of 'national' identities – British; and English, Irish, Scottish and Welsh – co-exist in Britain. Therefore it is no surprise that the nations in the state territory of Britain sustain separate cultural identities with strong attachments to their respective homelands (Hutnik 1985: 298–309). And the characterization by Hechter (1975), of Ireland, Scotland and Wales as internal colonies and peripheries of the English core, the dominant nation, therefore, seems to be not without substance.

France

France is almost always cited as an instance of state-building resulting in nation formation. The French Declaration of the Rights of Man and of Citizens proclaimed that 'the source of all sovereignty resides essentially in the nation, no group, no individual may exercise authority not emanating expressly there from'. It is clear that when the term nation is used the declaration is referring to the French state, because the French nation actually contained several nations or their parts – Alsations, Basques, Bretons, Catalans, Corsicans, Flemings and Occitanians. In fact, in 1789 half the population in France spoke no French at all, and even by 1863 about 20 per cent of the population did not speak what was considered to be French in official circles (Hobsbawm 1990: 60). Eugen Weber (1976) reported that most people living in France were not conscious of being French until long after the Revolution. Finally, the expansion of the mass media carved out recognizable cultural identities, which lay between the national and the local, leading to a growing sense of powerlessness among citizens and groups living in the peripheral regions (Berger 1977: 175–7).

Two post-war events have shaken the belief that France is 'one and indivisible': the Algerian War and the movement of May 1968. The non-Muslim Algerians claimed that they were French citizens and nationals because they were descendants of migrants from the metropolis and because they spoke French. If speaking the language is the measure of 'Frenchness', by extending the same logic the non-French nations in the territory of France could argue that they are not French as the language had been imposed on them. But there is a snag. According to the Evian Accords of 1962, French Algerians could be French citizens only if they returned to France. Those who resided in Algeria could not be French citizens, even though they were culturally and linguistically French (Beer 1977: 146). Thus, the Evian Accords made a distinction, perhaps unwittingly, between citizenship and nationality; the former was seen as a legal notion, residence within the state territory being an essential condition for citizenship, and the latter as a cultural notion, irrespective of the place of residence. Conversely, in the case of non-French nationals residing within the state territory, they could be citizens of France without being French nationals. However, there is a complication brought about by the process of ethnification. For example, although 200,000 French citizens claimed that they were Basques in the 1970s, only 80,000 spoke Basque (Beer p. 143). This divergence between nationality and nation-ness could be seen as a product of state-building, in which case the territory of the non-French nations within the state of France is not French territory even though these nations speak the French language.

Following the above logic, non-French nationalists of France pointed out that Brittany became part of France only in 1532. Alsace was attached alternately to France and Germany for centuries. The whole of southern France, inhabited by Occitanians, was joined to France after the terrible crusades of the Albigenses. These nations did not join the state of France of their own volition; they were victims of conquest and violence. And even those who argue that the Occitanian movement has a multiple agenda concede that it 'belongs to the great family of Third World nationalism', that it is a movement against 'the centralizing, capitalist and bureaucratic state' and that it is caused by the 'brutal domination of the centre over the periphery' (Touraine 1985: 157–75). The events of May 1968 reinforced the logic of these national aspirations, and accelerated the idea of national self-determination.

Among the different national movements in France, that of the Bretons is one of the most widely known and hence I will discuss this case briefly. The Breton national movement has two principal wings: political and cultural. The political wing is secessionist in orientation and has intermittently indulged in violent activities. It considers Brittany to be an internal colony of France, a view that has been reinforced by analysts like Reece (1979: 275–92). Breton nationalists claim to be socialists, and their ideology may be discerned from a 1969 declaration, part of which reads as follows:

> Recent events in Central Europe show that in Europe real socialism can only be independent and particular to each people. Our socialism . . . will be humanist, co-operative, federalist and communitarian, respectful of all human freedoms . . . If we are first and foremost nationalists and independentists, it is because we know that the construction of socialism requires the political liberation of Brittany and of the Breton society free of any foreign hegemony. Those in Brittany who call themselves socialists or communists but reject independence are only hypocrites, fools and traitors. (cited in Berger 1977: 170).

The cultural nationalists do not want an independent sovereign state of Brittany, but insist on maintaining their cultural identity within the French state. The most important aspect of the search for cultural identity may be discerned in the revival of the Breton language and literature in the post-war period. Although initiated by the cultural elite of Brittany, cultural revival seeps down to the bottom. One important indicator of this is the increase in the number of students offering Breton in the baccalaureate examination of the Academy of Rennes. In 1969 the number was between 150 and 180, but by 1975 it rose to 788. Another important indicator of the cultural revival is the popular interest in national music, dance and crafts (Berger p. 165).

It may however be noted that there are Bretons who reject even cultural nationalism. They belong to two groups and hold this position for entirely different reasons. First, those who take a statist position and fall in line with the Jacobin argument that cultural nationalism inevitably leads to secessionist movements and poses a threat to the integrity of France. They are willing to sacrifice the cultural identity of their nation for the stability of the French state. Second, those Bretons who renounce cultural nationalism because they have been subjected to an intense process of what I have called ethnification. One of Berger's respondents reported that although he used Breton in everyday informal interaction, and that he dreamt in Breton, it was an 'unnecessary language' because it was a source of trouble and humiliation when used in the public context (p. 166).

The source of his revulsion and self-pity for his own language ought to be located in the process of stigmatization to which the language and its speakers (the nation) have been subjected by French society and the state. During the Third Republic, 'no spitting and no Breton' was a very common form of graffiti in France. French cartoons conjured up the servant girl Becassine from Brittany, who symbolized the happy, stupid Breton to generations of French men. 'The Bretons were the servants, the prostitutes, the common fodder of France and escape from Brittany into French civilization was held out by schools to Breton children as the only route to dignity and self-respect' (Berger p. 166). Further, the Bretons were condemned as alcoholics and to get out of this pathological obsession they must 'renounce all that is most original, in their culture and assimilate into French culture and mores' (Reece 1979: 279). It is true that the French have not used force against the Bretons, but no opportunity was missed to emphasize 'the inherent superiority of French as a language of culture, progress, and social promotion' (Reece p. 280).

The state intervened to accelerate the process of ethnification. In 1905 Prime Minister Combes, a true Jacobin, prohibited the use of the Breton language in church, and he encouraged the citizens to enter into a 'sacred competition . . . to banish from all parts of France those jargons which are the remains of feudalism and the monument of slavery' (cited in Berger p. 167). While the Jacobin legacy has been appropriated both by the right and the left, occasionally the authentic character of France has been articulated. Thus spoke Alexandre Sanguinetti, a staunch Gaullist, in the National Assembly:

> It is no accident that for seven centuries monarchy, empire and republics have all been centralizers. It is because France is not a natural construction. It is an artificial political construction, for which the central power has always strived. Without centralization there could be no France. . . . in France there are several civilizations. And they haven't disappeared . . . (cited in Berger p. 167)

If so, France, like Britain, is also a multi-national state, assertions to the contrary notwithstanding.

Germany

The last case I propose to discuss from Western Europe is that of Germany. In fact, both Germany and Italy share a few common features: they fused citizenship and nationality, and defined nationality based on blood. Both developed aggressive nationalist tendencies

which degenerated into Nazism and facism; they were self-defined by
their national leaders – Mazzini, Mussolini and Hitler – as 'races'. The
degree of homogenization to which Italy was subjected may be discerned from the fact that when the country became a united political
entity in 1861 less than 3 per cent of its population used Italian in the
everyday context (Hobsbawm 1990: 61).

The most systematic effort to marginalize and liquidate a whole
people so as to achieve homogenization of the nation-state was undertaken by Hitler. Stalin did exactly the same, but for the opposite goal
– to dismantle the very idea of a nation-state. The targets of Hitler's
atrocities were different from the marginalized and/or ethnified nations of Great Britain and France. If the internality of the latter was
never in question, Jews and Gypsies and Slavs were clearly defined
and perceived as external to Germany; they were 'the other'. Slavs
were viewed as subhuman. Gypsies were imprisoned and enslaved.
But the Jews were non-human and were liquidated. To quote Yehuda
Bauer (1982: 89):

> Hitler saw the Jews as a kind of anti-race, a nomadic mongrel group.
> Because contact with Jews would corrupt German blood and culture Jews
> would be segregated, a segregation that led to the possibility of annihila-
> tion. ... In elaborating their concept of Jews as non-human, the Nazis
> described them as parasites, viruses or loathsome creatures from the ani-
> mal and insect world (rats and cockroaches). As a parasite force, the Jews
> corroded and would ultimately destroy, the cultures of their host nations.

Between 1933 and 1945 the Jews were eliminated from public life,
from the armed forces and from state education in Germany. They
were barred from the management of banks, prevented from owning
rural property, and their influence in the press was curtailed. Although predominantly middle class at that time, about 20 per cent of
the German Jews lost their livelihood. They were disenfranchised and
de-naturalized. The Nazis wanted them to leave Germany (Dawidowicz 1975: 57–60).

The Reich citizenship law of 15 September 1935 promulgated in Nu-
remberg stipulated the following:

> A Reich citizen is only that subject of German or kindred blood who
> proves by his conduct that he is willing and suited loyally to serve the
> German people and the Reich. The Reich Citizen is the sole bearer of full
> political rights as provided by the laws; only a Reich citizen ... can
> exercise the right to vote on political matters, or hold public office. Jews
> were even forbidden to fly the Reich national flag or to display the
> Reich colours. (cited in Dawidowicz 1976: 45–8)

The German state also intervened in the private life of Jews. Marriages between Jews and Germans and extra-marital intercourse between them were forbidden; marriages concluded abroad were also invalid. Jews were prohibited from employing German females under the age of 45 in their households according to the law concerning the protection of German blood and German honour (see Dawidowicz pp. 47–8).

It is clear from the discussion of Great Britain, France and Germany that they are not nation-states: first, in the sense that they have not achieved coterminality between nation and state; second, even if nation-states are defined as polities of high participatory possibilities, these three cases do not measure up because the smaller and weaker nations are not full-fledged participants, and at any rate they do not share this evaluation; third, because the dominant nations impose their language and culture on the dominated ones; and fourth, the internality of some of the social categories are questioned; they are not simply ethnified and marginalized, but also physically liquidated (as exemplified by the case of the German Jews).

The ideology of homogenization as implied in the notion of the nation-state and in operation for the past five centuries in Europe did not accomplish its avowed objective. And yet, the idea spread fast and was internalized by the political and intellectual elite almost everywhere. In the remainder of this chapter I will refer to a few cases drawn from different parts of the world so as to demonstrate the pernicious effect of the ideology of homogenization.

Middle East

If the basic anchorage of nation-state formation was language in Europe, in the Middle East and South Asia it was religion.[9] I will pursue the discussion with reference to Turkey to demonstrate how religious minorities are ethnified.

Turkey

The genocide of Armenians in Turkey in 1915 is the first well-known case undertaken in the twentieth century to bring about the homogenization of the 'national' population. Armenia was an ancient 'nation' crystallized in the sixth century BC. The Armenian homeland lay between the Black, Caspian and Mediterranean Seas on both sides of the Soviet–Turkish frontier. By the end of the fourteenth century the last Armenian kingdom had collapsed and it became a stateless nation. Under the Ottoman Empire, which expanded to its zenith by the

seventeenth century, the Armenians constituted the only prosperous
Christian community. While they enjoyed freedom of worship, they
could not use their language for purposes other than domestic conver-
sation and recitation of prayers. They remained largely anchored to
their historic homeland as peasants. Of the various subject peoples of
the Ottoman Empire, the Armenians were the most dispersed and by
the middle of the nineteenth century they no longer constituted a
majority in much of their historic homelands (Chalk and Jonassohn
1990: 249–89).

The multi-cultural Ottoman Empire gave a certain amount of freedom and autonomy to the religious minorities under the *millet* system. But the decline of the empire and the simultaneous spread of the
idea of the nation-state from Western Europe prompted homogenization. In Turkey this led to the genocide of the Armenian populations,
expulsion of the Greeks, impoverishment of the Jews and Turkifica-
tion of the rest (Cahnman 1944: 524–9). In contrast to the 'racism' of
the Nazis, the nationalism of Turkey was based on cultural assimilation. Members of minorities could become members of the majority by
adopting its language, culture and religion, which few did voluntarily. Even the progressive elements such as Young Turks were pursuing the goal of transforming the heterogeneous empire into a
homogeneous state based on the concept of 'one nation, one people'
(Chalk and Jonassohn 1990: 249, 259).

The Armenians formed a formidable obstacle in achieving this goal,
as they were the only non-Muslim group whose ancient homeland lay
in the very heart of Turkey. To give up this land would inevitably lead
to the dissolution of the Turkish state. The fact that Armenian and
Turkish villages co-existed peacefully side by side for centuries did
not in any way dissuade the nationalists from their homogenization
project. World War I provided an opportune moment for the Turkish
state to strike at the Armenian nation. But the Armenians, understandably, did not want to part with their sacred homeland. The
conflict between the two groups was 'a struggle between two nations
for the possession of a single homeland that ended with the terrible
holocaust of 1915, when a million and a half Armenians perished'
(Lewis 1961: 356).

The genocide of the Armenians eloquently unfolds the disastrous
consequences of the effort to create a nation-state, perhaps more than
the genocide of the Jews in Germany, because the Armenians were in
their ancient homeland. It also shows the untenability of defining
nation based on religion (see chapter 4), as the Turks and Armenians
shared a common homeland. Further, the Armenians did not seek to
establish their own state, they only wanted to preserve their cultural

identity, which was indeed deeply rooted in religion. They did not pose a threat to the Turkish state, particularly after 1908 when the regime of Abdul Hamid ended. In fact, a section of the Armenian leadership was in league with the Young Turks (Lewis pp. 210–11). Finally, the Armenians were reckoned as the 'people of the Book' in the traditional Muslim view, and they were the most loyal *millet* of the Ottoman Empire. And yet, the integral nationalism of Ziya Gokalp ignored it all (see below).

The Armenians did seek greater autonomy in internal matters and governmental protection against Kurdish designs. But they did not confront the Turks in any way, nor did they want to secede or join Russia. The Armenian 'programme was essentially one of reform within the Ottoman empire'. In fact, they believed that 'a complete separation of Armenia from Turkey was ethnographically and geographically impossible' (Davidson 1948: 483–4).

What then was the reason behind the ethnification and physical liquidation of the Armenians? Ottomanism hoped to sustain the empire by providing for cultural autonomy to all, regardless of religion and national origin. But the disintegration of the empire and the consequent secession of the Christian Balkans led to the crystallization of two competing orientations: pan-Islamism and Turkish nationalism. However, it was not possible to sustain pan-Islamism because first Albania and Macedonia, both predominantly populated by Muslims, revolted, followed by the Muslim Arabs. Consequently, Ottomanism and pan-Islamism were abandoned by 1914, and the Young Turks turned to Turkish nationalism.

In the first phase, Turkish nationalism assumed a pan-Turkish orientation called Turanism, according to which all the Turkic-speaking peoples shared a common culture and should be unified into one political entity. This meant constituting a new state spread far and wide – over the Russian Caucasus, Central Asia, Kazakhstan and the Crimea – and comparable in size to the Ottoman Empire, but without the irritating non-Muslim minorities. Although the project did not take off, it did intensify Turkish nationalism among Ottoman Turks. Conversely, it eroded the confidence of the minorities such as the Armenians to continue to exist as culturally distinct groups within the projected Turkish nation-state.

The ideologue of Turkish nationalism was Ziya Gokalp who conceptualized integral nationalism, while the architect of the Turkish nation-state was Mustafa Kamal who tried to create a homogeneous nation. The Greeks and Turks were exchanged, and the bulk of the Armenians left Turkey gradually (Heyd 1950: 132). To Gokalp, a nation was 'a society consisting of people who speak the same language, have had the same education and are unified in their religious, moral and aesthetic ideals – in short, those who have common culture and religion'. Non-Turkish people such as 'Greeks, Armenians and Jews who lived in Turkey were Turks only in respect of citizenship but not of nationality . . . they would remain a foreign body in the national Turkish state' (cited in Heyd pp. 63, 132). Even those whose ancestral homeland was in Turkey were outsiders because they were not Muslims; that is, the nationals were defined as ethnies. Thus, the ultimate rationale of the genocide perpetrated on the Armenians was the homogenization of the Turkish ate.

South-East Asia

I will discuss the case of this region with special reference to Indonesia and the Philippines. In the case of these two island states of South-East Asia, religion and language conjointly assume saliency as instruments of ethnification.

Indonesia

Indonesia is often cited as a successful case of welding a multitude of islands (13,000) into an integral state. The majority religion (Islam) and the second major religion (Hinduism) co-exist with substantial harmony. The source of tension between the predominantly Christian East Timor (West Irian) and the Indonesian state is often wrongly referred to as religious. In fact, it is a national struggle on the part of the people of East Timor for sustaining their identity and extending their autonomy.

The dominant island of Indonesia, Java, hosts the sprawling capital Jakarta. The major national groups are the Javanese, Sundanese, Minangkabau, Minahasan, Amboinese, and Bataks. The Bataks consist of four clans whose identity has firmed up only recently and yet they 'resented the invasion of their homeland by outsiders who did not speak their language, did not follow their *adat*, (customary law), and were not members of one of the four Simalungun clans' (William 1970: 59). Thus the insider–outsider dichotomy and the consequent conflict between nationals and ethnies was not absent in Indonesia. But there is a hierarchy of ethnies. Those who have an accredited homeland within Indonesia are ethnies only in the homeland of some other co-citizens. The 2.5 million strong Chinese community, which played and still plays an important role in the economic context, constitutes an ethnie in the country as a whole, although it settled in Indonesia over a century or more earlier. Many have married Indonesian women and most of them do not speak any of the Chinese languages. And yet, hardly a third of this community has Indonesian citizenship (Skinner 1963: 97–117).

Be that as it may, it is the imposition of a common language that has led to the eclipse of a large number of national languages of Indonesia. Malay, brought by the Muslim traders of the Malacca strip (now in Malaysia), has been the lingua franca of the Indonesian archipelago for several centuries. Malay was renamed as Bahasa Indonesia and made the official language in 1945. At that time only about 10 million people spoke the language, of which only 3 to 4 million were native speakers. By the early 1970s some 30 million spoke Bahasa Indonesia in contrast to some 60 million who spoke Javanese (Whiteley 1971: 62). Although this is in contrast to the European situation (e.g., Great Britain, France), where the language of the bigger nations became the lingua franca, the fact remains that Indonesia's 'national' language is largely alien to the majority of the people.

Philippines

The Philippines consist of 7,100 islands. The biggest city, Manila, located on Luzon Island, is the capital. The Malay immigrants, the Barangays, brought Islam to the Philippines long before Western colonization. But the country was thoroughly Hispanicized during the period of Spanish colonization (1521–1897). The most important mark of this is that the Philippines is the only Christian majority (94 per cent) country in Asia, in which Catholics predominate. However, with American colonization (1898–1946) English replaced Spanish as the primary language. After a relatively short anti-colonial struggle, the Philippines became an independent state in 1949.

Four national identities have crystallized and exist in contemporary Philippines: Tagalog, Ilocanos, Visayans and Mindanao – the last being invariably referred to as Muslims in most writings. The Tagalog homeland is Luzon and Tagalog is the major language of Manila. In the 1960s it was spoken as a mother tongue only by 21 per cent of the population (Grossholtz 1964: 80). The Ilocanos mainly inhabited the coastal strip of north-west Luzon but gradually spread to the hills. The Visayans occupy the island between Luzon and Mindanao; they speak a number of dialects which are, however, mutually intelligible. The Visayan is an aggregative identity, labelled so in urban Manila and rural Mindanao, but in their homeland they assume different identities – Cebuanos, Waray-Waray, Ilongos. Their large-scale migration to the sparsely populated Mindanao lands began during the period of Spanish colonization and continued through the American

period. This process continued as the state in the independent Philippines also encouraged migration to the Mindanao homeland. By the
early 1960s there were more Cebuanos in northern Mindanao than on
Cebu island.

The resistance by Mindanaos, predominantly Muslims, against the
colonization of their homeland by Cebuanos, largely Christians, has
been instantly labelled a Muslim rebellion in the press, and in popular
and social science writings. But it is actually a conflict between nationals and ethnies, and it continues to this day. The importance of Mindanao resistance can largely be understood in the context of the
tremendous value placed on land by the Filipino peasantry. Explain-
ing the resistance of the people of Apayao, the Isnegs, against the
government acquisition of land for development projects, McLean
(1980: 40) writes: 'For hundreds of years they lived in Apayao. Every
hectare of land has belonged to a particular family, whether they are
farming it that year or letting it lie fallow. In former years ... the
penalty for trespassing on Isneg land was death.' The fact that the
Mindanao Muslims, the descendants of ancient Malay immigrants,
have Muslim Malaysia and Indonesia as their cultural reference
points provides an easy excuse to label them as 'anti-national', that is,
anti-state. But the fact that Cebuanos identify themselves with Christianity, a religion that entered the Philippines long after Islam,
becomes an advantage given the hegemonic Christian ethos. That is,
irrespective of the time and mode of entry, the dominant religion
becomes the 'national' religion and the religion of the minority is
stigmatized.

Tagalog was chosen as the base language of the Philippines in 1937.
But it was labelled as Pilipino in 1955 to mollify the non-Tagalog
linguistic groups. In 1939 only 25 per cent of the Filipinos spoke the
language, but by 1960, 44 per cent did. During the same period the
English speakers rose from 27 to 40 per cent (Parole 1969). Even as
the Filipinos are gradually becoming bi-lingual – speaking English and
Pilipino – the vast majority of the population is likely to lose its mother
tongue. Once again, it is the same story. The homogenization project of
the state has deprived people of their basic cultural identities.

Africa

The salient element in the social identity of Africa is 'tribe'. Like the
island states of Indonesia and the Philippines, the scale of the constituting units is small and therefore the formula 'for each tribe its
nation-state' is not a viable option. There are some 6,000 tribes in
Africa. In Nigeria, the biggest and the most complex of African states,

there are 250 identity groups, the 3 largest constituting 60 per cent of the population. Tanzania has 120 groups, the Ivory Coast 60, and the Gambia, with a population of less than 1 million, has 8 groups. Out of the 50 African states 29 have less than 5 million and 13 have less than 1 million population each. Even in terms of area they are not always big: 13 states have less than 30,000 square kilometres (see Hughes 1981: 122–47). Be that as it may, as I have suggested in chapter 2, this is not a sustainable argument against tribes being considered as nations. The difficulty arises when the European idea of the nation-state is applied mechanically to the African situation.

European colonialism in general not only denied that African tribes are nations, dismissing them as peoples without history, but artificially and mechanically joined several of them into one administrative and/or political unit. The artificial division and grouping of African tribes has played havoc in post-colonial Africa, and has not been accepted by African nationalists and intellectuals. The political boundaries created by the colonial administration are, nevertheless, continued by African political leaders for reasons of expediency. And the question posed by King Mutesa II of Baganda remains unanswered and pertinent even today:

> I have never been able to pin down precisely the difference between a tribe and a nation and see why one is thought so despicable and the other is so admired. Whichever we are, the Baganda have a common language, tradition, history and cast of mind. While we stood alone, we were accepted as the most civilized and powerful of the kingdoms. Does this justify our being totally dominated by our neighbours, unnaturally yoked to us as they were by Britain? (1967: 78–9)

That is, all tribes may not be nations, but some could be. On the other hand, the aggregation of tribes in one administrative unit or polity will not make a nation. And this is precisely what Awolowo, an important political leader of Nigeria, meant when he wrote: 'Nigeria is not a nation. It is a mere political expression. There are no "Nigerians" in the sense that there are "English", "Welsh" or "French" ' (1947: 47–8). Thus viewed, most contemporary African states are multi-national or multi- tribal. But the dissection of the same tribe into two or more administrative or political units has further complicated matters. This is so precisely because people have a strong sense of attachment to their homeland and, furthermore, those who intrude into it are invariably viewed as ethnies – that is, outsiders. I will discuss the situation in Africa by focusing on a sample of cases of conflicts between insiders and outsiders.

It is useful to keep in mind that there was a hierarchy of ethnies in colonial Africa as elsewhere. Those who were perceived as political oppressors (Europeans) or as economic exploitors (Asians) were qualitatively different from those fellow Africans who were drawn from a different tribe or clan and whose homeland was the same or in the neighbourhood, usually contiguous, and who were competing for new opportunities. Therefore, Kautsky's quip: 'Why does one tribe in the Congo think of a government dominated by another tribe as less alien than a government dominated by Belgians?' is frivolous (1962: 37).

Generally speaking, the Europeans and Asians gradually left (except from South Africa) after de-colonization. And when they did not, they were expelled. For example, in 1959 the European population in Uganda was 10,000 and the Asians who dominated trade and commerce totalled 72,000. During the colonial period both were powerful, but once de-colonization set in they lost their political importance. By 1972 Asians had been expelled and the Europeans had withdrawn. In Tanzania's big towns the cultural division was between Arabs, Asians and Africans, a situation that was rendered redundant by the 1964 'revolution'. The Arabs left and the Asians were expelled and those who were native to Africa were accommodated. In 1948, at the peak of their presence, the Asians constituted 61 per cent of the population of Jinja, Uganda's second biggest town, and the Europeans made up 12 per cent. By the mid-1970s the town had become overwhelmingly African. This in itself is ample proof that there is a basic distinction between insiders and outsiders. The latter, be they immigrants, sojourners or even settlers, will leave for their own respective homelands or some other hospitable locales in the wake of political animosity; the former will not. And if a group flees to escape persecution from its own homeland, the hope is to return or to find a new homeland. It may be noted here that when the Europeans and Asians left Africa, ethnic Africans also left for their respective homelands, but *within* Africa. Thus, Malians left Upper Volta, Ugandans left Kenya, Dahomeans were expelled from the Ivory Coast and Nigerians from Ghana (Young 1976). Thus the ideology of the nation-state was harmful not only to non-Africans, but it threatened the fellow African ethnies too.

Rwanda and Burundi

The recurring, in fact continuing, conflicts between the Tutsis and the Hutus in Rwanda and Burundi, two neighbouring states, is well known. The two states were ruled together by Germans from 1885 to 1918, after which they became a Belgian trust territory. Although the Tutsis were in a minority both in Burundi (15 per cent) and in Rwanda

(10 per cent), they were the ruling group. When there was a wave of demonstrations against them in the 1960s they started feeling insecure. In 1962 Rwanda became independent and a republic, and the Hutu majority assumed political power. They started to persecute the Tutsis, killing some 20,000 in 1963–4; as many again left the country (Meisler 1976: 227–32). Burundi also became independent in 1962, but as a kingdom to be ruled by a chief. This chief was overthrown in 1966 by Tutsi army officers of a clan other than that of the ruling chief. The Hutus were trying to assert themselves as a majority, but were ignored or quelled. In 1972, in retaliation after a Hutu uprising, the government, run by the Tutsi minority, killed an estimated 100,000–200,000 Hutus. The killings selectively concentrated on three categories of people: those in government jobs, including the military; those with some wealth; and the educated – students and teachers in high schools and universities (Meisler pp. 227–32).

There are important differences between Rwanda and Burundi. In giving an account of this, Lemerchand (1970) points out that Tutsi domination was achieved through a long process spanning over several centuries, the critical point of transition being the fifteenth century when a Tutsi could establish his kingship in Rwanda. By 1900 Rwanda had achieved a remarkable degree of centralization. In addition, Tutsi elements were spread, albeit thinly, fairly evenly almost everywhere in Rwanda, so that the central state authority, manned by fellow Tutsis, had support. This also gave birth to a uniform system of stratification throughout the country. The situation in Burundi was different. The Tutsis were concentrated in a few pockets, and the rest were very thinly dispersed, which did not give them the required striking or resisting power in Burundi.

In his exhaustive study Lemerchand's explanation seems to me to have been geared mainly to understanding Hutu violence against the Tutsis in Rwanda in 1963–4 and why it was absent in Burundi. But by 1972 the situation had changed dramatically. In spite of their assumed lack of striking power, the minority Tutsi government indulged in the systematic killing of the Hutu majority in Burundi. And yet, Lemerchand persists with his explanation (see 1993: 151–71) because he notes that there was hardly any traditional hatred between the Tutsis and Hutus in Burundi compared with the situation in Rwanda. He seems to suggest that the Tutsi violence against the Hutus in Burundi was reactive, and that the Rwanda revolution, which created a Hutu republic (in Rwanda), had left a deep psychological impact on both; presumably it demoralized the Tutsis but was a morale booster for the Hutus. But Burundi too is a Hutu republic, in that 84 per cent of the population is Hutu. Therefore, we need to look elsewhere to locate the crucial variable. Religion does not provide an answer because both the tribes are highly Christianized and, indeed, of the same denomination – Catholics. They have a common language (Kirundi) and the same type of social organization.

The racial explanation is often pressed into service because there are phenotypical differences between them (see Meisler 1972: 227–32; Lemerchand 1970; 1993: 151–71). The Tutsis are tall, slender and of a lighter skin colour than the Hutus who are short, stocky and darker – a Bantu people. The Tutsis are pastoralists, while the Hutus are farmers. It is argued that the Tutsis developed a superiority complex and the Hutus internalized inferiority. Therefore, the Tutsi minority could dominate over the Hutu majority. But the 'racial' explanation is not admissible for two reasons (at any rate it is different from the racial conflicts between whites and blacks). First, most inter-tribal conflicts in Africa are between people who have the same phenotypical features. Second, even apartheid with all its atrocities could not lead to a permanent internalization of an inferiority complex by the blacks in South Africa, even though it was perpetrated by the Europeans, who are distinctly different as a race.

What then is the crucial variable which can explain the animosity between the Tutsis and the Hutus? I suggest that it is to be located in the fact that the Hutus are insiders (nationals) and the Tutsis are outsiders (an ethnie) in Burundi and Rwanda. Both Lemerchand and Meisler have acknowledged this fact, but I am afraid they missed its crucial importance. The Tutsi minority came to the region some 400 years ago from the north, that is, Ethiopia; they were an invading pastoralist tribe. Although they could establish their dominance, they could not institutionalize their hegemony either in Burundi or in Rwanda. I am making this point because in noting the difference between the two countries Lemerchand concluded that the Tutsis of Rwanda formed a hegemonic caste whose values were diffused throughout the society. In contrast, they did not possess this all-pervasive moral legitimacy in Burundi (1970: 472–3). And yet, in Rwanda the Tutsis were attacked by the Hutus in the early 1960s and the Tutsi retaliation occurred in Burundi. The fact that the Tutsis are an ethnie and that their claim to Burundi and Rwanda as their adopted homelands is not conceded by Hutus, who look upon the territories of these states as their ancestral homeland, is at the root of the conflicts.

Other African Cases

If the Hutu–Tutsi conflicts have inter-state manifestations, many other inter-tribal conflicts are intra-state in orientation. In most cases the conflicts found their natural habitat in urban areas, particularly in those towns and cities that expanded due to rapid industrialization. Thus in Kinshasa, a town in Zaire, the primary polarization was between the Kongo and migrants from up-river Ngala. Kinshasa is at the fringe of the Kongo cultural territory (nation) but the Kongo believed it to be their exclusive territory, over whose resources they had a natural claim. By the mid-1940s the firm position of the Kongo was threatened for three reasons. First, Lingala, the up-river lingua franca which served as the link language of the urban areas for the Ngala, was standardized. In contrast, the language of the Kongo continued to have at least four variants. Second, the Kongo earned the wrath of the colonial masters for their involvement in two major collective protests in 1921 and 1945. In contrast, Ngala was certified for good conduct by the Catholic mission and hence favoured by the colonial administration. Third, Lingala was used as the language for primary education, which gave a tremendous advantage to the Ngala people in terms of occupational mobility. These facts ought to be seen against the backdrop that the Kongo accounted for 82 per cent of Kinshasa's population in the 1950s (Young 1976: 167–74). The threat posed by Ngala united the Kongo, and the main claim to their legitimacy was that they were the sons of the soil and the Ngala were outsiders (ethnies).

The Luluva–Luba conflict in Zaire had the same basis. The two groups are culturally identical and speak the same language. But although they co-existed harmoniously for at least a century, it was as peoples each with their own distinct homeland. In fact, till the mid-1940s Luba agricultural immigrants were readily welcomed to the Luluva territory, and given land and women in marriage. However, at the time of colonial penetration the Luba group was economically disadvantaged and the Luluva became prosperous, although both were in the slave and ivory trades. Gradually, the Luba immigrants started competing with the Luluva natives in economic and political contexts. As a result, hostile confrontations between them started, and intensified by 1958. Luluva attacks against Luba began in October 1959 in Katanga, and at least 50,000 Luba went back to their homeland. From 1958 to 1963 the population of the Luba homeland of South Kasai increased from 332,620 to 1,348,030, most of them returnees. This was largely the result of the expulsion of Luba from the Luluva rural areas (Young pp. 175–7).

In the Copperbelt also the conflict was between Luba-Kasai and the native people, although Lubas from another area (Shankadi) too were present there. The Luba-Kasai came to the new mining centres such as Lubumbashi, which was founded in 1911, to avail themselves of the new opportunities. Far surpassing the native people in education, they could enter white-collar employment and get acknowledgement for their industry and intelligence. They also 'behaved well' and became pro-European. The notion of 'authentic Shabans', which excluded the Luba-Kasai, was invoked in the late 1950s by the native people. The attitude towards the Luba-Shankadi, counting about 18 per cent of the Lubumbashi population in 1950, was left ambiguous, partly to focus on the Luba-Kasai as strangers and as illegitimate intruders and partly to get the support of the Luba-Shankadi. The political mobilization of authentic Shabans had two main objectives. First, to stop the policy of favoured labour recruitment towards outsiders that was pursued by (European) companies. This policy, according to authentic Shabans, thwarted the intellectual and material development of the Katanga tribes, 'the genuine people' of the land. Second, they believed that the authorities were indulging in a deliberate policy of planting the people of Kasai in Katanga towns so as to crush the people of Katanga. Clearly, the Lubas were viewed as strangers from Kasai, so much so that in 1962, at the time of Shaba secession, the UN had to repatriate the Luba-Kasai temporarily to their accredited homeland (Young pp. 177–81).

Rural Nigeria

Although the theatre of the insider–outsider conflicts is largely the urban centres, rural areas are not exempt. I will illustrate the national ethnie conflicts in rural areas with two cases from Nigeria. The colonial state of Nigeria was created on 1 January 1914, ignoring geography and the bases of identity groups of the region. It had some 250 identity groups (tribes, clans, regional groups) incorporated into it by the British colonial official, Lord Lugard. When the country became independent on 1 October 1960, 80 per cent of the population lived in rural areas.

Nigeria is the most populous country in Africa, with a population of over 60 million. It has three distinct cultural regions, dominated by three of its biggest nations. The semi- nomadic Hausa tribe, constituting about 60 per cent of Nigeria's population, lives in the underdeveloped north. The possession of a distinct language and conversion to Islam has given the Hausa a specific identity. Western Nigeria is the homeland of the educated and urbanized Yorubas, who still are largely animists. Eastern Nigeria is the homeland of some 14 million Ibos (in mid-1960s) who converted to Christianity in large numbers in the early twentieth century. Industrious and mobile, the Ibos spread far and wide in the territory of the Nigerian state and took advantage of the new economic opportunities. Understandably, the Hausa majority felt intimidated by the presence of the Ibos in their homeland. In 1966 alone some 50,000 Ibos were killed in the north, as a result of which many others returned to their homeland. Given their religious differences, the source of conflicts between the three groups is invariably traced to religion. Meanwhile, the fact that the Ibos were migrants from the Nile Valley a few centuries ago is conveniently ignored. That is, while the conflict is essentially one between nationals and ethnies, it is referred to by some as a confrontation between different religious collectivities and/or between Nigerian nationalism and tribalism (see, for one example, Snyder 1976: 174–6). The problems here are of two types: first, the multi-national Nigerian state is simply labelled as a nation; second, there is a refusal to recognize the possibility that tribes could be nations.

The insider–outsider conflicts find their articulation even within the same region, as exemplified by the following case. According to the 1963 census figures, of the 275,623 Nigerians of Okitipupa Division in rural western Nigeria, 205,037 were the Ikale, a Yoruba people and the natives of the region. The rest were drawn from nearly a dozen Nigerian tribes, the most numerous being Urhobo (40,424) and Ijo (22,663). All others numbered less than 3,000. The Ikale are believed to have occupied the area around the fifteenth century when land was in abundance, whereas the earliest recorded immigration of Urhobo people, a tribe from mid-western Nigeria, occurred in the late nineteenth century. The chief occupation of the Urhobo was palm-oil production, and they were mainly settled in exclusive camps (Otite 1975: 120–3).

The Ikale farmers owned the land and tapped the shorter palm trees; meanwhile, the Urhobo tenants employed their skills in harvesting the taller trees, without which the resources would have remained unexploited. As tenants they had to pay an annual rent to tap the trees. Gradually, the Ikale landowners realized that the immigrants were substantially more prosperous than they were, and the younger Ikale adopted Urhobo technology and started to tap the taller palm trees themselves. Not surprisingly, a move to deny the tenants the right to tap palm trees started; in some cases landowners or their kin harvested trees for which rents had already been collected. This became a cause for conflict between the Ikale and Urhobo and the latter started returning to their natal homes. They had considered their stay in Okitipupa as temporary, and were not willing to make any capital investment in the host society. But they were willing to remain on a permanent basis if they were given equal access to land and local citizenship rights (Otite pp. 122–4), both of which were denied.

The following points are clear from this case. First, the Ikale and the Urhobo both agree that Okitipupa is the Ikale homeland. Second, the Urhobo defined themselves and are treated by the Ikale as outsiders, even after nearly a century of being in Okitipupa. Third, although both the Ikale and the Urhobo are citizens of Nigeria, they could be nationals or ethnies within the territory of the state depending upon whether they are inside or outside their own homeland. Finally, the insiders have an instant claim to their homeland, and it is difficult for the outsiders to gain the same level of legitimacy even after living there for decades or centuries.

The cases of conflicts that we have analysed from Africa are usually explained in terms of political hegemony (Tutsi–Hutu), modernization and industrialization (Kongo–Ngala, Luluva–Luba), resource competition (Ikale–Urhobo). These are certainly contributory factors. But what is common to all the cases (and many more examples can be added) is that they are contentions about homelands; the conflicts are between nationals and ethnies. The tribes everywhere have a strong sense of attachment to their ancestral homelands and intrusions into them are stoutly resisted if they have the striking power. Most of them do not have their own states; they may not even aspire to them. But by wrongly conceptualizing the nation as state, politicians and academicians have paved the way for their ethnification; making them outsiders in their own homeland. To add insult to injury the tribes have also been stigmatized as people without history and hence been disqualified for the act of self-determination. It is high time that they are rescued from this conceptual trap. The principle of self-determination is meaningless as it stands 'because the people cannot decide until somebody decides who are the people', to recall the pregnant statement of Jennings (1956: 56).

This brief survey of project homogenization initiated by the ideology of nation-state unambiguously demonstrates that the entire Old World – Europe, Asia and Africa – is plagued by it. And the project has a different trajectory in the New World, as we have seen in chapter 5. It is true that the salient dimensions vary across regions and civilizations – language in Western Europe, religion in the Middle East and South Asia, language and religion in South-East Asia, tribe in Africa. Although the collectivities that are ethnified differ in terms of their defining features, they are all nations – territorially anchored speech communities – with strong attachments to their homelands.

It seems appropriate to conclude this chapter by reminding the reader of the warning of Lord Acton which I quoted in chapter 2 (see

p. 29). He unambiguously held the view that the course of attaching nationality to state will bring about both material and moral ruin. But he is not alone in articulating this view. Statesmen who experience the problem of managing bi-national or multi-national states have come to the same conclusion. Thus Pierre Elliot Trudeau, a former Prime Minister of Canada, said: 'Except for a very small fraction of his history, man has done very well without nations . . . the tiny portion of history marked by the emergence of the nationstates is also the scene of the most devastating wars, the worst atrocities, and the most degrading hatred the world has ever seen' (1968: 157). This is in sharp contrast to what Graham Wallas attributed to European statesmen, quoted at the beginning of this chapter.

8

Immigration and the Chauvinism of Prosperity

In chapters 5, 6 and 7 I have dealt with the process of ethnification with special reference to three historical moments: European colonialism, proletarian internationalism and the project of homogenization enunciated and implemented by the nation-state. This chapter is devoted to a discussion of immigration, partly caused by the above three phenomena, but mainly occasioned by the economic prosperity – chauvinism of prosperity – experienced after World War II.[10] In the New World everybody was an immigrant to start with (save the First Nations), although with greatly differing social and economic statuses. In the Old World, in contrast, the distinction between the insider and outsider, the nationals and ethnies, was and remains sharp. The situation gets further complicated when the outsider has additional debilitating features such as a different colour (race) and/or culture (religion and language). Further, the historical background of the ethnic community influences the attitudes of the national community. In what follows I will briefly discuss the marginalization of three categories of immigrants to affluent Western Europe. These immigrants are the products of the demise of European colonialism, of the dismantling of the socialist states and of the rapid economic development of Europe after World War II.

Coloured immigrants

The European retreat from Asia and Africa started with the return of colonial officers and colonizers to their homelands. In the case of

Great Britain, France, Belgium and the Netherlands de-colonization also resulted in the immigration of 'natives', usually as workers from the former overseas territories. The legal status accorded to them depended on the policy orientations these countries pursued. Broadly speaking, one can discern three value orientations in this context. French colonialism was geared to assimilation irrespective of race and culture. The 1792 revolutionary decree declared that all men, whatever their colour, domiciled in French colonies were French citizens, and were entitled to all the rights assured by the French constitution. In contrast, the British policy assumed that races were distinct and different. While the British worked towards the creation of a Commonwealth constituted by diverse and independent peoples, the French wanted to create a homogeneous society of a single Greater France with Paris as the centre. As Emerson puts it (1962: 69): 'The roots of the difference in the two positions are to be sought in the British conviction that there are many breeds of men, each destined to develop along its own lines and the contrary French belief in the ultimate oneness of mankind.' The third value orientation can be seen in the Spanish–Portuguese approach, wherein, although informal intimacy with the coloured colonized peoples was encouraged to the extent of intermixture, a formal distance was kept, which manifested itself in benevolent despotism. Admittedly, these orientations have differing consequences when coloured people go as immigrants into metropolitan countries, but I will discuss only the British and French cases, because the problem in the Spanish–Portuguese context is not very acute.

Britain

The above differences in value orientation are reflected in legal provisions too. Thus, in Great Britain immigrants with British Dependent Territory citizenship or Commonwealth citizenship are recorded separately from all 'other' groups of foreign resident populations, although this formal distinction is devoid of any substance, as we shall soon see. But before that it is useful to refer to the magnitude of the immigrant population. The size of the Foreign Resident Population (FRP) in Great Britain in 1982 was 2,137,000, declining to 1,875,000 in 1990 when it accounted for 3.3 per cent of the total population. Of the nearly 1.9 million FRP of Great Britain in 1990, about 60 per cent were immigrants from former colonies in Asia or Africa. In 1990, according to the Labour Force Survey, 930,000 foreigners were working in Great Britain. The survey lists the ethnic and visible (non-white) minorities separately. In 1989 some 2.6 million (4.6 per cent) of the working population of Great Britain belonged to ethnic minorities, and most of them were from the Indian subcontinent (Fassmann and Munz 1992: 457–80). According to OECD statistics, there were 155,000 Indians, 55,000 Pakistanis, 38,000 Bangladeshis and 70,000 West Indians in Britain in 1990.

The paradox here is that these coloured immigrants who were Commonwealth citizens had no easy access to Britain, because the series of legal measures – such as the 1962 and 1968 Commonwealth Immigrants Acts, the 1971 Immigration Act and the 1988 Immigration Rules, which were introduced to restrict immigration – affected them also. The British Home Secretary provided the rationale for the 1962 act in the following terms. First, with no restrictions over a quarter of the world's population had the right to enter and settle in Britain. Second, the tendency for immigration from the new Commonwealth was steadily on the increase. Third, the anticipated economic recession would result in strain between immigrants and British nationals. Fourth, the scale of recent immigration had resulted in an 'intensified social problem' for the country (Miles 1989: 41).

The Labour Party opposed the bill introduced by the Conservative government on the grounds that it smacked of 'race discrimination', that the British subjects in the Caribbean had the right to enter and settle in the 'mother country' and that the history of British colonialism left the government with moral and legal responsibility for the post-colonial era. However, the bill was defended by the Home Secretary on the grounds that Britain was a small and densely populated country. A Conservative MP warned: 'Thousands are coming here from the West Indies; but if they wished to do so they could come here in their millions from India and Pakistan' (cited in Miles p. 42). The argument of the Labour MPs who opposed the bill was couched in racist tones too. One argued that the coloured folk were needed to run the basic services that the whites were unwilling to do. Another argued that the recorded rate of crimes committed by the coloureds was no higher than than that of 'our own people', as against the claim made by a Conservative MP that the coloured immigrants indulged in crimes 'out of all proportions' and committed the worst types of offences (Miles p. 43). Thus, it is clear that the discourse on the 1962 Immigrants Act was expressed in terms of race and colour, ignoring the legal status of the immigrants under reference as British subjects. They were perceived as outsiders or ethnies, both by the Conservative and Labour MPs, in spite of their differing ideological positions.

The debate over the 1988 Immigration Rules, which sought to abolish the right of British citizens born elsewhere in the Commonwealth, apart from those with a grandparent born in Britain, to enter and

settle in the UK, was equally suggestive of the insider–outsider dichotomy. The following excerpt from what two of the MPs who particip-
ated in the debate said makes it clear:

> There is much talk . . . about the reunification of families, a benign
> objective which I support. But if one family member has left his native
> land for Britain, we do not, as far as I know, prevent him from returning
> to the bosom of his family. However we are rightly anxious about who
> should have access to our country minimizing those from a different
> cultural background . . . Because of the way in which we have mis-
> handled immigration policies in the past, the damage done by mass
> immigration still poses a threat to the cohesion of our society. We face a
> number of social and racial problems . . . It does not matter in which
> section of the community the problems lie; they result from major
> changes to our country's racial content and from mass immigration.
> (cited in Miles pp. 48, 49)

Viewed against this background, it is no surprise that right-wing
extremism became active against coloured immigrants in Britain, as
elsewhere. The National Front (NF) of Britain was born in 1967,
through an amalgamation of three groups: the British National Party
(BNP) with 1,500 members, the League of Empire Loyalists (LEL) with
2,000 members and the Racial Preservation Society (RPS) with 500
followers. By 1974 membership of the NF peaked at 17,500. The new
recruits were from the Conservative Party, but most of NF's votes
came from Labour (Gable 1991: 245–6). The ideology of the NF was
initially anti-Semitic, but latterly it has become anti-black, calling for
the repatriation of the latter from Britain. 'A fundamental aspect of
National Front's ideology was, and remains, a type of nationalistic
racism, hostile to multi-culturalism and eschewing international en-
tanglements . . . that might be opposed to the interests of Britain as a
racial entity', and the supporters of NF demand 'the repatriation of
blacks as a solution to economic malaise . . . ', according to Husbands
(1988: 72, 75). However, it is wrong to assume that the anti-black
attitude is confined to the right-wing fringe. Mr Janman, a mainstream politician, echoing his predecessors of 1962 and 1988 said on
20 June 1990 in the British House of Commons:

> One in three children born in London today is of ethnic origin. . . . That
> is a frightening concept for the country to come to terms with. We have
> already seen the problems of massive Moslem immigration . . . Unless
> we want to create major problems in the decades or the century ahead
> we must not only stop immigration but must move to voluntary resettle-
> ment to reduce the immigrant population. (cited in Van Dijk 1993: 267)

Coloured immigrants from the erstwhile colonies move in order to improve their economic lot. They face considerable prejudice and discrimination in their everyday life. While those in the lower class are the worst victims, the middle class, or even the intellectuals are not exempt. Mr Braithwaite, who was invited to contribute to the special issue of *Daedalus* on 'Colour and Race', begins his essay thus:

> I am a coloured immigrant. In spite of my years of residence in Britain, any service I might render the community in times of war or times of peace, any contribution I might make or wish to make, or any feeling of identity I might entertain toward Britain and the British, I – like all other coloured persons in Britain – am considered an immigrant. (Braithwaite 1967: 496)

The coloured immigrant is likely to remain an ethnie in Britain because of his high visibility, which constantly reminds the nationals that he is not simply an outsider but was also a slave, subject and conquered. As we have noted in chapter 5, the African entered the colonial world as a slave and the South Asian as an indentured labourer, and they are still not dissociated from these stigmas of the past. This manifests itself in various ways. For example, they can find accommodation only in those sections 'that are already abandoned to immigrant invasion', many jobs advertised once carried the caution 'no coloured', and they are accused of 'hyper sensitivity' when they complain about discrimination (Braithwaite pp. 499–507).

Although most of the West Indians are Christians and regard themselves as 'Westerners', they are shunned by the British. In contrast, Asian immigrants are distinguished by their religion, whether Sikh, Muslim or Hindu, which manifests itself in differences in dress and dietary practices. On the other hand, there is a hierarchy of colour; the darker the colour the greater the exclusion. This too has worked against the immigrants from the West Indies. But when it comes to economic matters the coloured immigrants share a common plight: they are generally hired last and fired first. Finally, while class status partly moderated discrimination, in that the higher the class, the greater the possibility of inter-racial interaction, 'race' and 'colour' consciousness has persisted, manifesting itself in everyday interaction (Little 1967: 512–26).

France

France is Europe's second largest country of immigration. More than a million former French residents of Algeria had to be resettled in

France due to the dislocations caused by the Algerian War of Independence from 1954 to 1962. Those who returned from other former French colonies accounted for a further million. Thus, de-colonization brought at least 2 million French overseas residents back to their ancestral homeland. However, these immigrants were neither listed nor treated as foreigners, they were 'coming home'. Foreign workers in France were mainly recruited from the Mediterranean region – Portugal, Spain, Morocco, Algeria, Tunisia and Italy. Since the early 1980s, although the number of Moroccans and Turks has increased, the composition of the Foreign Resident Population (FRP) in France has changed little over time. Thus, of the 3,608,000 FRP in France in 1990 (6.4 per cent of the population) 18 per cent came from Morocco. The share of Italy and Spain (7 and 6 per cent respectively) declined, as many immigrants from these countries returned to their countries of origin (see Fassmann and Munz 1992: 457–80).

In spite of this demographic composition of 'immigrants' in France, the French debate on *jus soli* or automatic citizenship has concentrated almost exclusively on second generation Algerians. There is hardly any reference to the Portuguese, the largest category of immigrants. The focus of attention is on a people who are black, and on Muslims, although there is a high incidence of French citizens among them. Of the 2.5–3 million Muslims in France, 1 million have acquired French nationality (Brubaker 1992: 232). Apparently, it is dual citizenship – French and Algerian – that is under attack, because this leads to the de-sacralization of citizenship according to the French conception whereby citizenship and nationality cannot be bifurcated. The idea of dual citizenship, it is held, instrumentalizes citizenship. But the real issue seems to be the impossibility of assimilating the black Muslims (cf. Brubaker 1992).

In France, the discourse on immigration is deeply rooted in French nationalism and racism. In fact, the idea of a 'French race' got a new lease of life with the beginning of mass immigration. Working-class racism is nothing new in France. Italians, Poles, Jews and Arabs have faced discrimination in turn. Both employers and the state reserve skilled and supervisory jobs for those who are 'French', and unskilled jobs for immigrants, thereby creating a hierarchy of workers: 'Collectivities of immigrant workers have for many years suffered discrimination and xenophobic violence in which racist stereotyping has played an essential role' (Balibar 1991: 20). But what is new in racism in France is its spread to all social classes, 'and most notably the one which only recently represented in large part a force for transformation', and therefore should be 'regarded as a symptom of profound crisis' (Balibar p. 223). In this sense, what 55 per cent of the voters of

Jean-Marie Le Pen said, namely, 'the president of Front National is the only person who says publicly what many French people think privately', sounds authentic (see *Le Monde*, 4 November 1987).

The Front National (FN) could be viewed as an instrument of French racism, notwithstanding its anti-Judaeo-Christian and Marxist orientation, with its grand vision of history as chaos and man as a defiant being capable of unlimited possibilities (Johnson 1991: 234–44). In fact, it is not much of an exaggeration to characterize it as a single issue movement (Mitra 1988: 47–64). The salience of immigration as an issue in French politics is so marked that it has divided even the left. The official policy was contained in a programme that would 'legalize' the clandestine immigrants resident in France by giving them work permits and the right to vote in national elections. This move was supported by intellectuals and the middle-class left, but resented by the working-class left. Enfranchisement of immigrant workers was also opposed by the right, as it formed a vote bank for the left. On the other hand, the right tried to befriend the white worker, the traditional base of the left (Mitra p. 51).

In the 1984 European Parliament elections the key slogan of Front National was: 'Two million immigrants are the cause of two million French people without work.' The FN stuck to the slogan in the 1986 'national' legislative elections, and 46 per cent of their voters (as against a mere 8 per cent average of the entire electorate) felt that immigration was the single most important issue. The FN wants 'to give employment priorities to French nationals, to expel immigrants who were convicted of crimes or who lost their jobs, to refuse welfare benefits to immigrants and to deny automatic French nationality to those from France's former colonies' (Mitra p. 53). The anti-immigrant attitude, which is widely shared but articulated only by a minority, has the 'advantage' of taking an ambiguous view on the issue. This is evident in a statement made by M. Pasqua on 9 July 1986 in the French Parliament: 'The French are not racist. But facing this continuous increase of the foreign population in France one has witnessed the development in certain cities and neighbourhoods, of reactions that come close to xenophobia' (cited in Van Dijk 1993: 266). While denying that the French are racists, Pasqua provides the required justification for xenophobia.

It is not entirely correct to think that the hatred has crystallized only against the coloured immigrant in France. There is a general rejection of the outsider, as exemplified by slogans such as 'Give back France to the French'. However, within this framework there is a hierarchy of immigrants. Le Pen, the leader of Front National, articulated it thus: 'I like my daughters better than my neighbours, my neighbours better than strangers and strangers better than enemies.' But the imagery does not quite fit the reality. The neighbours are more acceptable only if spatial proximity co-exists with cultural and mental proximity. This is where religion plays an important role. The 'European' Muslims of Turkey and Bosnia, although neighbours, are worse than strangers, sometimes instant enemies. But the mental distance increases cumulatively if one belongs to a different race and religion. Thus, the Algerian Muslim who is a French citizen is a stranger and an enemy, but the Portuguese, the Spaniard, the Italian and the Greek who is only a European citizen is more acceptable as he or she is white and belongs to the European Christian brotherhood.

Our discussion of the condition of coloured immigrants in Great Britain and France from their erstwhile colonies should clearly demonstrate that they are ethnified social categories. This is also true of the coloured immigrants in the Netherlands and Belgium.

Victims of the Iron and Golden Curtains

In chapter 6 we discussed the victims of proletarian internationalism launched by the socialist state. Germany, which has had no overseas colonies since 1918, has been the major host country for refugees and asylum-seekers to Western Europe. Therefore, I will discuss the case of the victims of the Iron and Golden Curtains with special reference to the erstwhile Federal Republic of Germany (FRG) and the current unified Germany.

Between 1945 and 1950 nearly 12 million displaced persons came to the territory of FRG, that is, within the 1949–90 borders. Of these, over 3.5 million people were immigrants from the German Democratic Republic (GDR) before the construction of the Berlin Wall in 1961 (see Fassmann and Munz 1992: 462). But emigration from Central and Eastern Europe gradually diminished, thanks to the imposition of the Iron Curtain and the associated travel restrictions. Between 1955 and 1989 mass emigration occurred mainly as a result of political crises, as, for example, from Hungary during 1956–7, from Czechoslovakia in 1968 and from Poland during 1980–1.

When the Iron Curtain came down, and military blocks in Europe were dissolved, the flow of migrants accelerated once more. While in 1983 the number of asylum-seekers in the fourteen OECD countries was a meagre 76,000, by 1986 the figure had tripled. In 1991 alone some 400,000 people sought asylum in Western Europe. The total figure remained the same for 1992, but by then asylum-seekers from the former Yugoslavia constituted a substantial proportion of it

(Fassmann and Munz p. 463). For the present discussion it is of great importance to note that nearly 50 per cent of the asylum-seekers in Western Europe preferred to enter West Germany: in 1991 the number of people who applied for asylum in West Germany was 256,000. However, less than 5 per cent of the applicants were admitted. The situation was further complicated because of the return of ethnic Germans seeking resettlement in their ancestral homeland. This process was accelerated by the dismantling of the Iron Curtain. Thus, compared to 1984, those who returned increased tenfold within five years. The figure was 377,000 for 1989 and 347,000 for 1990. To conclude, between 1945 and 1992 West Germany received around 22 million displaced persons, refugees, labour migrants and their families, political refugees, asylum-seekers and ethnic Germans (Fassmann and Munz p. 463).

Given the magnitude of the numbers of outsiders who entered West Germany, there is some justification for the sentiment expressed by Herr Hirsch on 9 February 1990 in the German Parliament. He said: 'I know no other country on this earth that gives more prominence to the rights of resident foreigners as does this . . . country' (cited in Van Dijk 1993: 266). However, there is a sharp distinction between these people and the ethnic Germans who are welcomed back as blood brothers, although they might have been living outside Germany for generations, do not speak the language or lead a German lifestyle. In contrast, the Turks, who have been living in Germany for several decades, in some cases for over a century, speak impeccable German and have adopted the lifestyle of Germany, yet are neither accorded citizenship status nor accepted as co-nationals; indeed they are stigmatized and ethnified. This has been articulated in an extreme form in a letter to the editor which appeared in one of the newspapers in Germany.

> When . . . a Turk stupidly looks at me, my hands tend to hit him. They show archaic behaviour, they are illiterates from a completely alien, 'cultural' context and have Islam as their religion. Did Europe in 1683 conquer the Turks so that they now get children's allowance, rent allowance, social welfare, and return premiums . . .? The best policy for these Turks is: Kick in the ass and out. (cited in Van Dijk 1987: 233)

Even as one acknowledges the fact that in 1990, 320,000 Turks lived in West Germany, constituting 74 per cent of the Turkish citizens outside Turkey (Berlin is known as the second biggest Turkish city in the world), it needs to be noted that the sentiment expressed in the letter quoted above is one of extreme revulsion and contempt, and in stark contrast to the attitudes towards the ethnic Germans who are treated as returnees. In the light of the concepts I have employed, the Turks are ethnified, as they are not allowed to adopt Germany as their homeland, and the ethnic Germans are nationalized promptly because they 'have' German blood. But it may, however, be noted in passing that since 1991 administrative restrictions have been made more stringent and financial incentives less attractive even for the ethnic Germans. It appears that the privileged position accorded to *Aussiedler* (refugee) immigrants will be gradually curtailed.

During the years of cold war Western Europe and the rest of the democratic world chided Central and East European (CEE) socialist regimes for the restrictions they had put on the freedom of travel of their citizens, particularly outside their respective state boundaries. But the dismantling of the socialist states and the substantial increase in the immigrant flow that followed changed the idiom of discourse from the democratic rights of individuals to the economic disparity between the two Europes. In turn, this has meant that the poor cousin from across the border has come to be perceived as an economic liability in his status as an immigrant. That is, the Iron Curtain is being replaced by the Golden Curtain, to recall the evocative phrase in circulation in contemporary Eastern Europe (see Fischer 1992: 1).

In 1990–2 the German government signed a number of bilateral agreements with CEE governments providing for labour immigration from these countries. The period of employment stipulated can be as short as three months or as long as two years. But the immigrant worker is expected to return after the expiry of the period of contract, although provisions for applying again after a lapse of one year do exist. Agreements also fix quotas for each country. It is clear from these agreements that the immigrant labourer is not permitted to become a settler and that the number from any given country is controlled. These restrictions are evidently meant to prevent any future political problem. In 1991 the total number of workers contracted according to these agreements was 78,340; in 1992 it rose to 103,920 (Fischer p. 2). Other relevant provisions of these bilateral contracts for the present discussion are: workers can enter Germany only if there are employers who require their services; provisions have been made for German workers to emigrate for work to the CEE countries (which have not been availed of); arrangements exist for seasonal employment, over and above the fixed quota, if German and other European Union (EU) citizens are not available for work; and the possibility for workers from border states such as Poland to commute to Germany for work. As a result of all these provisions some 220,000 workers from the CEE countries found employment in Germany in 1991. This figure comes close to the number of asylum-seekers (256,000) who entered the country that same year. Thus a total of about 500,000 persons legally entered Germany in 1991 alone. In the same year about 8,500 illegal immigrants were retained at the German border (for the first eight months of 1992 the figure was 18,000). The provision for seasonal work leads to the legalization of clandestine work. Also, immigrants enter as tourists and stay on for work. In 1991, 37,300 cases of illegal employment of foreigners had been detected. Despite state restrictions, German citizens find it profitable to employ illegal immigrants, as their bargaining power for better wages is low. Thus, housemaids, craftsmen doing repair work, etc., in Germany today are very often Polish citizens. Some of these are very highly qualified persons who find the wages for manual work more attractive than the salaries they get as white-collar workers back home (see Fischer pp. 1–4). The economic gain, notwithstanding the erosion of their social and political status in the host country, is clearly in evidence.

In concluding the discussion on the plight of the immigrant workers from the CEE countries in Germany, the following points may be listed. First, such workers are considered for employment only after the vacancies are filled by German and other EU citizens. Second, it follows that they can get only those jobs that the privileged EU citizens refuse to take. Third, they are not in an open competitive labour market, in that they can come only if an employer in Germany wants them. Fourth, some of them enter Germany in a clandestine way (e.g., as tourists) or illegally, both of which reasons erode their bargaining capacity. Fifth, even when they are legal entrants they cannot search for jobs that suit their aptitudes and qualifications. Finally, they have no individual rights to apply for a working permit or legal residence. It can be seen that these immigrants are not only treated as ethnies (outsiders), but are also ethnified, that is, marginalized and consigned to the bottom layer of the society into which they have migrated, irrespective of their skills, aptitudes and academic training.

Victims of capitalism

The coloured immigrants' deprivation in Western Europe is cumulative because they belong to a different physical type, come from a different cultural background and get consigned to the lowest status group. Immigrant labour from the CEE countries is by and large of the same race and colour, shares the same civilizational background, but is intimidated by its previous political situation and present economic misery. In contrast, the guest workers who migrated to the affluent countries of Western Europe from Italy, Spain, Portugal, Ireland and so on, were poor Europeans who had much in common with their rich cousins.

The first large-scale recruitment of guest workers occurred after World War II. There was unanimity among the British politicians that immigration was unavoidable at that time. This comes out clearly from the following statement made by a Labour MP in 1947 in the British Parliament:

> Full employment means that people have a choice of jobs and when they have that choice I cannot conceive that there will ever be enough people who will choose the bottom jobs. There will always be a shortage of labour in the basic industries so long as there is full employment in a free economy, and that situation can only be overcome by a constant inflow from those nations where the standard of living is lower and where our bottom jobs appear to be jobs of luxury. (cited in Miles 1989: 34–5)

But the real issue concerned who was to qualify as an immigrant. The debate regarding this was littered with references to people of other 'races' and 'stocks' who were acceptable and assimilable even though they belonged to different nationalities. Pointing to past experience, a British Conservative MP noted: 'Many years ago when the population of this country was only seven millions we took no fewer than 100,000 Huguenots into this country, and we have very greatly benefited from doing so, and also from other foreign blood at different times in the course of history' (cited in Miles p. 35). In fact, a Labour MP chided the Home Office for its overly nationalistic approach and felt that: 'Our island population will be refreshed, enriched and strengthened if that process is carried through in an orderly and proper fashion.' As another Labour MP said, it 'would be of great benefit to our stock, would help raise the standard of living . . .' (see Miles p. 35). The policy should be pursued cautiously, however, because if the number of immigrants were to exceed a certain size there would be resistance 'on the part of the people of this country toward the immigration of a large body of foreigners', as another Labour MP warned. The minister in charge of labour justified the objections to immigration raised by trade unions as a rational reaction, and he was quick to remark that when 'it comes to days of unemployment, they will be the first to be dispensed with' (see Miles p. 38). As Miles concludes after a thorough analysis of the discourse on the rehabilitation of the displaced persons of World War II in Britain: 'acceptable immigrants were those who could not disturb, by virtue of their cultural attributes or their numbers, the cultural homogeneity and the reproduction of the defining characteristics of the British population' (p. 37).

The situation was not different in other affluent West European countries, and the guest worker continued to be welcomed with gusto for quite some time. To cite one instance, in 1962 Mr Armando Rodriguez, the one-millionth migrant worker to the FRG, hailing from Portugal, was accorded an official welcome at Cologne and was presented with a motorcycle. The German news magazine *Der Spiegel* reported this event in its cover story. And yet thirty years later persons like Mr Rodriguez were not 'guest workers' but simply 'foreigners' (Fassmann and Munz 1992: 457). In terms of my conceptualization the process of luring the migrant workers when the affluent countries needed them, but abandoning them later when they were not found to be useful or affordable, is to ethnify them. I will discuss the case of Belgium in this context, because it vividly highlights the distinction between nationals and ethnies on the one hand and different types of ethnies on the other.

The three national groups in Belgium are the Dutch-speaking Flemings, French-speaking Walloons and the small German-speaking minority. The conflicts between the Flemings and the Walloons are well known and still continue. The Belgian Germans are too small in number to have any bargaining power in the political context. But their internality to Belgium is not questioned by anybody. The proverbial and persisting tension between the Flemish and Walloons evaporates when they are juxtaposed with immigrants, particularly the non-white, non-Christian immigrants (see Blommaert and Verschueren 1992: 355–75).

In 1945 owners of mines in Belgium hired 60,000 Italians with government approval because local labour was not willing to take these jobs. Later, Italian and Spanish workers were hired in steel construction and service industries, and by 1960 this had become common. To start with, the foreign European workers were not perceived as a threat by the Belgians. Gradually, the catchment area of labour recruitment expanded from southern Europe to North Africa and Turkey, as the latter groups were willing to work for lower wages. By 1984, out of a total population of 10 million, there were 270,521 Italians and 55,952 Spaniards in Belgium. These ethnic groups and others from EU countries have become EU citizens; they have a dual identity, one enabling (citizenship) and another debilitating (ethnic). In contrast, the 70,033 Turks and 119,083 Moroccans are merely ethnies and not citizens (see Roosens 1989: 127–33). Thus there are three clearly identifiable groups: Belgians who are nationals and citizens; Italians, Spaniards and similar others who are ethnies and citizens of the EU; and the Moroccans, Turks and such others who are merely ethnies.

The critical difference between the immigrants to the New World from Europe, who abandoned their homeland to become settlers, and immigrants into the rich West European countries needs to be noted here. The latter came as temporary migrants and intended to return. In fact, as Italy and Spain became prosperous not only did many migrant workers return, but these countries became receiving countries too. The story is somewhat different in the case of the Turks and North African immigrants in Belgium. They experienced substantial economic prosperity, but were not inclined to undergo the process of naturalization, that is, to become citizens (Roosens p. 134). Their attitude may be characterized as sojourner ethnicity. Their children, born in Belgium, are second-generation migrants; they are 'natives' but not 'nationals'. They go to Belgian schools, and adopt the lifestyle of their Belgian peers. But, despite this, they are not integrated into the economy and are often denied equal opportunity. To complicate matters they also face opposition at home for adopting an 'alien' lifestyle. Thus, among the second generation there is often a search for an identity, an intense desire to return to the ancestral land and culture (Roosens pp. 137–8).

The deteriorating economic condition of Belgium by the mid-1980s, resulting in the unemployment of Belgian nationals, changed the attitude towards the immigrants. The latter came to be perceived as 'stealing' the scarce jobs. In this context, a hierarchy of ethnies clearly emerges. Those who are 'visible' (that is, in terms of race and colour) are the worst affected, and in the racist discourse physical features and cultural characteristics are often merged. The victims want to return to their ancestral homeland, but there are precious few material prospects back home. On the other hand, they refuse to be naturalized, as noted earlier, and want their language to be used in public education, and they also demand the right to vote. The combination of sojourner ethnicity and the demand for citizenship rights does not mesh well together. If this is the situation of the descendants of immigrant workers from North Africa and even Turkey the case of the second and third generation immigrants from Italy and Spain is somewhat different. They could pass as Belgians, as they are phenotypically the same and as they speak French and Dutch well. They lead a double life, publicly invisible in terms of their cultural identity, but behaving like Italians or Spaniards at home, creating an acute ambiguity about their identity. Those who do not take to this route aggressively assert their national cultural identity, often unsuccessfully, as they are in an alien land (Roosens pp. 140–1).

The situation is further complicated by the linguistic and religious composition of the resident population, particularly in Brussels. Some of the districts in Brussels have more than 40 per cent immigrants. To teach the students in their mother tongues would mean using several languages – Italian, Spanish, Turkish, Arabic – which does not happen. Islam has been recognized as an official religion in Belgium since 1974. This entitles Muslims to run schools organized on the basis of Islam, with full state subsidy. But more than 70 per cent of schools in Belgium are managed by Catholics, and Muslims also send their children to these schools. In Brussels and in a few other Belgian cities, more than 50 per cent of the students of Catholic schools are Muslim and in some this figure is as high as 90 per cent. In these schools the Catholic ethos prevails. In government-run schools it is mandatory to organize religion-based courses if a certain prescribed proportion of parents demand it. But such a regulation is not acceptable to Catholic-run schools even though they are subsidized almost entirely by the state (Roosens pp. 142–3). This means that the Muslim immigrant children who are educated in Catholic schools are gradually 'de-cultured' regarding their origins. The children of North African immigrants are the worst hit because they have the double disability of physical visibility (in society) and de-culturation (in schools). But the problem of de-culturation is no longer confined to ethnies, as some Belgians have converted to Islam. Thus, Flemish Muslims are gradually being ethnified, although they are nationals. This type of situation is not confined to Belgium, not even to Western Europe, but prevails in all regions that experience rapid economic prosperity.

Western Europe: policy and attitudes

I propose to conclude this analysis on immigration and ethnification with a short discussion on policies of governments and peoples' attitudes towards immigrants. As noted above, in Western Europe immigrants were welcomed, encouraged and subsidized to begin with, but gradually came to be hated and finally attacked and expelled. Summarizing the studies done between 1954 and 1956 regarding attitudes of and to migrants in Western Europe, Borrie observed a quarter of a century ago that the general public looks upon the foreign workers as a necessary evil and a productive asset in time of economic need, but a liability otherwise (1959: 169–73). This observation not only holds even now, but in several respects the attitude has grown more negative.

Among the conclusions that Rose (1969: 92–5) drew after a systematic study of migrants in Europe, the following are relevant for the present discussion. First, there are considerable variations among the receiving countries of Western Europe with regard to the measures taken to enhance the acceptance and integration of their immigrants. While France, Sweden and the United Kingdom have adopted favourable policies, Switzerland has done precious little. Second, inter-state agreements such as those of the then European Economic Community (EEC), the Council of Europe and the Scandinavian Free Labour Market created a hierarchy among workers. For example, Italians could freely travel to Germany and Belgium and they constituted about 80 per cent of the internal EEC migrants. This in turn meant that many more privileges were available to them as compared with migrants, say, from Spain or Greece. Further, when the host countries experienced recession the first to be expelled were workers outside the ambit of inter-state agreements. Third, private employers in Germany supplemented the efforts of the government to train and improve the reception of foreign workers. Among the receiving countries, Italy had the most effective programme for migrant workers and returnees. Fourth, inadequate housing and prohibiting the family of the workers to come to the host country were the most unpleasant features of the policy. A large proportion of migrant workers were either actually exploited economically, or thought they were being exploited. Rose observed that: 'despite the efforts of several countries and many groups' policies, programs and practices toward migrant workers cannot be considered as generally a favourable force toward the future integration of Europe' (1969: 95). This evaluation remains correct in that the immigrant worker in Western Europe, particularly from Asia and Africa, continues to be viewed not only as a foreign substance in the body politic, but also as an object of hatred, as is evident in the articulations by New Right organizations, movements and parties, as we noted earlier in this chapter.

As a finale to this discussion, it is instructive to recall here the relevant findings of the Eurobarometer Surveys of the European Community. The vast majority (over 80 per cent) of the respondents questioned each year during 1988–93 did not find the presence of people of another nationality, another religion or another race to be 'disturbing' in their daily life. Those referred to are immigrants from non-EU countries, particularly from Asia and Africa. There was also no discernible difference in the attitudes regarding the acceptance of immigrants from regions south of the Mediterranean or from Eastern Europe, as revealed by the surveys of 1991, 1992 and 1993. Nearly 60 per cent welcomed them with restrictions, that is, just as guest workers, but not as equals; a quarter did not welcome them at all and only a minority (12–15 per cent) welcomed them without restrictions. However, the surveys revealed a hardening of attitudes with regard to the rights of immigrants within the EU. Thus, in 1988, while 30 per cent of the respondents wanted the rights of immigrants be extended, 18 per cent wanted them to be restricted. In 1992, only 17 per cent wanted an extension of immigrant rights, while 34 per cent wanted them restricted. The remaining wanted to maintain the status quo or did not know what to do.

Although the immigrants in the EU as a whole totalled only 5–7 per cent of the total population and those from developing countries 2–3 per cent, an overwhelming majority of the respondents thought that they were 'too many' or 'a lot'. Thus, 84 per cent held this view in 1991, rising to 86 per cent in 1993. Even with regard to those who seek political asylum, the attitudes displayed by the respondents were not very encouraging. The surveys (1991–3) show that less than a quarter (23–4 per cent) welcome immigrants without restrictions, half (50–1 per cent) want to admit them with restrictions and 19–21 per cent do not want to accept them at all. Further, even the EU citizens are not welcome to 14 per cent of the respondents, while 46 per cent welcome them with restrictions. Only 35 per cent of the respondents welcome fellow EU citizens without any restrictions, according to the Euro-barometer Survey of 1993.

Finally, it is important to note who constitutes 'the other' in the perception of EU citizens. While the idea of a national or cultural other is nebulous, that of racial and religious others is clear. For example, according to the special survey on racism and xenophobia done in 1989, the blacks constituted the other race for 63 per cent of Germans, 29 per cent of French and 32 per cent of British; the yellows were the other race for 25 per cent of Germans and 7 per cent of British; and 39 per cent of French viewed Arabs as the other race. Generally speaking, Islam was identified as the religion of the other: figures from the survey showed this to be the case for 73 per cent of Germans, 52 per cent of French and 26 per cent of British. Jews made the second position, with 12 per cent each for Germans and the British and 9 per cent of French holding the view that Judaism was the religion of the other. For 17 per cent of British and 9 per cent of Germans it was Hinduism. It is also important to recall here that racial and religious others are often coalesced into one category specific to particular countries, determined by the large size of the immigrant community and its historical background. For the Germans the Turks, for the French the Arabs and for the British the 'Indians' (that is, those from former British India) constituted the other race or religion (see Commission of the European Community 1989).

Thus, notions of citizenship (European Union), nationality (Germany, France etc.) and of ethnies (those who are outsiders), are found in the conceptions of the respondents, although not discernible in the conceptualizations of social scientists. Among the ethnies, those from within Europe, Asia and Africa seem to constitute a continuum in terms of their acceptability. Admittedly, the process of ethnification impinges unevenly on these different categories, but the most adversely affected are those drawn from different physical types, those who profess different religions and those who speak non-European languages. The co-existence of these features in the case of particular categories renders them victims of cumulative ethnification. In the case of Western Europe, these are North African Muslims and South Asian Hindus, Muslims and Sikhs.

Part III
Towards a Rapprochement
Concepts and Reality

9

Reconceptualizing Nation and Nationality: The Importance of Territory and Language

I indicated in chapter 1 that the manner in which conceptualization is attempted has profound implications not only for the explanation of social phenomena, but also for human welfare. Both proletarian internationalism practised by multi-national socialist states (see chapter 6) and the homogenization attempted by democratic states (see chapter 7) have inevitably led to the ethnification of substantial populations within the territories of these states. How do we escape from this impasse? The first requirement is to provide a plausible conceptualization that takes into account the changing empirical situation, and the second is to evolve an appropriate policy and to implement it scrupulously. The present task is confined to the first of these requirements, and in undertaking it I will begin by referring to three traditions employed in the definition of nation and nationality.

The three traditions

Of the three traditions discussed below I will deal with two of them only very briefly because they are already discussed frequently, they are positions of particular individuals, and they are not very pertinent for the present purpose.

In Joseph Stalin's well-known and widely read work, *Marxism and the National Question*, which he wrote in 1913, four essential features of a nation are identified. These are: a common territory, language, economic life and a 'psychological make-up manifested in a community of culture'. The last of these is vague and it is extremely difficult to specify those aspects of psychological make-up that are conducive to the formation of a nation. The same problem is shared by the notion of 'national character' which several later writers have employed to define nation.

Accepting common economic life as a defining feature is problematic because a nation could be divided into two or more states (as was the case with the two Germanys and Vietnams, and still is the case with the two Koreas) resulting in the two parts of the same nation developing two different modes of economic life. Further, a large number of nations may share a common economic life featured by the nature of ownership, management of property and mode of production, if not style of consumption. This commonality of economic life was shared to a large extent by the erstwhile command economies and contemporary capitalist economies. And both enveloped and still envelop a large number of nations. This leaves us with the two features of common territory and language, which are the only two necessary conditions for a nation to emerge and exist, as I will endeavour to demonstrate in this chapter.

Generally speaking, there is consensus among authors on the point that the first essential prerequisite for a nation to emerge is territory. But there are two sets of authors who are major exceptions to this, represented by two Austro-Marxists and a Polish sociologist. This is the second tradition to which I am referring. Viewed in retrospect, it seems to me that these efforts were tuned to meet the specific difficulties posed by the empirical situations analysed by these authors: territorial dispersal and intermixture of national populations within the Austro-Hungarian state in the first case, and the division of Poland between different states in the second case.

The Austro-Marxist theorists Karl Renner and Otto Bauer advocated a concept of nationality entirely independent of territory, and viewed nations within multi-national states as mere associations of persons. This idea, which was articulated in the first decade of the twentieth century, held that while state administration should be centralized, culture should be left to be nurtured by each component nationality. Consequently, these theorists defined nation as an association of people who share the same culture (see Seton-Watson 1977). In the same vein the Polish sociologist Znaniecki (1952) has argued that nationality (and hence nation) can exist without territory, culture or, particularly, language being the crucial element.

There are several difficulties in this argument. First, the authors tend to conflate state and nation. Second, they do not distinguish between the different meanings of territory – legal and moral – in the context of state and nation. Third, a dispersed nation, even if it forms a cultural association, would find it difficult to maintain its cultural ethos and would find it nearly impossible to maintain its distinct identity. Fourth, several nations may use the same language (as do, for example, all the nations of the British Isles) and yet retain their separate national identity. Fifth, the same language (e.g., English, French, Spanish, Portuguese) is used by different nations drawn from the Old and the New Worlds. Finally, if a nation is defined as a dispersed collectivity without a territorial base the distinction between nation and ethnie will be obliterated. Therefore, I want to affirm that one cannot conceive of a nation without its own territory.

The third tradition of conceptualizing nation is the one that focuses on and in fact over-emphasizes the psychological dimension. There is an array of distinguished scholars in this category, but I will rest content by referring to just two of them. One is Rupert Emerson, who stated:

> The nation is a community of people who feel that they belong together in the double sense that they share deeply significant elements of a common heritage and that they have a common destiny for the future. ... The nation is today the largest community which when the chips are down effectively commands men's loyalty, overriding the claims both of the lesser communities within it and those which cut across it or potentially enfold it within a still greater society, reaching ultimately the mankind as a whole. ... In this sense the nation can be called a 'terminal community'. (1962: 95, 96)

There are two main problems in Emerson's conceptualization. The first is that the characterization can equally fit several other communities. The second is that he conflates state and nation. As I have discussed both these issues earlier (in chapters 4 and 3 respectively), I need not repeat them here.

The other author I want to refer to here is Walker Connor, who is in fact the most ardent advocate of conceptualizing nation in essentially psychological terms. Connor maintained that: 'Nation ... refers to a human grouping whose members share an intuitive sense of kindredness or sameness, predicated upon a myth of common descent' (1984: xiv). Later, he claimed that: 'the essence of a nation is intangible. This essence is a psychological bond that joins a people and differentiates it in the subconscious conviction of its members, from all other people in a most vital way' (1994: 92). Nation is a kinship group featured by the notion of shared blood, actual or fictive, 'what ultimately matters is not *what is but people believe is*' (p. 93). 'The essence of the nation . . . is a matter of *self*-awareness or *self*-consciousness' (p. 104). A nation 'is a group of people who feel that they are ancestrally related. It is the largest group that can command a person's loyalty because of felt kinship ties; it is from this perspective the fully extended family' (p. 202; italics in original).

Having defined nation largely in psychological terms Connor castigates those scholars who focus on objective factors: 'Failure on the part of the scholars to appreciate the psychological well-springs of the nation most certainly contributes to the tendency to undervalue the potency of nationalism' (1994: 204). On the other hand, he commends the political leaders for their capacity to fathom the psychological depth of national sentiments. And he is absolutely right in saying that nationalist ideologues and political leaders have plumbed the emotional attachment of people to mobilize them into collective actions.

It is, however, necessary to caution against manipulating emotional sentiments in the rising tide of nationalism. Nazism and fascism in Europe, and linguistic, religious, racial and tribal chauvinisms both inside and outside Europe have crystallized precisely because the nation is defined predominantly in emotional terms. We have already referred to several of these articulations in chapters 6, 7 and 8. Let me recall just one more here. In his *Biography of a Nation: A Short History of Britain*, Enoch Powell, who was a prominent member of the British New Right, writes:

> There is no objective definition of what constitutes a nation. It is that which thinks it is a nation. . . . Self-consciousness is the essence of nationhood . . . This phenomenon of national consciousness remains almost as mysterious as that of life in the individual organism. . . . This living thing, mysterious in its origins and nature, is perhaps the most difficult subject of purely human enquiry . . . (cited in Nairn 1981: 270)

The definitions of Emerson, Connor and Powell are perilously similar and one should note the implications of this way of defining nation. First, it allows for the possibility of extreme intolerance towards co-nationals, even though they may have co-existed for several decades or even centuries in the same ancestral or adopted homeland, because they belong to another race, religion, tribe or language. This is what is happening in Bosnia, the Kashmir valley and Rwanda. Second, it encourages the tendency to consider as co-nationals those who left the ancestral homeland centuries ago, even though they may not share any common 'national' characteristics with those who stayed back, as in the case of returnees to Germany, Italy or Japan. Third, such a conceptualization cannot adequately distinguish between those who continue to live in their homeland (the Germans in Germany, the Japanese in Japan) and those who have migrated (the Germans in the USA and the Japanese in Peru) and have become settlers.

The crucial importance of territory

For the reasons listed above I am persuaded to insist that a common territory is the first necessary condition for the formation of a nation. And there is a near consensus on this point. Barker holds that 'the true nation has a home' and he adds, 'A territory comes first for a nation' (1948: 14–15). Sturzo thought that a nation cannot evolve its individuality without stable geographical contiguity (1946: 13). Carr conceded that nation embodies 'such natural and universal elements as attachments to ones native land and speech' (1945: 40). Justifying the need for a Jewish homeland, Ben-Yehudah asserted: 'The nation cannot live except on its soil' (cited in Anthony Smith 1979: 50).

Smith notes that the solidarity of a nation is based on the possession of its exclusive 'homeland' and the 'national mission is to build the nation on it'. The nationalist aspiration is geared to 'territorial unity and cohesion' and a contiguous territorial 'homeland' (1979: 3, 48). To press the importance of the territory for the nation and the emotional link with the homeland, Smith elaborates on the significance of exile, external and internal: 'Exile is the ultimate in degradation for a nationalist but there is also an inner exile which can be felt in one's "own land" . . .' (p. 118). The US blacks and Jews who lived as a 'ghost' people in other lands experienced inner exile. Referring to Jews in particular who lived on 'spiritually as a nation' although their nation was long since dead, he quotes Pinsker (1882) approvingly, 'a people which is at home everywhere and nowhere, must everywhere be regarded as alien' (cited in Smith 1979: 119). Indeed, Smith reinforces the primacy of territory for nation when he writes 'a nation without homeland is almost unthinkable' (1981: 35, 63).

It may be noted here that psychological or emotional attachment is always *to* something – an object, a person, a value, a party, an institution. In the case of nationalism, the object of that attachment is primarily the national homeland, which is a moral entity. The national territory carries with it a baggage of items – history, heritage, language, religion, race – which may or may not be crucial. But it is important that the analyst identifies the *differentia specifica* between the object of analysis (here nation) and the other cognate phenomenon (ethnie), which shares most of the characteristics. From the articulations listed above it is abundantly clear that the notion of homeland is the irreducible minimum for a nation to emerge and exist. Thus, instead of the subjective essentialism of those who latch on to the psychological dimension, I suggest an objective minimalism.

Although Connor has emphasized, or, in fact, over-emphasized the psychological and emotional dimensions of nation, even he has noted that 'ethnonational groups tend to populate distinct territories' (1994: 146). The national territory is homeland, fatherland, motherland, sacred land, ancestral land, native land to which a person belongs, with which he or she emotionally identifies, where fathers and mothers died and are buried. Sometimes the phrasing itself unfolds the symbolic significance, as in 'Mother' Russia, Deutschland, England (that is land of angels), or Kurdistan (Connor 1994). In India the national land is reverentially designated as Mother India and the poet Rabindranath Tagore characterized his Bengali homeland as *sonar Bangla* (golden Bengal). Thus, the content of psychological and emotional attachment to the nation is primarily an attachment to the homeland. That any piece of territory cannot be transformed into a homeland is well illustrated by the insistence of the Jews who want to return to their ancient ancestral homeland. A Jewish oblast was created by the Soviet state in 1934 near the Chinese border, but the effort to attract Jews to this 'homeland' did not succeed (Connor 1984: 221, 248). The British offered the Zionists a portion of Uganda as a possible site for their homeland. This offer was discussed and rejected by the Eighth Zionist Congress in 1904 (Seton-Watson 1977: 396).

Attachment to one's homeland is not a matter of poetic imagination or scholastic construction, but something genuinely felt by the people at large. Noting the specificity of Scottish nationalism, despite Scotland's economic and political 'integration' within Britain, Esman refers to an attachment 'to a territory where their ancestors had shaped a separate civilization' (1977: 254). Even Connor locates the specificity of Irish nationalism not in Catholicism, as is widely but wrongly believed according to him, but in the sense of belonging to the Irish national territory. To make the point he quotes a newspaper report published on 16 August 1969, which reads thus:

In Ulster, especially, much of the tension dates to the seventeenth century. After yet another round of fighting the Irish Catholics, the British encouraged Englishmen and Scotsmen to settle in Northern Ireland and tame the Native. The Native Catholics have hated these invading Protestants ever since – not only as Protestants but also as outsiders with different customs and greater privileges. (cited in Connor 1994: 45)

After a comparative analysis of what he calls 'new nationalism', Snyder concludes: 'The same basic psychological drive, seeking security in the system of homelands, fatherlands and motherlands' informs all of them (1976: 136). That is, the emotional content of nationalism to which Emerson, Connor and several others are referring is not free-floating and homeless, but firmly anchored to an attachment to a homeland. If this is not recognized and scrupulously adhered to, it can create enormous conceptual confusion and human misery. The Catholic Croats, the Orthodox Serbs and Bosnian Muslims have a common language and a common ancestral homeland. But all three claim that they are different 'nations', presumably based on religious differences and the emotional attachments emanating out of this. The consequences of accepting the claim is clear and loud. This predicament of course is not confined to these people, but is shared by many, hence my contention that nation formation cannot be based on religion (see chapter 4).

If territory is such a fundamental dimension of the nation, dissociation of a people from the national territory should create a new social category. This is the rationale behind the distinction between the nation and the ethnie. In fact, Anthony Smith does distinguish between nation and ethnie based on the territorial dimension. He writes: 'a nation by definition, requires a "homeland", a recognized space and ecological base . . . whereas an ethnic community, let alone category, can maintain its sense of belonging or its distinctive cultural characteristics without such a territorial base' (1981: 69). And yet he does not adhere to this distinction, as we have noted in chapter 3.

Why is it that the crucial importance of territory is ignored or forgotten by some analysts of nation and nationalism? Before I answer this question it is necessary to revert briefly to the notion of nationality. This concept has two referents in Marxist-Leninist literature. One is a people who have not yet achieved or may never achieve nationhood. The other is a segment of a nation living outside the state in which the major body of the nation resides (Connor 1984: xiv–xv). There are two main difficulties in accepting this conceptualization. First, this mode of defining nationality implies that it is a label given to unsuccessful nations. This notion, seen in conjunction with the idea of people without history (see chapter 6), inevitably results in the construction of a hierarchy of nations, an unacceptable proposition, certainly to 'lesser nations'. Second, this definition cannot cope with the complex empirical reality. For example, if a nation is more or less equally divided between two states (e.g., Korea, Bengal, Punjab), do the two parts continue to be nations or have they become nationalities? What happens if a nation does not remain as a single body but lives in two or more different states, like the Basques or the Kurds? What is the term to be used to identify those who are dislodged from their national territory (e.g., the Armenians or Kashmiri Pandits), or are rendered a minority in their ancestral territory through state-sponsored colonization, as might happen in Tibet and Tamil territory in Sri Lanka, or as happened in some of the Soviet republics? Clearly, we need a conceptualization of nationality that has a positive connotation and that can take into account the variety of empirical situations.

Alter suggests that a social group that defines itself as an ethnic minority or that renounces the aspiration to establish its own separate state, if it strives for cultural and political autonomy within a federal framework, should be defined as a nationality (1985: 18). His conceptualization also implies a hierarchy in terms of power in that those nations with their own sovereign states are full-fledged 'nations' and others are merely cultural minorities. I have argued all along that the conflation between state and nation should be avoided at all costs, and that it is not necessary for a nation to have its own state in order to maintain its cultural integrity. Finally, those segments of the nation that live outside their accredited homeland are conceptualized as ethnies in this study. Nationality should therefore be viewed as an identity anchored to the entity called nation. In such a conceptualization there is no hierarchy of nations.

The eclipse of territory?

The importance of territory as a sociological phenomenon has been largely eclipsed by two others, those of community and class. I will develop the analysis here with reference to community, reserving the discussion on class for chapter 10. In analysing the importance of territory I will follow the lead given by Agnew (1989: 9–29) and draw upon and extend his analysis of place to territory. In the all-pervasive dichotomous constructions in Western social science, community and society are conceptualized as polar opposites. 'Community begins as a moral value; only gradually does the secularization of this concept become apparent in sociological thought in the nineteenth century' (Nisbet 1966: 18). Endowed with moral value, the community was juxtaposed with society, an entity infused with amoral value.

Community is used in three different senses in contemporary social science analyses: as a territorial entity (village, city or nation); as an agency which commands and imparts a 'we feeling' irrespective of physical locus and distribution of population (religious, lingustic or racial communities); and as a complete social system (the little community) in that it constitutes a 'cradle to grave' arrangement, to recall the tempting phrase used by Redfield (1955). But more often than not all three meanings are intertwined in the use of the concept of community. Thus, Nisbet writes:

> By community I mean something that goes far beyond mere local community. The word as we find it in much nineteenth- and twentieth-century thought encompasses all forms of relationships which are characterized by a high degree of personal intimacy, emotional depth, moral commitment, social cohesion and continuity in time. Community is founded on man conceived in his wholeness rather than in one or another of his roles, taken separately, that he may hold in social order. It draws its psychological strength from levels of motivations deeper than those of mere volition or interest and it achieves its fulfillment in a submergence of individual will that is not possible in unions of mere convenience or rational assent (1966: 48).

Admittedly, Nisbet is heir to a long sociological tradition, beginning with Tönnies and Durkheim and followed by many others, giving birth to dichotomies such as rural–urban, folk–urban and the most widely used traditional–modern. This mode of conceptualization was the necessary product of an unwarranted assumption, that is, that the ongoing process of urbanization and bureaucratization brought about by the Industrial Revolution had led to the eclipse of the community and given birth to a national society which involved 'secondary contacts over wide geographical areas' and 'considerable mobility', according to S. P. Hays (cited in Agnew 1989: 12). But soon the assumption was found to be wrong, the primary group was 'rediscovered' in the industrial-urban setting and the tradition–modernity dichotomy was pronounced to be a misplaced polarity (Gusfield 1967: 336–51).

Notwithstanding the above pronouncements, the conceptualization of the community–society dichotomy left its telling impact on social science, and several generations of analysts almost uncritically accepted it, nurtured it and left a formidable baggage of scholastic heritage behind. What is pertinent for the present discussion is the persisting belief that the world is changing from a territory-based system of community to a system of de-territorialized national society. I must hasten to add here that the assumed de-territorialization is not only a physical, but also a moral phenomenon. It is believed that modernity amoralizes, if not immoralizes, the traditional locality-based community. Thanks to earlier revolutions in transport and

communication and the more recent developments in high technology and mass media, it is possible to maintain and nurture one's
national feelings and sentiments irrespective of one's physical location, and hence the glib talk about long-distance nationalism (see, for
example, Anderson 1992: 3–14). Understandably, the nation came to
be cognized primarily as a psychological phenomenon dissociated
from territory.

In other words, those who conceptualize nation exclusively or predominantly in psychological terms perceive and define it as a community that perpetuates a 'we feeling', but which has either lost or has
no need to sustain its territorial anchorage. Further, nation is not even
a complete social system encapsulating the human individual in the
totality of his or her activities. The national community has become a
partial social system, as individuals have emotional identification
with their 'fellow-nationals' living anywhere. Yet it effectively commands men's loyalty, overriding the claims of both 'lesser communities' and of the 'greater society', to recall the phrases of Rupert
Emerson; in the words of Walker Connor, it is a 'fully extended
family' sustained by 'felt kinship ties'. As I see it, this is an untenable
mix. For sustaining men's loyalty, commitment and affection, the
nation should be primarily a territorially anchored moral community.

This, though, is not a unilinear process, or a one-directional flow.
The dialectics between the territorial community and the sentimental
community become evident in two different ways. One of these is the
creation of a homeland for a territorially dispersed community. The
most eloquent example of this is provided by the Jewish case. Although dissociated for 2,500 years from their ancient ancestral homeland, the yearning for it did not die out. The reason for this cannot be
fully explained by anti-Semitism and the holocaust, although both
provided irreversible motivations and accelerated the process. But in
the wake of Zionist impulses and movements the Jews left for Israel
even from lands that had domesticated and nurtured them for centuries (e.g., India). And sojourner ethnicity, the yearning to go back to
Israel, is evident even among post-Zionist and prosperous immigrant
Jews in the USA. In other words, the domestication of a territory is a
prerequisite for the formation of a nation by a people. Conversely, the
idea of a common homeland and its territorial base may gradually
expand or contract. The first will happen primarily because of the
amalgamation of several national segments into a larger unit, and the
second when a large nation splits into several smaller ones. The point
is, the idea of a homeland is not a static one. More importantly,
individuals and groups do adopt new homelands, without which the
very notion of the New World or a settler nation is untenable.

The community–society dichotomy and its successor the tradition–modernity dichotomy were viewed with diametrically opposite moral visions. For Comte the disappearance of community and its pristine values and the incursions made by society and its impersonal values were matters to be lamented. In contrast, for Spencer community was a coercive and intimidating factor on individual autonomy (Agnew 1989: 11). Durkheim (1893) tried to provide a balance between society and community. He argued that it is possible to combine both social integration and individual autonomy through organic solidarity brought about by the division of labour in modern societies. Max Weber (1968) attempted to rescue the attendant confusion by suggesting that community and society are but ideal types and models and therefore should not be mistaken for concrete societies. But in contemporary social science, community and society, and traditional and modern societies are taken to be concrete entities.

Consequently, the passage of territory-based community was bemoaned by traditionalists and celebrated by the modernists. The disappearance of the tyranny of the primary group articulated through and by the local community was a welcome development for the consolidation of the 'nation', which was a wider community. Presumably, the national community lost its territorial base, but retained its community sentiment and 'we feeling'. This seems to provide the rationale for conceptualizing the nation in purely, or predominantly, psychological and emotional terms.

There is yet another reason why the importance of territory tends to be ignored in the analysis of nation and nationality. Western epistemological dualism implied in dichotomous constructions such as community and society assumes the displacement syndrome. Which is to say that in the inevitable movement from community to society the latter ineluctably replaces the former. In other words, if territory is important for a community, it cannot be so for a society. Further, if community values persist, they should be forcefully exorcized, as they constitute a formidable obstacle in the process of modernization, 'nation building' being an important project in this context. Thus, both the teleological track of social transformation implied in dichotomous constructions, and the demands of social engineering required for 'nation building' conjointly relegated the sociological significance of territory to the background. To cap it all, the current refrain, namely globalization, is believed to transcend the notion of territory.

This presumed displacement has not occurred, and several analysts have testified to it. For example, Tilly maintains that communities, that is, durable populations, anchored to localities have not declined, that 'local ties have diminished little or not at all, extra-local ties have increased' and that the present evidence is inadequate to claim that 'urbanization produced an absolute decline in community solidarity' (1973: 236). As I have argued elsewhere (Oommen 1967: 30–48), the community–society pair does not constitute a dichotomy, but falls at best on a continuum, and social transformation occurs more often than hitherto recognized through a process of accretion and not displacement (Oommen 1983: 111–36; 1992b: 131–9). If so, the presumed decline of the importance of territory is not a fact; it is an assumption, and a flawed one at that. And as we have seen earlier, particularly in chapter 7, national populations are very intimately attached to their homelands – be they ancestral or adopted.

Let me recall some empirical evidence with regard to the attachment of national populations to their territory. In 1851, 95.5 per cent of the people living in England were born there. In 1966, this figure had come down to 90.5 per cent. The corresponding figures for Wales (for 1851 and 1966 respectively) were 88.2 and 82.9 per cent and for Scotland 91.2 and 90.8 per cent. The situation in the two Irelands is very similar, although the Irish are said to be a migrant people. In 1851, 94.4 per cent of those living in Northern Ireland were born there. The 1966 figure was 90.5 per cent. For the Republic of Ireland, the corresponding figures were 99.3 and 97.5 per cent. As we can see, the difference in the national populations of the British Isles did not vary much over a period of 115 years. And most of the Irish emigration was to the USA. In 1852, 84 per cent of Irish migrants went to the USA (in 1902 the figure was 85 per cent), which they adopted eventually as their new homeland (Rose 1970: 7). There is no evidence to suggest that the situation in regard to spatial mobility is changing. These data are particularly pertinent because Britain was the mightiest colonial empire and British citizens had accessibility to a vast territorial space enveloped by those colonies.

Finally, it is not true that the contemporary world is filled with eager migrants in search of better economic prospects. Fear of marginalization may dissuade people from migrating. The Slovakian nationals were unwilling migrants. Their psychological attachment to the national territory and homeland made them reluctant seekers of employment in the Czech homeland, even when Slovakia was a part of the multi-national Czechoslovakia (Connor 1994: 155). Needless to say, in the wake of the break-up of the state Slovak nationals quickly retreated to their homeland. This is by no means exceptional.

It ought to be clear by now that the belief that the centrality of territory has been eroded due to industrial urbanization and modernization is based on certain unwarranted assumptions, and it can be sustained only by ignoring vital empirical facts. In the case of nation formation, territory is the first prerequisite. Thus viewed, a nation should be conceptualized as a people who consider a given territory to be their homeland irrespective of their background, whether in terms of race or religion.

The relevance of language

The second basic prerequisite for nation formation is language, as I have suggested earlier. Once again there is no consensus among scholars on this point, and at least part of the disagreements can be traced to the original sin, namely, the conflation of state and nation and on insisting that the nation-state is the ideal polity. Thus, Ernest Barker avers that 'a group may form a nation without possessing a common language' and refers to Switzerland and Britain as 'nations'. And yet he concludes: 'all who belong to one nation tend to speak the same language and a common language becomes the more necessary to the spiritual unity of a nation, as the spirit of a nation plumbs greater depths' (1948: 12, 13, 14). Incidentally, the situations in Britain and Switzerland are not comparable. In Britain the constituting nations lost or renounced their languages and English has become the common language through which they plumb the spiritual depths. In Switzerland, not only have the four part-nations retained their respective languages, but they are all recognized as 'national' languages, while three of them are also 'official' languages. Further, in everyday interaction the German-Swiss speak in their language and the French-Swiss respond in their language. This involves not only an accommodation of others' languages, but also the acquisition of competence in them. Be that as it may, Barker's ambivalence can be traced to his anxiety to designate Britain as a nation, while in fact it is a multi-national state. And multi-national states need not always be multi-lingual, as exemplified by the case of Britain. There, only Wales is bilingual; others have become practically mono-lingual.

If Barker's conceptualization is based on the experience of Britain, that of Znaniecki (1952) is anchored to the experience of Poland. Although the territory of Poland was divided across three states between 1795 and 1919, the Polish *narod* (that is, nationality) did not disappear. As nation is distinguished by its culture (and language being the nucleus of culture), the nation could not have disappeared, even as the national territory was divided up, according to Znaniecki. Once again, the division of a national territory into compact areas need not result in the disappearance of the national culture and language, unless of course the nation is deliberately subjected to a process of ethnification. On the other hand, the territorial dispersal of a national community may invariably result in the loss of its language in spite of considerable resilience.

The proverbial case here is that of the Jews. Having been absent from their homeland for 2,500 years, they lost their mother tongue and gradually developed at least three distinct linguistic variants. Those who spoke a form of Spanish were known as Sephardim as against those who spoke Polish, the Ashkenazi. The third variant, the Yemenite, was Asian. Although the Asian variant became prominent in the wake of the Zionist movement, Hebrew, the ancient ecclesiastical language of Jews, became the natural candidate for the national language (Seton-Watson 1977: 402–3). This happened in spite of the fact that Ashkenazi (known also as Yiddish) was spoken by almost 80 per cent of the Jews and the old Hebrew was spoken by hardly any. But within a decade thousands of immigrants to Israel learned Hebrew. Therefore Hobsbawm's contention that 'National languages are ... almost always semi-artificial constructs and occasionally ... virtually invented' (1990: 54) is an exaggeration. But the pertinent question to ask is why some of the invented national languages such as Hebrew came to be accepted, while others (e.g., Swahili, or Sanskrit) were rejected. Further, it is significant to note here the process at work, namely, an ethnie returning to its homeland and adopting a common language and transforming itself into a nation. If it does not or cannot create a homeland, in all probability it may not retain its language, as witnessed in the case of the gypsies.

The fact that the loss of homeland invariably results in the loss of one's mother tongue is illustrated by the Sindhi speech community (Hindus), who came to India from their ancestral homeland in West Pakistan in the wake of partition. They were dispersed into several urban centres of India. Within a few decades they lost their mother tongue largely because they had no territorial enclave. It is of great relevance to note here that there was no persecution or discrimination of the Sindhi speech community. On the contrary: with fewer than two million speakers, Sindhi is recognized as one of the seventeen 'national' languages of India, although several other languages whose numerical strength is much superior are not accorded any such recognition. That is, even when legal recognition is granted, a language may not survive if it does not have a home, a territorial anchorage. It is this combination that makes for the nation. Incidentally, the Sindhis of Pakistan (Muslims) who continue to live in their ancestral homeland are demanding a separate state based precisely on this, that is, their linguistic identity.

However, even when nations retain their ancestral homeland, they may renounce (e.g., Scots) or not succeed in retaining (e.g., Irish) their language. In such cases there is every possibility of bilingualism or diglossia emerging. In the case of bilingualism the mother tongue, which is a distinct language, is retained for informal use and may even develop its own distinct literary tradition. Diglossia emerges when the difference between the language used for official or formal purposes and the language used at home is merely dialectal. That is, retention of a homeland provides a greater possibility of retaining ones tongue. The reverse is not true.

Finally, it may be noted that the relationship between language and territory is not unilinear. While the Scots abandoned their language despite remaining in their ancestral homeland, the Hindu Sindhis had to abandon it because of their expulsion from their homeland. But the Catalans retained both their territory and their linguistic conscious-ness. Vilar captures this fact well: 'It is without a doubt because they spoke Catalan that the Catalans were able to preserve a group consciousness. But it is above all when they have most keenly felt this group consciousness that they have refused to forget Catalan' (1980: 573).

Interestingly enough, identical views on the importance of language in characterizing nation are held by those who hold diametrically opposite ideological positions. As is well known, both Mazzini and Herder thought that language constitutes the inner core of the nation. According to Herder: 'Language expresses the collective experience of the group', and 'every nation has its own inner centre of happiness as every sphere has its own centre of gravity' (cited in Anthony Smith 1981: 45). Stalin was equally unequivocal: 'a national community is inconceivable without a common language' (1940: 5). Paradoxically, in spite of the crucial role he assigned to language, it was language that had to be liquidated because nationalism and socialism were incompatible. Hence this utopian vision of the role of language:

> After the victory of socialism on a world scale . . . we will have . . . hundreds of national languages from which at first the most enriched zonal languages will emerge as a result of lengthy, economic, political, and cultural co-operation of nations, and subsequently the zonal lan-guages will fuse into one common international language, which will of course be neither German, nor Russian nor English, but a new language which has absorbed the best elements of the national and zonal lan-guages. (Stalin n.d.: 46)

That is to say, it is one thing to recognize the primacy of a dimension (here language) and quite another to retain it. For the nationalist, a nation without language is inconceivable; for a socialist, the nation is an unwanted entity to be exorcized from the body politic for the cause of socialism.

The fundamental flaw widely shared both by nationalists and socialists is that linguistic homogeneity fosters an ideal polity. Both try to liquidate linguistic heterogeneity, althogh they traverse different routes. The assumption that linguistic homogeneity fosters an ideal polity attained universal acceptability thanks to the ideology of the nation-state. After reviewing the two 'cross polity' surveys regarding the linguistic situation based on the Yale Human Relations Area Files, Joshua Fishman made a candid comment (1968: 60), which deserves to be quoted at length:

> One cannot help but come away from this recitation of findings with the decided impression that linguistic homogeneity is currently related to many more of the 'good' and 'desirable' characteristics of polities than linguistic heterogeneity. Linguistically homogeneous polities are usually economically more developed, educationally more advanced, politically more modernized and ideologically-politically more tranquil and stable. They more frequently reveal orderly, libertarian and secular forms of interest articulation and aggregation, greater division of governmental powers, and less attraction toward personalismo and charisma. All in all, linguistic homogeneity characterizes the state in which primordial ties and passions are more likely to be under control, cultural-religious homogeneity and enlightenment are advanced, more modern forms of heterogeneity via associational, institutional and political groups are fostered, and in which the good life is economically within the reach of a greater proportion of the populace.

Thus viewed, homogenization becomes not only an ideal worth pursuing, but also a self-fulfilling prophecy. But what are the facts on the ground? Of the 114 polities analysed in the two studies, 52 are linguistically homogeneous and 62 are heterogeneous. The linguistically homogeneous category in fact includes a few linguistically heterogeneous states, such as the United Kingdom and the United States. That is, a polity is viewed as linguistically homogeneous if it has one predominant language which is the official language of the state. This is not a correct characterization. However, a more important point that Fishman brings out (p. 62) is that, of the 52 linguistically homogeneous polities, only 27 have achieved very high or medium levels of gross national product (GNP). Conversely, of the 62 linguistically heterogeneous polities, 15 do have very high or medium levels of GNP. Admittedly, the lack of fit between linguistic homogeneity and heterogeneity and GNP is vivid. Further, some of the polities that are homogeneous and with very high or medium levels of GNP were not democracies (e.g., Argentina, Chile, Hungary, Poland, Cuba) at the time of data collection and analysis. Conversely, some of the linguistically heterogeneous polities with low or very low GNP were democracies (e.g., Ceylon, India).

It is evident that neither in terms of the level of economic development, nor in terms of democracy was the ideal of homogeneity found to be worth pursuing. It is true that the surveys were preliminary and their findings tentative. But the implications of these findings have not been confirmed since, and the lack of isomorphism between societal homogeneity, economic development and political democracy is widely noted. If this really is the case, the doctrine of homogeneity and its institutional vehicle, namely, the nation-state, should be given a decent burial. And yet, the central tendency in Europe even today is to believe that different people do not like to live together, and that homogeneity is a prerequisite for the building of viable societies, and that the current East European nationalism is the equivalent of democratization (Blommaert and Verschueren 1992: 372–3).

In the institutional arrangement that I am suggesting the linkage between state, nation and the ethnie is neither axiomatic nor eternal because it is based on a processual relationship. As a result, one can apprehend adequately the stages involved in an ethnie becoming a nation, and a nation either aspiring to become a state or renouncing such an aspiration. Conversely, the reverse process of states dismantling nations and dissolving them into ethnies can also be discerned. Finally, nations in multi-national states may opt out through a process of secession. One can thus visualize five end-products of this process, namely, nation-states, multi-national states, poly-ethnic states, combined multi-national and poly-ethnic states, and states for a national segment.[11] This position is in contrast to the prevailing tendency (at least which prevailed until recently): the insistence on laying down the teleological track for ever and predicting the inevitable emergence of nation-states. The importance of language ought to be situated in this context instead of pursuing the dogma of 'homogenism', to recall the apt phrase of Blommaert and Verschueren (1991: 503–31).

Admittedly, nation-states and states of national segments do not face any language problem; they are mono-lingual entities. But this is hardly a solace, as most states in the world today are not mononational. However, the empirical reality is not quite as simple. In the Middle East, the Arabic speech community is divided into fifteen states in each of which at least 85 per cent of the population is Arabic-speaking. But the remaining population belongs to non-Arabic speech communities. Similarly, in Latin America fifteen states have 80 per cent or more speakers of the Spanish language. Once again, the non-Spanish speaking groups drawn from the Amerindians have a strong presence. The poly-ethnic states of the New World, generally speaking, do not really face any serious problem in this context, as their linguistic communities do not have territorial anchorages. If they do acquire a territorial base they become bi- or multi-national states and face linguistic problems, as exemplified by the case of Canada. The ethnies in multi-national states do not usually have the required legitimacy (as they have not become settlers and have not yet identified with the new land as their homeland) or striking power to make serious demands based on their linguistic identity. Thus, an acute linguistic problem is actually posed by the nations in multi-national polities. I will now turn to analysing this problem.[12]

Language, nation and state

The assumptions and value orientations that inform the present analysis are the following. First, experience the world over clearly demonstrates that in order to bring about participatory development communication is imperative. Second, adequate and appropriate communication is possible through the languages of the people, that is, their mother tongues. Third, if they are going to be viable and effective at different levels, administrative units ought to be coterminous with communication units, that is, linguistic areas. Fourth, generally speaking, when language is directly linked to a specific territory it provides the basis for a common lifestyle and communication pattern. Fifth, most languages, irrespective of their graphemic status, are capable of effective communication in the context of everyday life. Sixth, while it may not be possible, nor even desirable, to establish separate administrative units for all the linguistic areas wherever it is viable and feasible (based on population size, financial viability, territorial spread) it is preferable to establish such units. Finally, if compulsory primary education is imparted through the mother tongue, this single step will substantially contribute to the eradication of illiteracy and should lead to more efficient communication, thereby accelerating the process of development and democratization.

Keeping the above considerations in mind, it is necessary to identify the contexts in which denial of language rights exist. On the basis of available evidence and experience we can list four situations. First, subaltern communities (tribes and peasantry) inhabiting their traditional homeland might be denied the opportunity to use their mother tongues either because the languages are not spoken by many people, or because they are not 'developed', development being viewed in terms of absence of scripts and/or inadequacy of vocabulary. Second, the requisite facilities for retaining linguistic competence at the required level may not be made available to groups that are small and dispersed as a result of voluntary migration to an alien cultural milieu in search of better economic prospects. In a third situation people involved in large-scale migration or dislocation due to religious persecution, political intolerance or war might be denied the opportunity to retain their linguistic competence. There are several possible scenarios under this rubric: the dislocated persons are settled or come to inhabit a contiguous uninhabited territory wherein they constitute the exclusive population; they live side by side with their own speech communities, which are made up of citizens of another, usually neighbouring, state; they are dispersed into a vast territory, usually in urban centres, where they remain small minorities.

The fourth situation occurs when a territory is colonized, either in a government-sponsored operation, or when an enterprising dominant collectivity does so in search of economic opportunities. Government-sponsored internal colonization occurs under two conditions: when a peripheral or minority collectivity with a territorial base shows recalcitrant tendencies by demanding greater political and/or fiscal autonomy; and when such a community demands secession from the polity so as to constitute an independent sovereign state. Under both these conditions government-sponsored colonization by culturally dominant collectivities is used as an instrument to marginalize and ethnify the nationals. Internal colonization, irrespective of its source and motivation, may and often does lead to a situation of denying the cultural freedom of the local people, an important element of which is the decimation and destruction of their language.

The efforts made by multi-lingual states to create a 'communication community' are essentially of three kinds. First, there is the liquidation of all languages other than that of the most influential linguistic collectivity, which leads to the assimilation of all linguistic minorities into a dominant group. Second, disallowing the languages of the minority groups for formal purposes such as education and administration which leads to their marginalization. Third, the legal recognition and development of all those languages that have a critical minimum number of speakers, particularly when they have a territorial base, promotes linguistic pluralism, that is, the dignified co-existence of numerous languages. Which of these strategies a multi-national state should pursue to deal with a particular national language or languages would depend upon its size and dispersal, economic resource base and political clout, historical association and symbolic value, the bases for creating administrative units and the quantum of material resources available. That is to say, the issue of language rights cannot be considered as one divorced from concrete empirical situations.

A serious difficulty in handling the language problem is the tendency to make it an ideological issue, to make it an ingredient of 'nationalism', that is, to link language with state-building and designate it as nation-building. More often than not when most analysts refer to national languages what they actually mean is the state or official language; this is the logical corollary of the conflation of state and nation. Instead, if the distinct difference between state and nation is clearly recognized, it would be easy to understand that in a multi-national state there would be as many national languages as there are nations. But for a number of reasons it may not be possible or feasible for all national languages to be official languages. Once this is conceded it is possible to visualize the co-existence of a multiplicity of languages within the same state territory. These languages or sets of languages may serve different functions in differing contexts and levels.

It is estimated that there are some 6,170 languages spoken in the world today (Grimes 1988: vii). If the ideal of the nation- state were to be relentlessly pursued, there would be so many states and national-isms in the world that even its staunchest supporters would shudder. At present there are only around two hundred states in the world, from which it is clear that most of them must have several spoken languages. Similarly, even an incurable pluralist may not want 6,170 'nations' in the world, although he may want as many identity groups to exist. In other words, while language is an important element of nation, it does not mean that all speech communities inevitably and automatically constitute nations or even aspire to do so. However, this does not mean that particular speech communities cannot become nations.

The situation is more complex in Africa, where tribes constitute the basic building-blocks, and in island states such as Indonesia and the Philippines. In both cases the scale of the constituting units is rather small. But Bahasa Indonesia and Pilipino are accepted as 'national', that is, official languages in their respective states. In Africa, the inter-tribal conflicts could also be linguistic conflicts. And yet no clear pattern exists. Rwanda has substantial linguistic homogeneity, with 90 per cent of the population of Kinya-Rwanda speaking one language. This is in contrast to Cameroon, which has a five million population but one hundred languages or dialects. Tanzania comes in between, with 80 per cent of the people speaking closely related Bantu languages of which Swahili is the dominant one.

In spite of Rwanda's substantial linguistic homogeneity, the country is beset with chronic conflicts which are not linguistic. Cameroon's stupendous linguistic heterogeneity, on the other hand, has not produced conflicts commensurate with that heterogeneity. Finally, notwithstanding the dominant position of Swahili in Tanzania, the linguistic issue is yet to be solved. Herein lies the need to distinguish between language as an object of emotional attachment irrespective of its utility, and language as an instrument that fosters unity and mobility of different peoples, individuals and groups. The nationalist uses language as an emotional symbol to mobilize people into collective action. What needs to be done is to help people to perceive language as a cultural capital to make material advancement.

To illustrate the difficulty in considering all speech communities as nations, let me refer to the Indian case, the most polyglot polity in the world today. The number of mother tongues listed in the first three censuses of independent India varied substantially and are not always reliable: 782 in 1951; 1,652 in 1961; and 1,019 in 1971. Obviously, the enormous variations in the number of speech communities (around 30 per cent) over a period of twenty years is suspect. However, the figure has been around 1,000 since 1971, with the stabilization of the situation after the linguistic reorganization of Indian states. Be that as it may, according to the 1951 census as many as 650 speech communities out of 782 (83 per cent) had only 10,000 or fewer speakers. Admittedly, these small speech communities themselves may not be aspiring to any specific identity, let alone national identity. At the other end of the continuum only 59, or barely 8 per cent of the mother tongues had 100,000 or more speakers. By 1971 the number of languages with 100,000 or more speakers had reduced to 43, or little over 4 per cent of the mother tongues spoken. Most of these speech communities may be looking for a specific cultural identity, but not necessarily as nations. If they are territorially concentrated, most of them may want to have some sort of local self-government. Only the very big speech communities – those with a population of a million or more – would want to be recognized as nations. They may demand a politico-administrative arrangement within the federal set-up, or may even want to secede from the state. But there are only about 25 of them in India today.

It is not my intention to make a fetish of the size of speech communities as a factor in developing national identity. But I want to insist that the problem posed by the polyglot character of many polities in Asia and Africa does not automatically constitute a problem for 'nation building'. The real problem faced by these polities is the artificial dissection of many nations, even when they count a million or more persons each, and their allocation into different politico-administrative units either within a sovereign state or across different sovereign states. This was first done by the colonial state and subsequently perpetuated by the 'national' state. More often than not it is the division of the legitimate motherland of speech communities that has created conflicts. Both 'socialist' and 'democratic' states have done this, as I have demonstrated in chapters 6 and 7.

To conclude the discussion, the following points, which are supported by existing studies, may be listed. First, there is no such thing as an eternal attachment of a people to a language or an ineluctable spirit that informs it. Language shifts are quite common (see Tabouret-Keller 1968: 107–27). Second, there is a variety of multi-lingual situations in terms of their permutations and combinations. They do not all pose problems for consolidating nations and states (see Rustow 1968: 87–105). Third, the degree of language differences does not automatically lead to conflicts, for a variety of reasons, prominent among which are that not all language differences are taken into account, and that even as the differences are noticed they may not result in conflicts: 'language creates identity and discontinuity. It unites and it divides' (Blommaert and Verschueren 1992: 370). Fourth, even when the difference between two languages is minimal, it may lead to intense conflicts. Conversely, languages with substantial differences may peacefully co-exist. Fifth, not all linguistic conflicts are national and even when language differences are minimal it may result in nationalist strife (Anthony Smith 1971: 184–5). What I am trying to say is that language in itself and by itself is not a factor in making or breaking nations. But in conjunction with territory it often becomes so. Further, linguistic homogeneity may often be a facilitating force to consolidate a nation. But this does not mean that plurilingual nations will not emerge and exist, although it is true that they are often beset with nationalist disharmony sparked by language.

What way out is there from this continuing malady? The first firm requirement is to de-ideologize the task of state-building and to stop calling it nation-building. In Connor's (1994) eloquent and appropriate phrase what is really done in the name of nation-building is actually nation-destruction. The second requirement is to recognize that nation is a tangible entity definable in terms of concrete objective characteristics such as a common homeland and a language. That is, nation is not simply a sentimental community as Connor or Emerson make out, or an imagined community as Anderson avers. Third, the above implies that all those who belong to a common homeland – ancestral or adopted – should be recognized as constituting a common nation irrespective of their racial, religious or linguistic background, which is to say that the very idea of homogeneous nation-states ought to be abandoned, both because of its empirical untenability and its ideological unsustainability. Finally, the importance of communication for developing a participative polity should be squarely endorsed as a prerequisite. In spite of this, multi-national polities should have several national languages even if they limit the number of official languages to a workable minimum.

Once again the first step towards this is appropriate and clear conceptualization, although this cannot solve the extremely complex problems that we face in the context of nation, nationality and nationalism. It is useful to recall here that there was a time when a wide variety of democracies – one-party, people's, popular, direct, representative, basic, and of course multi-party – existed, and everybody, even the worst authoritarians, claimed to be 'democrats'. Today there is a virtual consensus about what constitutes democracy, namely, multi-party polities, and there is a near universal endorsement that this is the value to pursue. We need to do the same for nation and nationality. This is what I have attempted to do.

10

Class, Nation, Ethnie and Race: Interlinkages

In chapter 9 we noted that the two concepts that dominate contemporary social science are community and class, relegating most others, including territory, to the background. We have already discussed the importance of territory in the context of nation. What remains to be done is to discuss the relationship between class and nation. But since there is a widespread tendency to subsume race under ethnie, as well as to treat ethnicity as the basis of nation, it will be useful to discuss the relationship between race, ethnie and class as well. Such a discussion is also important to understand the complex system of inequality that prevails in multi-racial and pluri-ethnic societies. This will also serve as a prelude to our discussion on citizenship in chapter 11.

Nation as class

In discussing the relationship between nation and class we must begin by noting the three different ways in which this relationship is conceptualized. These are: class as nation, class across nations and class in nation. Perhaps the first well-known case of considering class as nation is found in Disraeli (1926: 76) when he refers to the situation in eighteenth-century England as that of:

> ... two nations between whom there is no intercourse and no sympathy; who are ignorant of each others habits, thoughts and feelings, as if they were dwellers in different zones, or inhabitants of different

planets; who are formed by different breeding; are fed by different food, are ordered by different manners and are not governed by the same laws, the rich and the poor.

Similarly, Marx refers to the division of the French nation into two: the nation of owners and the nation of workers (1977: 144). To refer to classes as nations provides them with an emotional content and facilitates their mobilization into collective actions. But to consider nation and class as interchangeable units is clearly misleading. Since nation contains several classes, such a usage confuses the part for the whole. However, a variant of this usage has re-surfaced lately in the notion of 'internal colonialism'. If classic colonialism alludes to domination by an external agency, internal colonialism occurs within multi-national states. The first notable contribution in this strand of thinking was made by Hechter (1975). In its bare essentials Hechter's theoretical claim was that the survival of nationalism depended on a stratification system that gives cultural distinctions political salience. Modern industrialization creates and accentuates inequalities between the nations within a multi-national state, giving birth to a cultural division of labour among them. In this process the core nation achieves dominance over the peripheral ones, turning the latter into colonies of the former.

The empirical case on which Hechter based his theory, namely, that of Great Britain, did not entirely fit the bill, as Scotland had been as much an industrialized nation as England since the eighteenth century, although Southern Ireland was a clear example of internal colonialism. Hechter later reformulated the notion of a cultural division of labour, which presumably gave birth to a system of hierarchical stratification. In the new version (1985: 17–26) Scotland is viewed as occupying a ladder in a vertical stratification system due to segmental cultural division of labour. Thus viewed, the occupational class categories into which the nations are stratified are not hierarchical but vertical. This provides for the possibility of colonized nationalities filling 'occupational niches' specific to them, which may not be inferior to those occupied by the colonizer nations. This reformulation has weakened the sharp dichotomy between the colonized and colonizer nations within a multi-national state. Further, the Act of Union with Ireland came into force only in 1800, and in 1921 most of the Irish island became the Irish Free State, independent of British rule, leaving only six counties of Northern Ireland as internal colonies. In contrast, both Wales and Scotland have been part of Britain since 1536 and 1707 respectively. Thus viewed, the latter nations should have provided more apt instances of internal colonies as compared with Ireland. But the point to be noted for the present purpose is the proclivity to treat nations as if they are classes.

The same strand of thinking is evident in Nairn when he writes that 'nationalism is as a *whole* quite incomprehensible outside the context of . . . *uneven* development (1981: 96; italics in original). The proposition does not make it clear as to which type of nation – more developed or less developed – will respond through nationalism. But as Nairn is writing about the 'neo nationalisms' of Scotland, Wales and Ireland within the multi-national state of Great Britain, it is safe to assume that he is alluding to the nationalisms of weak and small nations. This makes the empirical base of the proposition weak, as strong and big nations within multi-national states also take to nationalism when it is necessary and 'beneficial' to them. But the story of nationalism is more complex. In the case of Scotland, to which much of Nairn's analysis is anchored, renunciation of the state and hence the absence of state-seeking nationalism characteristic of nineteenth-century Europe can be traced to beneficial effects. In preface no. 1 of the *Edinburgh Review* 1755, Scotland's union with England is defended as follows: 'The memory of our ancient state is not so much obliterated, but that, by comparing the past with the present, we may clearly see the superior advantages we now enjoy, and readily discern from what source they flow.' In addition, William Robertson wrote in History of Scotland in 1803, 'that 1707 agreement had admitted the Scottish commons to a participation of all the privileges which the English had purchased at the expense of so much blood' (both cited in Nairn p. 109).

In other words, the union with England clearly benefited Scotland; this benefit was largely unearned; and the trade-off was renunciation of state and not nation. This accounts for the dormant state-seeking nationalism of Scotland. Presumably it became animated when Scotland perceived a material advantage in dissolving the union, a situation that arose with the discovery of North Sea oil in the mid-twentieth century, leading to the crystallization of a new nationalism (Esman 1977: 251–86). Viewed either way, it is not uneven development as such that explains the emergence or absence of nationalism, but the 'material advantages' that particular nations perceive in having specific political arrangements.

Even so, is it legitimate to conclude that nationalism and material interests and, concomitantly, nation and class are interchangeable categories? Gellner seems to think so. He holds the view that it is the coterminality of cultural differences and class divisions that gives birth to nationalism.

Classes however oppressed and exploited did not overturn the political system when they could not define themselves 'ethnically'. Only when a nation became a class, a visible and unequally distributed category in an otherwise mobile system did it become politically conscious and activist. Only when a class happened to be (more or less) a 'nation' did it turn from being a class-in-itself into a class-for-itself, or a nation-for-itself. Neither nations nor classes seem to be political catalysts. Only nation-classes or class-nations are such. (1983: 121)

This heroic effort to equate nations and classes does not, however, quite fit the facts on the ground. First, even homogeneous nations, those rare entities, not to speak of multi-national states, are multi-class. Second, the class–nation relationship postulated by Gellner is meaningful only in multi-national states. But he does not recognize such entities, they are simply designated as nation-states, nay, nations. Third, Gellner insists that nationalism is a 'modern' phenomenon brought about by industrialization. Therefore, his explanation cannot account for the existence of nationalism and nation formation in pre-industrial, non-industrial and post-industrial societies, in all of which the phenomenon can be found. For these reasons one must recognize the basic difference between the two phenomena – class-in-itself and nation-in-itself – and their respective transformations into class-for-itself and nation-for-itself. If and when the nation-in-itself is transformed into a nation-for-itself, it has to be an *all-nation* phenomenon because the enemy is an outsider. When the enemy is outside the nation but inside the state (that is, within a multi-national state) such a 'nationalism' is a response to internal colonialism. In contrast, the transformation of a class-in-itself to a class-for-itself is a *part-nation* phenomenon, as the enemy is within the nation and the state. The class-for-itself fights against other class or classes within the nation-state. In other words, the relationship between class and nation – and hence class struggle and national struggle – is contextually conditioned and not a given state. The national struggle is a reaction against the domination over an entire people and is well captured by Touraine when he writes: 'Here it is not a class but a territorial collectivity, whether regional or national, that is defending itself against an external domination' (1977: 427).

Class across nations

Statements such as 'the proletariat has no fatherland' or phrases such as 'proletarian internationalism' in Marxist-Leninist literature imply that class is a cross-national phenomenon. Marxism maintains that the real building-blocks of society are classes, and the most persistent conflicts are between classes that cut across nations. Further, in the Marxist perspective nationalism was mainly a device invented and resorted to by the bourgeoisie to divert the attention of the proletariat and to blunt the edge of class conflict between it and the proletariat. The *Communist Manifesto* declared: 'The working men have no country. We cannot take from them what they have not got.' But to capture a country, that is, to possess property, the proletariat must acquire political supremacy for which it should become the leading class of the nation, nay, constitute itself as the nation, according to the Manifesto. This means that to be national, to belong to the nation, ownership of property is a prerequisite; the propertyless are 'a-national'. The propertyless proletariat is hence placed in a privileged position so as to cut across national boundaries and participate in cross-national class struggles. But the contingency of the success of class struggle and the consequent embourgeoisement of the proletariat and its subsequent nationalization had not been fully anticipated or accounted for. Indeed, this is precisely what was to happen: the nationalization of the proletariat!

Those who consider class as a cross-national, indeed a world category, view not only nations but also races and ethnies as classes in the final count, because the 'fundamental political reality' of the contemporary world is the existence of a capitalist world economy and of 'class struggle' within it (Wallerstein 1979: 181, 230). Further, 'As a status-group category, race is a blurred collective representation for an international class category, that of the proletarian nations.' And, in addition, 'Race is a particular form of status-group in the contemporary world, the one which indicates rank in the world social system' (Wallerstein 1991: 199, 200). Thus status groups, races and ethnic groups are all ultimately 'blurred collective representations' of class categories.

For Marx, the bourgeoisie was facilitating the demise of nations and nationalism: 'National differences and antagonisms between peoples are daily more and more vanishing, owing to the development of the bourgeoisie to freedom of commerce, to the world-market, to uniformity in mode of production and in the conditions of life corresponding thereto' (1932: 340). If both the proletariat and the bourgeoisie are undergoing the process of de-nationalization, what is it that distinguishes them? Indeed, it is none other than the vanguard role assigned to the proletariat in the context of revolution, a role that is bound to be transnational. But as we have noted in chapter 6, the proletariat is utterly nationalistic and fought for the national cause in the German Democratic Republic, Hungary, Poland and Czechoslovakia in the 1950s. It fought against the USSR, a socialist state, which was a national enemy.

In contrast to Marxism, nationalism holds that the essential human groupings are nations, and therefore the basic cleavages are between nations. To the nationalist, class is an artificial phenomenon and class conflict is an invention of the Marxists to divide nations and to sap them of their vitality. Ignoring this stratagem, the nationalists must unite and protect the nation. What Theodore Napier rhetorically asked fellow Scots in 1909 is typical of the nationalist spirit: 'When will Scotsmen cease denominating themselves as conservatives, unionists, and liberals and become Scottish Nationalists instead?' (cited in Hanham 1969: 134).

I have juxtaposed the Marxist and nationalist positions sharply to bring out the line that each takes vis-à-vis class. It is clear that the Marxists want individuals and groups to abjure national identity and embrace class identity. In contrast, nationalists want people to assert their national identity by basing it on assumed common descent and kinship and by ignoring class divisions. Both are untenable positions because they ignore the fact that individuals and collectivities have multiple identities. Further, they assign primacy to one identity – to class by the Marxists and to nationality by the nationalists. But the fact is identities become salient only in particular contexts. Thus, national identity assumes saliency in inter-nation interactions, and class identity becomes salient in intra-nation contexts.

What form do classes take in multi-national states? Classes of multi-national states are cross-national coalitions drawn from the different units. It is in this context that one comes across the 'cultural division of labour' and 'occupational niches' specific to particular nations. But if we are to understand the class situation in the multi-national state as a whole, we have to conceive of it in coalitional terms. In the event of the break-up of such polities, classes of all hues and levels identify themselves with their respective 'nations'. This was what happened when Pakistan, Yugoslavia, Czechoslovakia and the Soviet Union broke up. It is quite possible, however, that an immigrant collectivity identifies itself with the nation, in the midst of which it settles down by adopting it as its new homeland, as we have seen in the case of a section of Russians in the Baltic republics (see chapter 6). Thus, the classes in a multi-national state are often precariously perched between the nation and the cross-national class category into which they belong. But when the chips are down they have to choose one of the nations in order 'to belong'.

Those who consider class as nation invariably consider nationalism to be a phenomenon prevalent among the economically deprived 'nations'. Economic exploitation is viewed as the mainspring of nationalism resulting in the national movements of the Third World, and uneven development is seen as the basis of nationalism in the case of weak and smaller nations within politically independent multi-national states. But as I have noted in chapter 1, the tripartite division of the world is unsuitable for understanding the phenomenon of nationalism. Some authors (e.g., Van den Berghe 1970: 244–7) would even contest the designation 'national movements' for liberation struggles of the Third World, and would contend that these are nothing but 'territorialisms'. But territoriality is the most important element of nation, as I have argued in chapter 9. Some anti-colonial movements were national, in that particular nations conducted the struggle alone. If several nations together formed a colony, they conjointly strived for decolonization. Even when the nations that constituted the colony continue to remain in one state, their nationhood does not wither away. But the familiar mistake of conflating state and nation has resulted in the instant labelling of post-colonial states as nations. The moment we acknowledge this it will become clear that most post-colonial states are multi-national and not mono-national.

To come back to the point regarding the inadequacy of the tripartite division of the world in the context of nationalism and colonialism, it is not only the colonies of Asia and Africa that fought for freedom. The colonies of the Americas also fought for freedom from their respective mother countries, which invariably turned out to be an exercise in severing the umbilical cord. While in the case of Latin America the settler-majority populations occupied compact areas and got themselves divided on the basis of languages – Spanish and Portuguese – the pattern is quite different in the USA. Finally, it would be extremely difficult to sustain the argument that it was economic exploitation of the colonies in the Americas, specifically in North America, which triggered off the liberation struggles. This is clearly exemplified in the case of the United States.

Migrants drawn from a variety of places and backgrounds and occupying a common territory can emerge as a well-knit society only if they acquire political authority over the territory. The American War of Independence provided this much-needed cementing force. But it is important to remember that there was no basic difference between the colonial master and the subjects (at least the most significant of them, such as the WASP) in terms of religion, language, race, colour, or perhaps even culture. The mother country was territorially alien and politically inimical, but culturally affined. That is, the American freedom movement was essentially instrumental in orientation, but not expressive in content. It represented an effort on the part of the immigrants to assert their territorial, political and economic independence, but not their cultural autonomy. To recall the pregnant phrase of Max Lerner, it was an exercise in 'the slaying of the European father' (1957).

When one considers the motive force behind the national movements of the small and weak nations within politically independent multi-national states, one does not notice any pattern from the perspective of uneven development or class exploitation. Let us look at some cases from different contexts. The nationality policy of the Soviet Union was clearly addressed to the issue of equality between national republics, and special efforts were made to boost the economic development of backward regions:

> Throughout the Soviet period, the party has ensured higher economic growth rate in the non-Russian republics than the average for the country as a whole. In 1968, growth of industrial output for the Union was 79 times the 1913 level, but in Kazakhstan it was 125 times, in Kirghizie 152 times, in Armenia 146 times and even higher in some autonomous republics . . . The party and the state set aside a relatively larger share of capital investments for the national areas so as to raise them to the level of advanced nations. (Gililov 1972: 61)

If the above statement is taken as correct, it is clear that the Soviet state made extra efforts to boost the development of economically backward nations, and the income disparity between the different nations may gradually have been reduced. If so, economic disparity alone cannot explain the nationalisms that arose in the erstwhile Soviet Union. In fact, there is evidence to suggest that national consciousness crystallizes and intensifies precisely when the economic conditions of nations improve. This is illustrated by the Slovak case. After an exhaustive study of Slovakia, Steiner concludes: 'Economic dissatisfaction is not always the main source of nationalism; very often nationalism becomes overt with the improvement of economic conditions. Slovak nationalism would have existed and grown even if the country had no reason to complain of unjust economic treatment from Prague' (1973: 132). This seems to apply to Slovenia also, a constituent nation of the former Yugoslavia. Then again, it was not only the weak and small nations, but also the strong and big nations of the former socialist block that articulated their nationalism. The Great Nation chauvinism of Russia, of the Han people, of Serbia and so on, illustrates this. What these nations had articulated was not class, but national solidarity.

In Western Europe both economically backward and economically well-off nations within multi-national states express their resentment against 'oppression' by the dominant nations. The more well-known cases of economically developed nations are the Basque, Catalan, Scottish and Flemish nations. In fact, in the Flemish case the nationalist wave started mounting when they started tasting economic prosperity, while in the Scottish case it was the anticipated economic prosperity, thanks to the discovery of oil, that triggered off nationalism. The persisting squabbles between the French and Germans in Switzerland are not anchored to economic disparity between them. In India, the Sikhs are the most economically prosperous religious community (save the Zoroastrians) and yet the demand for a separate Sikh homeland (nation) and state crystallized. Viewed from the other end, the Hindus of India and the Sinhalese Buddhists of Sri Lanka, both dominant communities, are acutely 'nationalistic' as compared with several other religious communities within these multi-national states. The point is, nationalism is not exclusive to those 'nations' that are materially deprived; it can as well crystallize among the economically prosperous but culturally or politically deprived 'nations' if they perceive that there is a distinct advantage in having an exclusive nation-state. But this perception itself is something that changes over a period of time, as we have seen in the case of Scotland.

The belief that inequality and nationalism are closely related is not confined to Marxists or leftists. A wide variety of analysts, irrespective of their ideological background, hold this view. I will cite just three authorities. Karl Deutsch closes his study of nationalism and social communication with the following eloquent sentence:

> Not before the bottom of the barrel of the world's large peoples has been reached, not before inequality and insecurity will have become less extreme, *not before the vast poverty of Asia and Africa will have been reduced substantially by industrialization and by gains in living standards and in education – not before then will the age of nationalism and national diversity see the beginning of its end.* (1953: 165; italics in original)

The belief embedded in the above statement – that with equality across nations nationalism will erode, and with inequality it will increase – has not come true. Nor is it true that with increasing equality the world will become more 'integrated', as Myrdal thought: 'Only when all these underprivileged nations with their great multitude of peoples with different racial features, color of skin, religions, folklores and cultural heritages have risen to equality of opportunity will the world become integrated' (1956: 320). The same sentiment is expressed by Nash. According to him, ethnicity 'is not likely to disappear so long as there are nations, inequality and perceived injustice in the way the good things of the world are distributed among the people of the world' (1989: 128). Inter-nation (which is actually inter-state in the citations above) equality will not lead to the demise of nationalism or integration of the world, because the assumption in the above statements that the trade-off between equality and identity is possible and will take place is a false one. People want to have both equality and identity, and one of the main sources of identity in the modern world is the nation; national identity is one of the persisting collective identities, in spite of modernization and globalization.

In the final analysis classes can effectively operate (and they do) only *within* nations. But nations come alive when social categories are viewed as insiders (nationals) and outsiders (ethnies) which are not class categories. However, when there exists coterminality between nation, ethnie and race on the one hand, and class on the other, the intensity of conflicts aggravates. In a multi-national state, wherein a multiplicity of nations and ethnies co-exist, the saliency of class recedes to the background. This alone accounts for 'internal colonialism' in multi-national states. That is to say, if classes constitute layers in a mono-national society, nation is a unit vis-à-vis other nations. This is not to deny the existence of a small category of global bourgeois capitalists. But this aggregative category is an artificial one, like that of global citizens (see chapter 11).

To conclude, each nation is divided into several classes. The effective operation of class differences occur within and not across nations. More than that, class difference also operates within races and ethnic groups. Given this fact, it is necessary to develop this discussion with specific reference to a multi-racial and poly-ethnic society. And there is no society more suited for this purpose than that of the United States of America. But before I attempt this task a few general remarks are in order.

Race, ethnic groups and class

The relationships and interlinkages between race, ethnic groups and classes is the subject-matter of a large number of studies. Generally speaking, the present trend is to posit race and ethnicity on the one hand and class on the other, as two master identities, with the one subordinating the other. Further, the tendency to subsume race under ethnicity is widespread and I have argued in chapter 3 that this conceals vital empirical facts and renders conceptualization and explanation troublesome. As Van den Berghe suggests, 'class, race and ethnicity are all important types of social cleavages; . . . no matter how much they might overlap empirically, their analysis is impoverished by lumping them together; and . . . there is no *a priori* reason to expect one type to be more basic, more important, or more salient than the others' (1978: xiv–xv).

That these categories overlap empirically is pointed out by several analysts. For example, in modern-day France the word 'immigrant' is a 'catch-all category' under which all foreigners are labelled indiscriminately, as Balibar notes. And yet there is a hierarchy of immigrants. In Paris a Portuguese is more an immigrant than a Spaniard, although less so than an Arab or a black. A Briton or a German will rarely be an immigrant, although a Greek is one as compared to them. If Spanish and Moroccan workers are invariably immigrants, the Spanish capitalist or even the Algerian capitalist need not be (Balibar 1991: 221). This is an accurate description of the relationship between race, ethnicity and class, although Balibar also subsumes race under ethnicity. If we paraphrase this description into our conceptual terms, we would arrive at the following propositions. First, some ethnies, that is, outsiders (e.g., Britons and Germans) are equals, but others (e.g., Greeks, Spaniards and Portuguese) are unequal vis-à-vis the nationals, that is, the French. The unequal ethnies experience greater difficulty in de-stigmatizing themselves as immigrants compared with the equal ethnies, but they can and often they do, especially if they belong to the middle or upper classes. Second, a category that is ethnic as well as different in terms of race (e.g., the non-whites) and/or religion (e.g., the Muslims, or Jews) will find it very difficult to overcome de-stigmatization, although this is partly possible if they are in the upper class. That is, an immigrant's class status is inextricably intertwined with other identities, notably race and religion.

The class element persists even after substantial miscegenation. Thus, in much of Latin America there do not exist two distinct groups – Negro and white – and consequently racial discrimination is not sharp. In fact, racial boundaries shift over a period of time through miscegenation. For example, in Mexico the native population has declined from 99 per cent of the total in 1600 to 11 per cent in 1950. The hybrid types variously referred to as mestizos, ladinos, cholos and the like are becoming the mainstream physical types in Latin America. Even persons belonging to the same nuclear family are accepted as belonging to quite different racial types. The very cognition regarding particular physical types vary. Therefore, passing from one 'racial' type to another is usual, possible, not to be protected by secrecy and does not call for withdrawal from one's own group (Harris 1974). Commenting specifically on the Brazilian situation, Harris writes: 'A Brazilian is never merely a "white man" or a "coloured man"; he is a rich, well educated coloured man or a poor, uneducated white man; a rich well educated white man or a poor uneducated coloured man' (p. 61). If this is the case, it is untenable to talk about linkages between race, ethnicity and class, ignoring the specificity of particular empirical situations.

We might therefore consider three possibilities representing a rigidity–fluidity continuum in the context of race–class relations: fluid race relations, but a rigid class system; both race relations and the class system being rigid; and, rigid race relations, but a fluid class situation. Although Brazil has a fluid situation in race relations, it has only a few blacks in the upper class and most blacks are poor. In contrast, South Africa's race relations and class situation are rigid. It can be seen, then, that a fluid race relations situation does not lead to the disappearance of class stratification, although it would facilitate limited class mobility, as in Brazil. On the other hand, rigid race relations accentuate class polarity and income disparity, as in South Africa (see Worsely 1984: 240). Thus Banton's distinction between the two-category (dichotomous) and integrated (continuum) race relations situations is useful, but not adequate.

Banton's two-category system is characterized by the following points: an exclusion of the lower category from possible competitions, despite the merits of the individuals who constitute it; racial prejudice that tends to be more emotional and directed to all members of the lower category; an ideology that approves the preservation of race; a consciousness of discrimination that is continuous and obsessive; a lower category that reacts collectively and tends to organize collective actions; and it offers no legitimate means of crossing the colour line. In contrast, in the integrated order prejudice leads to avoidance and the maintenance of social distance; prejudice itself is intellectual and aesthetic; ideology is pro-assimilation; culture is more important than race; consciousness of discrimination is intermittent and individuals may try to compensate for their deficiencies by initiating the lifestyles of social superiors; class prejudice operates in conjunction with race prejudice; and people's reaction against racial prejudice tends to be fused with class struggles (Banton 1967: 277–8).

This contrast does not capture all aspects of the empirical reality. For example, even in the most rigid race relations system, namely, that of South Africa, the presence of intermediate categories such as the coloureds and Indians complicate matters. Further, the case of the USA comes in between the two-category and integrated systems, in that while race relations are certainly rigid, as in the two-category system, a section of the blacks are somewhat 'integrated' through the policy of affirmative action, which has given birth to a black bourgeoisie. This does not mean that the black middle class in the USA is not discriminated against on the basis of race. While they may escape institutional racism, the blacks continue to be victims of everyday racism.

With these clarifications in mind, let me turn to a specific discussion of the United States. But before that one more caveat is called for. I have defined ethnies as outsiders to society. Several segments of the American population still define themselves as outsiders, as exemplified by black nationalism (see chapter 4) and sojourner ethnicity among the Jews. It is true that among both these categories there are also substantial segments who are nationals, that is, those who consider the USA as their homeland. In other words, both Jews and blacks have ethnies and nationals among them. What distinguishes them is, respectively, religion and colour. Therefore, a comparison of the US Jews and blacks should bring out the race–class and ethnicity–class linkages.

The US situation

In 1980, over 75 per cent of the US population was white, incorporating a large number of ethnic groups, the most numerous ones being the British (20 per cent), German (15 per cent), Irish (8 per cent) and Anglo-American (6 per cent). All other white ethnic groups constituted only 4 per cent or lower of the population. The blacks counted for 9 per cent and the Asians (yellows and browns) together accounted for merely 2 per cent (see Jiobu 1990). Given the hierarchy of race and colour, as well as the numbers involved, the conflict-ridden race relations obtained largely between the whites and blacks, apart from the occasional flare-ups in certain localities (e.g., the attack against the browns (Indians) in New Jersey by whites or against the yellows (Koreans) in California by blacks.

It is necessary to have a brief look at the trajectory of race–class relations in order to understand the current articulations about it. Dollard (1937) found that most blacks were from the lower class – although there was a small black middle class, there was hardly any black upper class; most whites were middle class; and while the black middle class consisted mainly of ministers and school teachers, the white middle class comprised businessmen and professionals. Not surprisingly, Myrdal could conclude: 'Any reasonable criterion used to describe the white lower class would, when applied to Negroes, put the majority of the latter in the lower class' (1944: 700).

However, over the years the US blacks have been experiencing upward mobility and there are reports of narrowing income gaps between them and the whites. According to one estimate, the income of black males was 61 per cent of that of whites in 1955, 68 per cent in 1970 and 71 per cent in 1981 (Farley 1984: 60). But there are contrary reports. For example, it is claimed that there was a decisive deterioration in the condition of the US blacks in the 1980s; their median real family incomes declined in 1987, while those of whites increased. A 1988 study revealed that the net worth of white households averaged ten times that of the black households (Perlo 1988: 55–60).

The limited levelling of incomes between racial groups is attributed mainly to education. Therefore, it is useful to consider the role of education in this context. In the USA, even when the median level of education of racial groups is the same, their median annual income varies. For example, for Anglo-Americans it is $8,800, but for blacks it is $6,900 (Jiobu 1990: 54). That is, the same level of education does not ensure the same level of income. There are two reasons for this. First, the quality of schooling. It is well known that there exist enormous variations in the quality of education in the USA, and the higher the socio-economic status, the greater is the possibility of securing a better quality education. Thus, class differences *per se* lead to unequal access to high quality education within the same race. But even when there is no income difference and even though the school system is 'open' it may lead to unequal access to quality schooling between different races, thanks to residential segregation.

Second, even for those who do not achieve a high quality education, discrimination in employment may still exist because, even as institutional racism stands abolished through legislations, everyday racism does operate. Further, patterns of neighbourhood, location of firms and so on, which are not legally regulated, influence the flow of information and accessibility to jobs. The numerous unintended and invisible interfaces between race and class are not always recognized by most analysts.

Understandably, analysts have taken diametrically opposite positions while discussing race–class relations. For example, Wilson writes: 'Race relations in America have undergone fundamental changes in recent years. So much so that now the life chances of individual Blacks have more to do with their class position than with their day-to-day encounters with whites' (1978: 1). And yet Wilson has admitted in his later work that under-class families are mostly black urban male-headed households and that there are almost no blacks in the upper class (1987: 156). According to Boston, the black bourgeoisie is less than 1 per cent, although the black middle class constitutes about 15 per cent of the total population. But the bulk of them are from the working class, accounting for 84 per cent (1988: 8).

Thus, there is agreement that there are hardly any capitalists among the blacks and that most of them are in the working class. The question is why? To answer this one must situate the US Negroes historically.

The major source of accumulation of capital among the Negroes during the period of slavery and soon afterwards was land owner-ship. By 1860, there were around 488,000 free blacks in a population of 4.5 million who had accumulated about $50 million worth of wealth (Harris 1936:9). But with the defeat of the reconstruction policy, they were deprived of both land and capital, and at the same time dispos-sessed of the judicial and political mechanisms with which to protect their economic interests. This was a lethal blow to the emergence of a viable capitalist class among the blacks. Further, the availability of capital in the USA was extremely restricted for black entrepreneurs. In 1971, the assets of black-owned banks constituted less than one-tenth of 1 per cent of the assets of the white-controlled banks. And yet, 40 per cent of the loans secured by black businessmen were from 'black' banks. There was also a black economic enclave, which had three distinguishing features. 'First, its enterprise evolved mainly before the Civil Rights era and were constrained to operating in an environ-ment of racial segregation. Second, ... their clientele was black, al-most exclusively. Third, these constraints tied the fortunes of entrepreneurs of this segment to the economic, political and social developments of the black community' (Boston 1988: 39).

But since the 1960s this pattern has changed and the identification and affiliation of black entrepreneurs with the black community be-came weaker, as they came to be dependent on whites economically. Thus, not only could the blacks not develop any racial hegemony in certain regions and occupations, but even in their own racial enclave they had become ineffective, unlike the Jews (see below). In fact, the main source of upward mobility for the blacks today is government employment, thanks to affirmative action. Between 1970 and 1984 the US government employed approximately 45 per cent and 65 per cent respectively of the blacks who were professionals, managers or ad-ministrators (Cherry 1989: 212). But as long as they remain employees, not employers, the blacks cannot generate the required economic resource or possess the necessary political clout to help their own community.

After an incisive analysis of inequality based on occupational class distribution, Jiobu concludes that the most distinctive division is be-tween the whites and non-whites: 'Most white groups are under-represented or at parity in the lower strata while most non-white groups are over represented. In the under-class alone, five of the six over-represented groups are non-white while eleven of the thirteen under-represented groups are white' (Jiobu 1990: 64).

Viewed against this background Blauner's observation has a ring of authenticity. He writes:

> Racism excludes a category of people from participation in a society in a different way than class hegemony and exploitation. The thrust of racism is to dehumanize, to violate dignity and degrade personalities in a much more pervasive and all inclusive way than class exploitation . . . Racist oppression attacks selfhood more directly and thoroughly than does class oppression. (1972: 146)

More recently, Pinkey has observed: 'Black people are the victims of oppression because of their racial heritage, not because they are separated from whites by class differences. Indeed, in matters involving the two races upper-class blacks fare no better than do poor blacks. In the eyes of the white Americans, race is the salient factor in relation with blacks' (1984: 53).

There is clearly a link between race and class. As racial boundaries are hard and difficult to break, it is nearly impossible for individuals to compete as individuals and succeed in so far as they are drawn from races that are subjected to cumulative oppression. In contrast, ethnic boundaries are relatively soft and hence individuals may often succeed in achieving upward mobility. This is illustrated by the case of the US Jews. To start with, it may be noted that the Jews were discriminated against only in certain sectors even in Europe. For example, they were discriminated against in politics, which seems to have contributed to their achieving excellence in commerce, scholarship and the arts. The Napoleonic legal code in the nineteenth century was a milestone in this context:

> The Jews had every reason to feel grateful to Napoleon. This act by opening to the Jews the doors of trades and professions which had hitherto remained rigidly barred to them, had the effect of releasing a mass of imprisoned energy and ambition, and led to the enthusiastic – in some cases over-enthusiastic – acceptance of general European culture by a hitherto segregated community. (Berlin 1972: 25)

In fact, the American Jews did not face any such discrimination compared with their European counterparts. Several factors are listed to explain Jewish exceptionalism. First, their positive cultural traits, such as love for learning, hard work, aversion to alcholism, cleanliness and rejection of crime, are believed to explain their upward mobility (see Chiswick 1983: 313–35). But this attributed cultural determinism is not sustainable. For example, the Jewish quest for modern education is largely confined to the second generation Jews, after the community had experienced an initial economic success largely because of self-owned and managed family businesses. At any rate, considerable differences in educational disposition existed between Ashkenazic and Sephardic Jews. Second, the educationally inclined Ashkenazic Jews took to religious education, which was not necessarily conducive to the internalization of secular values required for modernization (Slater 1969: 359–73). Therefore, Mazrui's suggestion that Jewish success in the intellectual field is due to their Talmudic tradition, as compared with blacks who have had limited intellectual achievements, seems to be an exaggeration (1978: 19–36). Finally, in the early days Jews accounted for a disproportionately large amount of crime and the Jewish family was not adequately stable (Steinberg 1981).

What was, however, specific to Jewish immigrants was the high proportion of skilled workers among them (Steinberg 1981). Furthermore, many more Jews were owners and employers as opposed to workers, compared with other ethnic groups (Lestchinsky 1946: 391–406). Consequently, a disproportionately large number of them were self-employed. Anti-Semitism being the nodal point of discrimination against Jews, in the economic context this could have been manifested mainly in the hiring process. But as they were mainly self-employed, it did not adversely affect their economic prospects. Further, there was an entrenched German Jewish elite present in the USA which supported the new immigrants economically and politically (Dobkowski 1979).

Bonacich (1973: 583–94) argued that the Jews attained 'middleman' minority status in the USA, which brought in economic prosperity. But their sojourner outlook was an obstacle to the development of lasting relationships with members of the surrounding society, which invited political flak because they were perceived to have mainly financial interests in the host society, and no political commitment to it. This united the workers and capitalists of the host society against the sojourners, and discrimination began when the latter monopolized middlemen positions. This in turn led to insulated ethnic economic ties and the consequent emergence of the ethnic market.

The argument that the Jews had sojourner attitudes has been contested by many. Waldinger points out that assimilationism was an important goal of the Jews in the USA (1986: 249–85). That is, they wanted to merge into the cultural mainstream and acquire a class status, relegating their ethnic identity into the background. Further, Jews were active in trade unions and movements for social change and championed the demands of black civil rights (Liebman 1979). These authors argue that it is not correct to think that the Jews had a sojourner attitude.

At any rate, Jews achieved the middleman minority status only after World War II. According to the census of 1900, less than 20 per cent of Jews who were gainfully employed were owners, managers or peddlers, while 60 per cent were blue-collar workers (Goldberg 1947). They were not middlemen everywhere; in Russia their middlemen position was modest, although among the Jews of Russian ancestry in the USA it was substantial. In 1940 only 27 per cent of Jews in the labour force were self-employed, owners or managers, while 65 per cent were clerical and industrial workers (Lestchinsky 1946: 391–406). The number of Jews who were professionals, self-employed, owners or managers rose from less than 35 per cent in 1935 to more than 60 per cent by the mid-1970s. That is, they attained middleman status only two generations after immigration to the USA (Cherry 1989: 209). In contrast, the blacks were only negligibly represented in the self-employed sector of the economy (see Frazier 1962).

The purpose of this comparative analysis of the US blacks and Jews is to bring out certain general points. Whether or not a collectivity experiences rapid upward mobility or extremely limited mobility depends on the following. First, the mode of incorporation of the collectivity into society. This has varied enormously between the US blacks and the Jews; the former were brought in as slaves and subjected to considerable oppression and stigmatization; the latter came as migrants, mostly searching for economic opportunity and/or political freedom. The basis of the discrimination to which the Jews were subjected was qualitatively different, in that anti-Semitism was an ideology that grew out of being despised because of their religion and their economic success. Second, the salient identity of the blacks is racial, while that of the Jews is ethnic; if the boundary of the former is very hard and difficult to break, the ethnic boundary is soft and is relatively easy to cross. Third, the Jews gradually became capitalists, entrepreneurs and self-employed, thereby facilitating their acquisition of political and cultural visibility, although they constitute a mere 3 per cent of the US population. In contrast, a capitalist class did not emerge among the blacks and the main source of their mobility was government employment; their resources were not only limited, but not even functional to achieve political power and cultural visibility. Although the blacks constitute nearly 10 per cent of the US population, they do not have the political clout commensurate to their numbers. Understandably, the class position of the Jews and the blacks in the US varies enormously.

I have attempted to unfold the relationship between race, ethnie and class and their reciprocal relationships. I want to suggest that any attempt to subsume the notion of race under ethnic groups would camouflage the specific oppressions rooted in racism and the difficulties faced by non-whites to cross class barriers. In contrast, given the relatively soft boundaries between ethnic groups it is not very difficult to break them and achieve equality. These propositions have profound implications for the analysis of citizenship, which is an instrument of equality, as will be shown in the discussion which follows in the next chapter.

11

Reconciling Nationality and Ethnicity: The Role of Citizenship

Both nationality and ethnicity have positive and negative connotations in the social sciences, as we have seen in chapter 2. In contrast, citizenship does not carry with it any pejorative connotation: it always had and continues to have a positive meaning. In fact, it is the state that creates 'second-class citizens' or non-citizens that is disparaged, not the victims who may have been denied citizenship. The battle for achieving universal citizenship has been a continuous one, characterized by the progressive inclusion of new categories – women, lower classes and youth – even in homogeneous societies with democratic states. However, there is no consensus about the content and meaning of citizenship.

Today a wide variety of subjects is analysed from the perspective of citizenship; for example, authoritarian polities, cultural minorities, environmental degradation, ecological crisis, gender issues, poverty, participatory democracy, supra-national developments, unemployment, underclass and, of course, national identity and ethnicity. The present concern is mainly confined to delineating the relationship between citizenship, nationality and ethnicity. But a few clarificatory remarks are in order before we start that discussion.

The concept of citizenship

For Marshall (1965), social citizenship (which crystallized after civil and political citizenship, was the crowning glory of the progress of the idea of citizenship. But today we have advocates of active, democratic, cultural, communitarian, earth, European, ecological, environmental, gender-neutral, global, individualistic, liberal, participatory, race-neutral, republican, neo-republican, and world citizenships, to list a few. Admittedly, this babel of labels confuses rather than clarifies the content and meaning of the concept. Some of these adjectives do not refer to citizenship status, but to the intensity of involvement (e.g., active and participatory) of citizens. Some others are annexing new territorial bases for the citizens – European, global and world – or are assigning new responsibilities to the citizen, as in the case of environmental and earth citizenships. Still others are stuffing the concept with new content, as in the case of cultural or ecological citizenship. Finally, most are providing value-orientations to the concept, be it race or gender neutrality, republicanism, democracy, communitarianism or individualism. It is evident that there is a need to delimit the meaning and content of citizenship. I shall attempt to do so with special reference to the present theme of our concern, namely, the relationship between citizenship, nationality and ethnicity.

I have noted at the very outset in chapter 1 that these three notions can only be properly understood in their processual relationships, and that they are anchored to the entities of state, nation and ethnie respectively. That is, the notion of citizenship is meaningless without its anchorage, namely, the state. Therefore the notions of global or world citizenship do not sound authentic without a world or global state, which is nowhere on the horizon. While it is true that the state has surrendered some of its authority to inter-state, supra-state and intra-state organizations, and consequently the conventional idea of sovereignty as indivisible has come to naught, one may safely assert that the state will not wither away, and it cannot be wished away. This is not to deny the possibility of different levels of citizenship wherever governments exist – local or federal. Thus, the same person can at once be a European Union citizen, a German citizen, and a citizen of one of the *Länder* in Germany, or a US citizen and a citizen of California. But the full blossoming of European Union citizenship is possible only when the union becomes a multi-national federal state. Hence, even presuming that there could be different levels of citizenship only one of these would assume centrality, depending upon the context.

The foregoing discussion raises three points. First, the overburdening of the concept of citizenship makes it not only plastic, but also ambiguous. Second, it is necessary to specify the unit to which citizenship is anchored. Third, the content of citizenship needs specification. I will discuss these points successively.

The first point may be profitably discussed with reference to the notions of global and ecological citizenship. Falk (1994: 127–40) argues that global citizenship is in the making for three basic reasons. First, the reverberations of events occurring in one part of the world, particularly in the economic context, inevitably impinge on the rest of the world. While this is largely true in a general sense, it is important to keep in mind that such events impinge with unequal intensity on populations of states with different levels of development (e.g., Mexico or the USA), on those that belong to entities with common economic arrangements (e.g., residents of the European Union) or on those that are more or less equally developed (e.g., Japan and the USA). This imbalance is often of such a wide range that it does make qualitative differences. While it acutely affects some states, it scarcely affects others. More importantly, the reverberations are both negative and positive, as in the case of the devaluation of currency. While such 'global' events make people aware of their existence in an interdependent world, they increase the awareness of dependence in some and that of dominance in others. And neither dependence nor dominance contribute to the making of authentic citizenship, which is and ought to be an instrument that engenders equality.

Another indication of the emerging global citizenship mentioned by Falk is transnational activism. The typical players of this persuasion are the global reformers, the business elite and the managers of environment, whose activism articulates itself in trans-state regional political consciousness, such as those relating to the European Union and/or even in global consciousness. None of these activists function, nor do their deeds operate vis-à-vis a state, and hence it is inappropriate to designate them as citizens or label their actions as those of a citizenry. They are actors in a reluctantly emerging global civil society. But more often than not the incipient global civil society is dominated by the people of a few states and, indeed, by just a handful of citizens within those states.

Finally, Falk lists the ecological imperative, which again is not anchored to a state or to a group of states. State territories and ecological areas rarely coincide. In fact, the appropriate unit of ecology is a geographic region which sometimes contains several state territories, or occasionally one state territory may have several such regions.

Van Steenbergen (1994: 141–52) elaborates the discussion on ecological citizenship and mentions three current approaches to it. The first of these is exemplified by increasing inclusion, which in itself is of a positive orientation. But one should have some criterion of inclusion and exclusion in regard to rights and duties of citizens. In 1792 Thomas Taylor, the Cambridge philosopher, published (anonymously) his book *A Vindication of the Rights of Brutes.* It was a satirical response to *A Vindication of the Rights of Woman* by the pioneering feminist Mary Wollstonecraft. In 'equating' women and brutes Taylor would be instantly condemned today, even by arch-reactionaries and conservatives. On the other hand, two centuries after the publication of Taylor's book there are ecologists who argue for animal rights, in particular of those animals with higher intelligence such as chimps and dolphins, which of course is nothing new to those who are familiar with the Jaina philosophy that emerged in India in the sixth century BC.

Logically, one can extend the argument to plants too, that is, to all living entities. The Indian scientist J. C. Bose has established that not only animals but plants also have life; they respond to music. Astrophysicists like Chandrasekhar may extend this logic to the stars, because they too have a 'life'. Thus one may extend 'rights' to the entire cosmic order. Yet one cannot deny the existence of three qualitatively different entities: material objects, which are capable of only reactivity (e.g., iron and magnet, water and sodium); living entities, which are capable of responsiveness (animals and plants); and human beings who alone are endowed with reflection, the facility to make judgements, although it is not developed in them all. While unborn human beings, insane or imbecile persons, or children below the age of consent can have rights, they are not in a position to make judgements. Therefore, the current tendency of ecologists to expand 'the notion of citizenship . . . to include parts of nature other than humans', and the extension of citizenship rights to all 'living beings' (Steenbergen 1994: 145) ought to be viewed with some circumspection, as I see it.

The second strand in the ecological approach assigns the responsibility to nurture nature as well as human society to humans. That is, ecological citizenship extends the notion of human responsibility to the natural world, challenging the primacy of society over nature. But the point is that animals and some humans are not equipped to discharge this responsibility. Therefore, they cannot be ecological citizens. Even environmentalists concede that only human beings are endowed with the capacity to choose their attitude to environment, as distinct from animals. At any rate, responsibility to nature is a human responsibility and need not be confined to citizens. Not all humans are necessarily citizens everywhere; aliens and ethnies should also have a responsibility to nature.

In the third approach, the global dimension of ecological citizenship is emphasized. But the global dimension is not exclusive to the ecological citizen, it is shared by the global reformer, the business elite and the manager of the environment, that is, by all those types of global 'citizens' listed by Falk to whom I have referred above. The orientations of these global citizens vary dramatically. For example, the ecological citizen of Steenbergen's conception is an earth citizen rooted in the national territory, but committed to nurturing the earth as a whole. In contrast, global business operators are high-flying 'sky citizens' indulging in high profit-making. And although they eat their breakfast in Berlin, lunch in London and sleep in Strasbourg at night, they need the Sprint or Visa card 'to call home'. Even here it is hard to conceive of citizenship without a territorial referent. In the case of a citizen this referent is the territory of the state, as opposed to the case of the national, whose attachment is to the territory of the nation. That these territories occasionally coincide, in which case these attachments may co-exist, should not confuse us. The possibility of dissociation of these territories and hence of these identities is perennial in the contemporary world (see Nielson 1985: 27–56). For this reason, the advocacy of 'transnational citizenship' by Baubock (1994) is also ambiguous and unsustainable. To conclude, there are no global citizens because there is not and perhaps there will never be a world state or government. There can, however, be a global civil society, although, of course, as of now it is virtually non-existent and only gradually emerging.

The second point I have listed is the need to specify the unit to which citizenship is anchored. As hinted already, it should be the state and the state alone that is a territorial entity with a legal base. As the territorial base of a state changes, so too does the composition of its citizenship. This is obvious when one considers the processes of unification and division of states. Only a European Union 'citizen' can participate and contest for the European Parliament elections. When the Soviet Union broke up the Soviet citizens disappeared and became citizens of one or other of the successor states. This was also the case of the citizens of Yugoslavia and Czechoslovakia. But in spite of the change in their citizenship status, individuals did not and could not change their national or ethnic identities. This may be illustrated with an example.

From World War II until today there have only been two cases of secession in the world – Bangladesh and Eritrea. The illustration I am providing is related to the first case. Let us consider the hypothetical case of Mr Rehman, a Bengali-speaking Muslim who lived in Dacca, now the capital of Bangladesh. On 14 August 1947 Mr Rehman was a British subject and citizen. On 15 August he became a citizen of the state of Pakistan. In 1971 he became a citizen of Bangladesh, although he still remains a Bengali-speaking Muslim. What has changed is neither his nationality nor his ethnic identity, but his citizenship.

The point I want to make is this. Whether new states emerge through a process of unification as happened in the case of Germany, or existing states are dissolved as in the case of the erstwhile Soviet Union, or new states are formed through secession, citizens are born instantly. That individuals and groups may be denied their citizenship by particular states based on their national or ethnic identities is well known. States cannot easily erase national and ethnic identities, but they can instantly confer citizenship. Which is to say that the state can both deny and confer citizenship. Therefore, to dissociate citizenship from its very source – the state – is to render the notion irrelevant and meaningless.

My third point concerns the need to specify the content of citizenship. There is no consensus on this point either. In fact, there is a persisting and acrimonious controversy over it. One set of writers emphasizes entitlements (e.g., Dahrendorf 1994: 10–19); others focus on obligations (e.g., Mead 1986). To Dahrendorf modern politics is about two themes: provisions and entitlements. While the former deals with growth and the widening range of choices, the latter is about access to provisions and citizens' opportunities. Dahrendorf holds the view that citizenship is a status to which any individual should be entitled irrespective of the value of his or her contribution to the economy, because it is a non-economic concept. The contrary view upheld by writers such as Mead sees the idea of unconditional entitlements as a sure invitation to bulge the rank of 'free riders'. Therefore, only those who pay taxes to the local authorities should vote (the argument in Britain) and those who receive welfare benefits should be willing to work; that is, it should be workfare instead of welfare (the articulation in the USA). In this view, the citizen's obligation is over-emphasized at the cost of entitlements.

The polarization of the debate on citizenship today is thus based on the notion of social citizenship upheld by the left, and the idea of an 'active citizen' who is expected to fulfil his social obligations to society, which is championed by the New Right. Clearly, both these views are one-sided and we need to inject a balance into them. The issue therefore should not be viewed as one of entitlement versus obligation, but one of combining the two wherever it is necessary and feasible. Dahrendorf rightly holds that if citizenship is turned into mere obligations of individuals, both the market and the state would nullify the very idea. Therefore, the idea that basic entitlements should be a given is beyond debate. This prescription is based on recent experience. In instances where entitlements receded to the background and provisions gained saliency, the size and the immiseration of the underclass grew. The much-heralded safety net of the market had too many big holes. The underclass lost access to the most critical segments of the market and society that were relevant for them – the labour market, the political community and the social network. They became a mere category, victims, indeed (1994: 13–15). Therefore, the real challenge is to 'citizenize' the underclass.

However, a citizen by definition cannot be a mere recipient. To be an eternal receiver is morally degrading, and to emancipate oneself from this condition one has to be a giver too. But those who are not equipped to give cannot be expected to give. And it is here that the New Right's prescription of active citizenship ought to scrutinized carefully. How can handicapped – physically and/or mentally – persons or children below (and the old above) certain ages be 'active' citizens? What seems plausible is that the able-bodied unemployed can be rendered active if appropriate conditions are created. This should do away with 'free riders' and, consequently, the alienated in the system, because they are two sides of the same coin. The free riders who consider themselves clever in the beginning gradually become morally degraded, even in self-perception. This is what a persisting recipient status does. In the light of this discussion I suggest that the problematique of citizenship is to be viewed in terms of its contexts and related contents. The contexts of citizenship may be identified at three levels – that of the Three Worlds, inter-state migration and the internal social milieu prevailing in particular states. I will discuss each of these successively.

Contexts and contents of citizenship

I have argued in chapter 1 that the tripartite division of the world and the nationality–ethnicity distinction do not hinge well together. But even in the case of citizenship rights the categorization is of doubtful value. Marshall's (1965) civil rights consist of liberty of person, freedom of speech, thought and faith, the right to own property, the right to conclude valid contracts and the right to justice. Political rights are mainly the right of franchise and the right of access to public office. Social rights, which are actually economic in content (Giddens 1985: 206–9), consist of the right to a modicum of economic welfare and social security, to a full share of the social heritage and to live the life of a civilized being according to the standards prevailing in society.

Even in First World democracies, the perceptions regarding the content of citizenship vary immensely. As Fraser and Gordon (1994: 90–107) note, Americans rarely speak of social citizenship because it implies rights and entitlements embedded in a contract and not charity wrapped up in institutional welfare benefits. Social rights which imply respect and equality rarely figure in public debates. Welfare is stigmatized, but work is sacralized; the public domain is demonized, but the private is sanctified. Unemployment is viewed as a private predilection and not as a manifestation of social policy or economic pathology. In contrast, civil citizenship is highly valued. The hero of civil society, created by civil rights, is the property-owning individual; civil society is exemplified by 'possessive individualism', to recall the seductive phrase of Macpherson (1974). In fact, as civil society is possessed by individualism, it is very difficult to liberate the body (civil society) of the spirit (individualism).

The robbing of social citizenship of its contractual character and viewing it as charity has several consequences. First, the beneficiary becomes a mere recipient of charity with no entitlements, a situation that is morally degrading. Second, the giver of charity assumes instant superiority and accumulates moral merit, the concern being the giver's entry into the other world and not the receiver's physical survival in this world. Third, since the giver and receiver are strangers, the recipient cannot demand charity, but can only solicit it. And 'the cultural mythology of civil citizenship stands in a tense, often obstructing relationship to social citizenship. This is nowhere more true than in the US, where the dominant understanding of civil citizenship remains strongly infected by the notions of "contract" and "independence" while social provision has been constructed to connote "charity" and "dependence" (Fraser and Gordon 1994: 104).

The consequence of this juxtaposition of social and civil citizenship in terms of charity and contract is manifested in the widespread belief in the USA that the opportunity for economic betterment is widely available, that social mobility is determined by the individual's efforts, and that, therefore, economic inequality is fair (Klugel and Smith 1986: 37). Further, the feeling that the recipients of welfare exaggerate their needs, cheat the state and avoid work is widespread. That is, Americans are far more concerned about the duties or social obligations of the poor, particularly those who receive welfare support, than about their rights: 'it is the moral fabric of individuals, not the social and economic structure of society, that is taken to be the root of the problem' (Wilson 1994: 53).

In a comparative study of nine West European countries regarding perceptions of poverty less than 25 per cent of the respondents, except in the United Kingdom where the percentage was nearly half, attributed poverty to 'laziness and lack of will power' (CEC 1979). That is, the attitude in the UK is fairly close to that in the USA about individual responsibility regarding poverty. And yet, there is a sharp difference between these two countries regarding the value orientations of citizenship. In the USA it is predominantly liberal and in the UK it is largely communitarian, although the two value orientations co-exist in both these countries (Conover et al. 1990: 1–33).

The empirical analysis attempted by Conover and his colleagues confirms the differing emphases in regard to citizenship rights; American respondents focus on civil rights, whereas British respondents focus on social rights, confirming the articulations of the analysts we have quoted. With regard to citizens' duties, the Americans focus on political responsibility, but the British responses 'contained relatively more communitarian elements'. The central elements in the identity of citizenship in the USA are freedom and individualism; in the UK these are a sense of belonging to the land, a shared heritage, and a national identity (pp. 7–24). That is, the conceptions of citizenship vary drastically not only within the so-called First World (the USA and Western Europe), but also between the UK and the USA. It is important to recall here that these two 'nations', the 'first nation' and the 'first new nation' of the world are widely believed to have common values and institutions; the latter is regarded as a replica of the former. I suggest that the motives for their differences should be traced to the fact that they are drawn from different contexts, the Old and the New Worlds, and the consequent variations in their making and modes of incorporating citizens.

Generally speaking, the difference between the First and the Second Worlds is striking with regard to citizenship rights in that civil and political rights were almost completely absent in the latter. The fact that the socialist state abolished individual ownership of property, seizing it all for itself, rendered civil rights largely irrelevant. Similarly, the moment for political rights disappeared because of the one party system and the installation of the *nomenklatura*, which totally dominated the system. On the other hand, while substantial weight was given to the welfare component of social rights, the right of small nations to a social heritage was effectively blocked by Great Nation chauvinism in the multi-national socialist states, as we have seen in chapter 6. That is to say that for the individuals of relatively homogeneous socialist states the possibility of maintaining the social heritage was substantial. This was also true of individuals who belonged to the dominant nations of multi-national states. Once again, the relevant point is that the differences within the Second World were substantial with regard to certain social rights.

In the case of the Third World the situation is more complex and mixed. The only thing more or less common to all of them is the absence of the citizen's right to even a modicum of economic welfare and social security. This is so not because of any ideological resistance from any section of the population (which was the case at least until recently), but because of the gross inadequacy of material resources at the command of Third World states. As for civil and political rights, some of the Third World countries have exemplary records in this, while the performance of others is as tainted as that of the Second World. The point again is that the states in the Third World cannot be put into the same basket as the Second World. The inescapable conclusion that one reaches is that the tripartite division of the world does not reflect the differences in and conceptions about citizen rights. In fact, differences within each of these worlds are as numerous as the differences across them. Hence, the appropriate unit to understand citizenship is an individual state and not a block of states.

The second context to influence the content of citizenship is inter-state migration. Baubock argues that immigrants should be regarded as members of the host society even if they intend to return to their country of origin, as membership is acquired gradually and is mainly a function of the duration of residence. This in turn is possible only if an open civil society exists which is not deeply fractured by class or ethnic cleavages: 'If a society is strongly segregated along cultural boundaries immigrants will indeed have to make a choice as to whether they want to become members by assimilating, and institutions of the receiving society will control this admission by defining the criteria of successful assimilation' (1994: 173).

There are several difficulties with this argument. First, if immigrants plan to leave, either for their homeland or for some other destination, that is, if they remain an ethnie, it is unrealistic to consider them as members of the host society. It may be the case that they want to leave precisely because they are treated as outsiders. In other words, whether the motivation to leave springs from their attachment to the homeland or from stigmatization in the host society, the fact remains that the immigrant has not become a member of that society. But this should not be viewed as an obstacle in accepting them as members of the host polity and in granting them citizenship rights and prescribing obligations. What I am suggesting is that to be a member of a society (that is, a national) is not simply a matter of voluntary choice, but also involves being accepted by other fellow nationals. In contrast, one can choose to be a member of a polity (that is, a citizen), and the authority of conferring citizenship rights can be invested in the state. In other words, one can be an ethnie as well as a citizen; nationality need not be a prerequisite to becoming a citizen. But whether or not this is possible is dependent on the very concept of citizenship that a state adopts. I will revert later to this.

Second, there is hardly any functioning civil society that is 'open' to immigrants whatever be their background. Those societies that come nearest to being so are deeply divided by class, ethnic and racial cleavages, precisely because they are heterogeneous. A democratic polity today by definition cannot be a homogeneous society because the former is open and the latter is closed. That is, a nation-state that fosters homogeneity is bound to produce a closed society. Several nations and ethnic groups can and should co-exist in a democratic polity, as this is the real test of openness. In the persuasive words of Dahrendorf: 'The true test of the strength of citizenship is heterogeneity. Common respect for basic entitlements among people who are different in origin, culture and creed proves that combination of identity and variety lies at the heart of civil and civilized societies. . . . Exclusion is the enemy of citizenship' (1994: 17).

Third, the prescription of assimilation as a prerequisite for the immigrants to become members of the host society is coercion, and is hence undemocratic. While assimilation often provides some material and symbolic pay-offs, the assimilated lose, or have reluctantly to renounce, their identity; they are compelled to destroy their 'society' so as to become members of the host society. The immigrants may do it because of their precarious material condition; it is precisely because of this that, while they often resent assimilation under coercion, they cannot always resist it, because of their inadequate striking power. They are captives of their helplessness.

Social milieu and citizenship

The third context in which citizenship rights are influenced is the internal social milieu of societies. I will distinguish between four broad types of societies – homogeneous, heterogeneous, hierarchical and plural (cf. Despres 1967). Even homogeneous societies are stratified along gender, age, class and kinship lines. But if a society's population is drawn from the same race, religion and nationality, it may be viewed as a homogeneous society. Citizenship was not a universally bestowed status in the beginning even in those societies, being the privilege only of the propertied male. However, one of the most distinguishing features of homogeneous democratic societies in the contemporary world is universal citizenship. This is not to deny that even in such societies the poor, the women and the youth are not always full-fledged citizens.

But the situation changes drastically when one considers the case of heterogeneous societies, that is, multi-racial, multi-religious, multi-national and poly-ethnic societies. In heterogeneous societies there is a greater possibility of inter-group inequality emerging and persisting. Nevertheless, it is conceivable and possible that heterogeneous societies may be constituted by groups that are equal. But in hierarchical societies group-based inequalities are institutionalized. This was the case in the entire New World, in which the First Nations were marginalized and the blacks were brought in as slaves. The worst case of institutionalized inequality prevailed in South Africa, where the settlers did not even constitute a majority. As for the Old World, the worst case of institutionalized inequality was that of the caste system in India. These societies were hierarchical in that lowly placed categories could not cross the social boundaries. But today in all these societies the erstwhile underprivileged are granted formal citizenship status irrespective of their background. It is equally important to remember here that, in spite of the depressed status of the erstwhile Indian 'untouchables', or the slave status of the American Negroes, neither of these groups was ever considered as an outsider to the system. This may partly be due to the fact that they were viewed as indispensable for maintaining the position of the privileged. To the extent that the internality of a category to society was not questioned, the possibility of that category achieving citizenship status was greater as democratic values spread. To put it differently, the prospect of citizenization of the underclass, the slaves or the 'untouchables' is greater if they are considered as insiders, that is, nationals. On the other hand, if they are also perceived as outsiders or ethnies, the prospect of their becoming citizens is limited.

This brings me to the fundamental feature of a plural society. A plural society is stratified like a homogeneous society; it is characterized by diversity like heterogenous societies, but it may or may not be hierarchical in that inequality need not be institutionalized in them. But one or more segments of the population in plural societies are not even considered as members of that society, and such segments are treated as ethnies. Ethnies are often immigrants, but some of those who are native to the land are subjected to a process of ethnification, like the First Nations in the New World, or some of the religious communities, particularly Jews and Muslims, in several contemporary societies. In so far as the notion of citizenship is linked to nationality, there is no possibility of these segments becoming citizens. There are two ways of getting out of this impasse. First, nationalization of ethnies: the prospect of this happening is bleak, partly because the nationals invariably do not welcome it and partly because the ethnies do not always want it, as it results in the eclipse of their identity. Second, citizenization of the ethnies: this means conferring citizenship status on the ethnies without insisting that they should become nationals, that is, without their undergoing the process of assimilation. This alternative allows for both the retention of their cultural identity and the acquisition of citizenship entitlements.

As I am not using the term plural society in the sense in which it is understood in contemporary social science, it is necessary to discuss the notion at some length. The classic description of a plural society by Furnivall reads as follows:

> Each group holds by its own religion, its own culture, its own ideas and ways. As individuals they meet but only in the market place, in buying and selling . . . There is a plural society, with different sections of the community living side by side, but separately within the same political unit. Even in the economic sphere there is a division of labour on racial lines. (1948: 304)

In the plural society of Furnivall, the co-existence of the different segments, usually of racial collectivities, one native and the other alien, is not voluntary but brought about through the force imposed by the colonial power from outside.

M. G. Smith (1971: 415–58), who later analysed and extended the notion of the plural society, lists three basic deficiencies in the conceptualization made by Furnivall. First, its total identification and restriction to the modern colonial situation and to multi-racial societies. Second, its co-related confinement to tropical latitudes. Third, its consequent restriction to the phase of European expansion and laissez-faire capitalism. Smith expands on the notion of the plural society and refers to pluralism as the condition in which there is formal diversity in the basic system of institutions such as kinship, education, religion, property, economy and recreation, but not government. This is so because, 'Given the fundamental differences of belief, value and organization that connote pluralism, the monopoly of power by one cultural section is the essential pre-condition for the maintenance of the total society in its current form' (Smith 1965: 86). That is, two or more 'societies' co-exist in one polity within which the dominant society has the monopoly of power. Smith distinguishes between three types of pluralism: structural pluralism, which connotes the differential incorporation of collectivities into a polity, but which is segregated into aggregates and characterized by institutional divergences; social pluralism, which involves the organization of institutionally dissimilar collectivities as corporate segments, whose boundaries demarcate distinct communities and systems of social action; and cultural pluralism, which consists of variable institutional diversity without corresponding collective segregation (1971: 444).

Cultural pluralism can exist, according to Smith, without social and structural pluralism, but these latter two cannot obtain without the former. Thus, the three types of pluralism may be placed on a flexible–inflexible continuum, as it were.

Van den Berghe contends that there are two types of plural societies: the democratic and the despotic. The latter type is ruled by a despotic minority whose rule lacks 'consensus on both values legitimizing polity and norms regulating political behaviour. Plural societies . . . are primarily held together by coercion and the latter largely results from the superiority of the dominant group in the technology of violence' (1971: 73). In contrast, democratic plural societies have a consensual value system enshrined in their constitutions and articulated through their institutions. While constitutional guarantees are important, what matters is the substantive realities of life. That is, legal and formal framework and guarantees are necessary but not sufficient, because praxeological gaps are bound to exist even in a democratic plural society. Hence, Berghe asserts: 'I believe that pluralism is intrinsically associated with conflict and relative lack of consensus and integration' (p. 79).

If Furnivall's conceptualization of a plural society was anchored to the empirical situation of tropical, colonial, multi-racial societies, Smith and Berghe refined the notion and extended it to other empirical contexts, such as slave and multi-racial societies, both colonial and non-colonial. In contrast to this there is another conceptualization of pluralism based on an entirely different type of empirical situation, that which grew out of a multiplicity of collectivities competing in the political arena through the instrumentality of parties and associations, institutions and mobilizations. The typical cases that represent such situations are the capitalist liberal democracies of Western Europe with its multi-national and religious populations, and the United States of America, which is poly-ethnic and multi-racial, that is, those that are termed the First World.

Two early exponents of this notion of pluralism are Shils (1956) and Kornhauser (1960), but their intellectual ancestry can be easily traced to Alexis de Tocqueville (1956). Having observed the persisting turmoil in the country of his birth, France, Tocqueville was eager to locate the sources of stable and successful democracy that obtained in the USA. He found that there existed a number of 'secondary powers', that is, voluntary associations, which, along with the autonomy of local authorities (e.g., muncipalities) served to prevent the authoritarianism of the central state and helped to stablize democracy. This is how voluntary associations are today recognized as countervailing powers which sustain political pluralism in democratic societies. In

Western Europe the major concern of the pluralists was, and continues to be, how linguistic and religious blocks can co-exist with socialist and liberal parties in a democratic polity through accommodation and compromise between elites drawn from a variety of contexts (see, for example, Lorwin 1971: 141–75; Lijphart 1980).

Theorists refer to two types of pluralism, the conflict model and the equilibrium model. The essential source of conflict in the first type, the despotic plural society as characterized by Berghe, is located in the fact that a demographic, racial and cultural minority dominates over the majority in every aspect of life. This domination is made possible through its economic and technological superiority, which necessarily breeds conflict between the two parties. The resolution of conflict is possible only by doing away with its very source, namely, the domination of the minority over the majority. Viewed historically, a large number of such societies have continued for a long time as 'stable' societies, the dominated majority rarely revolting against the dominant minority, either because the value of self-governance was not internalized by them or because they did not have the requisite striking power.

On the other hand, it is not true that societies grouped under the equilibrium model, the democratic plural societies, did not have any conflict. In fact, the thesis of political pluralism, which propounded the idea that 'integration' in the First World societies should be achieved through the multiple affiliation of individuals to a variety of institutions and associations, neglected, if not entirely ignored, the inter-group conflicts between the white Christian and the non-white, non-Christian segments of these societies. And conflict is more visible in the 'democratic' plural societies as compared with the despotic ones. Thus, conflict and equilibrium are common to both types of plural societies, and to label them in terms of one of these features is inadequate, often even misleading. Hence, we need to distinguish between two types of societies based on the quality of equilibrium that obtains in them. Despotic plural societies are characterized by coercive equilibrium and the democratic plural societies ought to be informed by consensual equilibrium. Admittedly, the real challenge faced by a democratic plural society is to create and sustain a consensual equilibrium.

On the basis of this discussion, I want to suggest that pluralism is not a fact, but a value orientation, which indeed is based on diversity and heterogeneity. Further, pluralism as a value ought to refer to the dignified co-existence of a multiplicity of groups – racial, religious, ethnic – in the same polity. That is to say, the real challenge of a plural society is to institutionalize pluralism. While in homogeneous societies individuals, occupational groups, classes, gender and age-groups constitute the building-blocks, in heterogeneous and hierarchical societies, racial, religious, caste, regional and linguistic collectivities will come to constitute additional building-blocks, often in combination with classes, gender and age-groups, thereby rendering them more complex. But none of these groups is considered as an outsider to the society. What distinguishes the plural society is that a segment of its population is considered as an outsider, and has a distinct identity assigned to it. The effort to homogenize heterogeneous and plural societies is an undemocratic project, as I have argued elsewhere (Oommen 1992a: 154).

First, to homogenize often means to establish the hegemony of the dominant collectivity, annihilation of the weak and minority collectivities, or at best their assimilation into an artificially contrived cultural mainstream, leading to the eclipse of their identity. Second, most state societies, as they are constituted, draw their population from diverse sources. Therefore, annihilation and assimilation entail endangering the principles of maintaining diversity and developing pluralism. Third, contemporary societies are constantly exposed to alien influences and hence characterized by frayed edges and loose textures. If anything, the ongoing process of globalization would intensify this trend. In such a situation the only viable option is to accommodate diversity, foster pluralism and nurture inter-group equality.

The point I am making is that the option before 'democratic plural' societies is not the escape route of homogenization, but the reconciliation of competing demands of equality and identity. In contemporary societies the instrument through which equality can be ensured is citizenship. Structurally plural societies deny citizenship; they consist only of masters, slaves and subjects. A socially plural society limits citizenship; it institutionalizes inequality. The culturally plural society does not deny or limit citizenship, but often intimidates citizens, and calls upon racial and cultural outsiders to shed their identity and assimilate if they want the status of full-fledged citizens. That is, to avail themselves of the entitlements of citizenship they are coerced to renounce their collective identity.

In terms of the conceptualization of plural society that I pursue, the 'democratic' societies of the First World are plural in that some segments within them are treated as outsiders to the society. Commenting on the condition of guest workers in the affluent West European countries, Bottomore (1971: 395) writes:

> The fact that these workers are citizens of another country, speak another language, and participate in a different culture, largely excludes

them from political life in the countries where they work . . . The most significant features are the growing heterogeneity of the working class as a result of ethnic diversity, and the creation of a distinct, socially isolated sub-proletariat.

Bottomore was referring mainly to guest workers from Southern Europe who were assimilable and could be gradually absorbed. But the immigrants drawn from Asia and Africa face formidable resistance and remain an alien element in the body politic. This is evident from what a British respondent said to Conover and colleagues when answering the question: 'Do you think of everyone born here as being a British citizen?':

> I'd like to think that, but I don't think I do. I'd like to think that all colours and creeds are British citizens. But I think in reality . . . I might say they are not. They come from another culture . . . I think I have a slight anti-feeling towards them if I am truly honest in that I feel they are invading our country. (Conover et al. 1990: 23–4)

On the other hand, not all British citizens are truly British. That is, they are not nationals. As another respondent said:

> Sikhs and Hindus and Muslims, they are born here, their children go to schools. And what I find very hard to understand is why they are living in such close-knit communities . . . as though they are living in Pakistan or India or whatever. I can understand them not saying that they feel British even though they are born here. (p. 23)

We have seen in chapter 8 that coloured immigrants, particularly those drawn from the lower class, cannot easily find accommodation in white neighbourhoods in Britain. This may partially explain why they are clustered in specific neighbourhoods. But the more important point is that, even though they are born and brought up in these countries and are citizens, they may not feel that they belong there. If so, to deny citizenship to those drawn from this background is to accentuate their alienation. This is the rationale behind the proposal to citizenize the ethnies. To nationalize the ethnie is a more complex process, as it entails not only their willingness but also acceptance by the host society. But extending entitlements of citizenship to those who are not nationals also often creates fierce resistance from nationals, because the ethnies are believed not to be committed to the system, they are cognized as free riders who are milking the host society to their advantage. Therefore, it is necessary to insist on entitlements to all, and obligations from those who are capable of it.

The balance between entitlements and obligations is necessary because if the population at large perceives a given ethnic category as an 'exploiter', animosity towards it would gradually crystallize. The European Jew was perceived as an outsider and exploiter to be expelled from the society. The under-class immigrants from Asia and Africa in Europe, even though not burghers like Jews, are yet cognized as free riders who have no responsibility towards the society. Such a perception is also widely prevalent in the USA vis-à-vis those of the non-white population in general, and the blacks in particular, who are welfare beneficiaries. Herein lies the significance of maintaining the balance between the rights and duties of citizenship.

Unlinking citizenship and nationality

I have argued that both empirical reality (heterogeneity of contemporary state populations) and the prevailing value orientation (commitment to democracy) militate against the linkage between citizenship and nationality. This suggestion, however, is not as startling as it appears. Habermas puts it succinctly: 'Citizenship was never conceptually tied to national identity' (1992: 4). Greenfeld and Chirot (1994: 79–130) identify three initial conceptualizations regarding the linkage between citizenship and nationality, while delineating the relationship between nationalism and aggression, which is an extension of Greenfeld's earlier attempt (1992: 11). It seems to me that these linkages were attempted to meet the specific requirements of state-building. The empirical reality has changed substantially due to the emergence of the New World, dislocation of populations wrought by socialist states, the failure of the homogenization project initiated by nation-states and the ongoing process of inter-state migration accelerated by modernization and abetted by globalization.

The English 'nation' was initially conceptualized as a collective of sovereign individuals; this later gave birth to the individualistic libertarian concept of the state. If individuals constitute the units of nation, citizenship and nationality could be bifurcated. Great Britain was thus conceived as a collectivity of citizens drawn from different nations – England, Scotland, Wales and Ireland. This conception was functional to its state-building. I have drawn attention to the persisting ambivalence in characterizing both Great Britain and its constituting units as 'nations' even among scholars, while in reality the former is a multi-national state and the latter are nations. Other examples of this type are Switzerland, the Indian Union and the emerging European Union. In contrast to this is the conceptualization that views nation as a distinct people, the collectivistic-ethnic nation. In this mode of conceptualization citizenship and nationality become fused, giving birth to the collectivistic-authoritarian state. The typical examples of this concept of nation are the German and Italian nation-states.

These two types of conceptualizations have given birth to two different criteria of membership in the national collectivity. Where nationality and citizenship are bifurcated, the former, at least in principle, is civic, that is, open and voluntaristic; it can be acquired. In contrast, where the two are fused, membership in the nation is inherent, that is, nationality has nothing to do with individual will and citizenship is inherited. One implies the other. The collectivistic nation and the multi-national state are patently contradictory to each other.

The third mode of conceptualization is a mutation of the two and is exemplified by the French case. In France an individual can acquire nationality, that is, citizenship, through a process of 'Frenchification' – learning the French language, receiving a French education and internalizing French culture, irrespective of race and religion. This in principle gives birth to a civic-collectivistic state fostering a community of citizens. However, as we have seen in chapter 7 there is a hierarchy of citizens and nationals even here; the white, Catholic, French-speaking citizens from France at the top, and the 'Frenchified' black Muslim 'immigrant' citizen at the bottom.

It is clear from the above analysis that unlinking nationality and citizenship is an imperative if the society is to be rendered open and if the polity is to remain democratic. This should not endanger the integrity of the polity because it is possible to construct a political culture dissociated from national and ethnic origins, but anchored to the principle of multi-culturalism as noted by Habermas (1992: 7). The British model, in principle, fits the bill. But in practice a variety of collectivities feel deprived – both nationals and ethnies. Thus Ireland, Wales and Scotland are characterized as internal colonies of the dominant English nation, although the nationals of these 'colonies' are full-fledged citizens of the British state. The lower classes from these nations may feel that they are 'second-class' citizens. If so, the predicament of the non-national citizens, particularly the coloured immigrants, who are also largely of the under class, can well be visualized. Granting citizenship will not necessarily lead to their being accepted as co-nationals, but citizenship entitlements will at least partially erode the stigma associated with them as ethnies.

The importance of the suggestion becomes evident when one notes that consensus about the content of citizenship and the provision to protect the poor from the depredations of the market have been eroded of late. The four reasons listed by Van Gunsteren for this erosion (1994: 36–48) may be paraphrased as follows. First, in the context of increased inter-state (the author refers to it as international) spatial mobility, citizenship has become an eagerly sought-after status. The logical corollary of this is resistance to the conferring of citizenship on ethnies – the issue of exclusion. Second, an increasing number of citizens has actually started to misuse, or is perceived to be misusing, their entitlement – the free-rider problem. Third, the state's authority has been gradually diluted both by supra-state and intra-state agencies – erosion of state sovereignty. Fourth, the liberating and enabling provisions of the welfare state have come to be discredited – the current emphasis on the free play of market forces.

To cope with the situation Van Gunsteren suggests a new type of citizenship, the neo-republican type, which draws its constitutive elements mainly from three models of citizenship – the communitarian, the republican and the individualistic (pp. 45–7). First, the citizen is to be viewed as a member of a public community: the republic, which in principle gives freedom to individuals to form communities, to join or to reject them – the communitarian element. This freedom to join the republic is not available to the ethnic groups and when they form their own 'communities', which indeed is a mark of estrangement and alienation from the republic, they are accused of opting out of the 'nation'. Second, there are elements of virtue to be drawn from the republican concept of citizenship: the competence to participate and the ethical commitment to play the role of citizenship are emphasized. But one can play the role of citizen only if and when one is assigned the status of citizenship. The problem faced by members of the ethnie is not playing the role of citizenship, but the very exclusion from this. The third model is citizenship as the primary office in the public community – the individualistic element. That is, to be meaningful, citizenship should be activated, it should be exercised. Once again, the role of citizenship being kept under suspended animation is not germane to the ethnies, but its very acquisition is. The notion of a neo-republican citizen as an autonomous and loyal individual capable of making sound judgement and fulfilling the double role of governor and governed, as Van Gunsteren constructs it, is applicable only to nationals and not to the ethnies. The problem of the latter is the very accessibility to citizenship.

It is appropriate that I close this analysis by referring to what T.H. Marshall, 'the father of sociology of citizenship', had to say on this theme. He recognized the basic contradiction between citizenship rights and market forces and the consequent contradiction between citizenship and class, which he considered fundamental and unsolvable (see Barbalet 1988: 94–5). Social citizenship was an instrument which provided at least limited succour to the disadvantaged. And Marshall's hope was to create 'a direct sense of community membership based on loyalty, to a civilization which is a common possession'. The content of civilization that Marshall talked about was material, and its key was mass production. He wrote in 1945:

> There has been going on especially in the last fifty years or so, a steady fusion of class civilization. . . . There was a time when the culture of each class was, as it were, a unique species. Mass production destroyed this isolation . . . There has been a progressive equalization of the quality of material culture . . . (cited in Barbalet 1988: 91)

The decline of feudal classes, the ushering in of civil and political rights and the emergence of a modern state which could weld together the different nations of Britain provided 'a sense of community membership and common heritage', according to Marshall. The process of integration that he had on the agenda was confined to the national community which had a civilization as its common possession. But as Young (1967: 10–18) observes, the persisting differences in language, diet, manners and customs, and education among the different classes in Britain indicate that cultural integration is far from consolidated even among the nationals.

Given the above, it is unrealistic to expect that a common civilization which embraces the multiplicity of nationals and ethnies will emerge even in a distant future; it is a wrong agenda to be pursued. This is so because even those members of the ethnie who are successful in acquiring material possessions comparable to those of the national upper and middle classes are not always viewed as co-nationals. Herein lies the limitation of Marshall's perspective based on the British experience, which cannot be extended at all to the 'plural societies' of the New World, nor retained for the Old World which is increasingly becoming not only heterogeneous but also plural. One must recognize the role of citizenship as an instrument that can reconcile the two identities of nationality and ethnicity and the competing demands of equality and identity.

Notes

1 This is a collection of nine papers by Walker Connor published between 1967 and 1993. For the sake of convenience I refer to the book which is published in 1994. But the reader should keep in mind that most of the ideas contained in the book were articulated by Connor well before 1994.

2 I prefer to use the term First Nations to refer to the indigenous peoples for two reasons. First, to distinguish them from the Indians of South Asia. Second, to allude to the fact that the term ethnie is inappropriate for them as they are living in their ancestral homelands, although, of course, they are subjected to the process of ethnification resulting in their marginalization (see chapter 5).

3 This chapter draws from and expands on Oommen (1994b: 26–46).

4 I introduced the term 'culturocide' in 1986 (see Oommen 1990b) to refer to the deliberate policy of destroying the cultures of particular peoples. Culturocide should be distinguished from the gradual cultural assimilation of immigrants through modernization. I prefer the term to others such as cultural genocide or ethnocide. The former is uncouth, as it implies a parallel between the liquidation of cultures and the physical annihilation of human beings. The latter implicitly equates nations and ethnies, both of which are cultural identity groups.

5 This section partially draws on Oommen (1994a 83–93) with the permission of the Editor, *International Social Science Journal*.

6 This section partially draws from Oommen (1994c: 455–72) which first appeared as an article entitled 'Religious nationalism and democratic polity: the Indian Case', *Sociology of Religion* 55(4), © Association for the Sociology of Religion.

7 This figure is problematic because the Indian census automatically counts all those who do not belong to one of the world religions as Hindu. In the British Indian census there was a religious category variously designated as 'animist', 'tribal', or 'primitive', which accounted for 2–3 per cent of the population, which would have amounted to about 25 million persons

those days. This category is absorbed under the rubric of Hinduism from the 1951 census onwards.

8 The sections on First Nations and Africans in the New World selectively draws from Oommen 1992a: 141–72 and 1989: 279–305. The material from 1992a is quoted with the permission of the Editor, *International Review of Sociology* (New Series) and that from 1989 is drawn from Melvin L. Kohn (ed.), *Cross-National Research in Sociology*, with the permission of Sage Publications.

9 As I have discussed the case of South Asia with special reference to India in chapter 4, it is not necessary to repeat it here.

10 The phrase 'chauvinism of prosperity' is from Habermas (1992: 13).

11 States of national segments exist when a nation is divided into two or more states (e.g., two Germanys before unification); or when one segment of a nation consists of a sovereign state (e.g., Bangladesh, Republic of Ireland) and the other segment (e.g., West Bengal, Northern Ireland) is attached to another sovereign state; or when different national segments are attached to different states (e.g., Kurds, Punjabis, Basques, etc.). Also see above, pp. 41–3.

12 As I have discussed a large number of empirical cases of culturocide with special reference to language, particularly in chapter 7, these need not be repeated here.

References

Abdulgani, Roselan 1955: 'Ideological background of the Asian-African Conference'. *United Asia*, 7 (2), 43–5.

Agnew, John A. 1989: *The Devaluation of Place in Social Science*. In John A. Agnew and James S. Duncan (eds), *The Power of Place: Bringing Together Geographical and Sociological Imaginations*, Boston: Unwin Hyman, 9–29.

Alba, Richard D. (ed.) 1985: *Ethnicity and Race in the USA: Toward the Twenty-first Century*. London: Routledge and Kegan Paul.

Alter, Peter 1985: *Nationalism*. London: Edward Arnold.

Anderson, B. 1983: *Imagined Communities: Reflections in the Origin and Spread of Nationalism*. Bombay: New Left.

—— 1992: 'The new world order'. *New Left Review*, 190, 3–14.

Angle, P.M. (ed.) 1958: *Created equal? The complete Lincoln–Douglas debates of 1858*. Chicago: University of Chicago Press.

Aron, Raymond 1966: *Peace and War: A Theory of International Relations*. New York: Doubleday and Company.

Ashworth, Georgina (ed.) 1980: *World Minorities in the Eighties* (vol. 3 in the series). Sunbury: Quartermaine House Ltd.

Awolowo, Obafemi 1947: *Path to Nigerian Freedom*. London: Faber and Faber.

Bacal, Azril 1991: *Ethnicity in the Social Sciences*. Coventry: University of Warwick.

Balibar, Etienne and Wallerstein, Immanuel 1991: *Race, Nation, Class: Ambiguous Identities*. London: Verso.

Balibar, Etienne 1991: 'Race and crisis'. In E. Balibar and I. Wallerstein, *Race, Nation, Class*, London: Verso, 217–27.

Banton, Michael 1967: *Race Relations*. London: Tavistock Publications.

Barbalet, J.M. 1988: *Citizenship: Rights, Struggles and Class Inequality*. Milton Keynes: Open University Press.

Barker, Ernest 1948: *National Character and the Factors in its Formation*. London: Methuen and Co. Ltd. (fourth and revised edition).

Barker, M. 1981: *The New Racism*. London: Junction Publications.

Barth, Frederick (ed.) 1969: *Ethnic Groups and Boundaries*. London: Allen and Unwin.

Baubock, Rainer 1994: *Transnational Citizenship: Membership and Rights in International Migration*. London: Edward Elgar.

Bauer, Yehuda 1982: *A History of Holocaust*. New York: Franklin Watts.

Bauman, Zygmunt 1973: *Culture as Praxis*. London: Routledge and Kegan Paul.

Beer, William R. 1977: 'The social class of ethnic activists in contemporary France'. In Milton J. Esman (ed.), *Ethnic Conflict in the Western World*, Ithaca: Cornell University Press, 141–58.

Bell, Daniel 1975: 'Ethnicity and social change'. In Nathan Glazer and Daniel P. Moynihan (eds), *Ethnicity: Theory and Experience*, Cambridge: Harvard University Press, 141–74.

Berger, Suzanne 1977: 'Bretons and Jacobins: reflections on French regional ethnicity'. In Milton J. Esman (ed.), *Ethnic Conflict in the Western World*, Ithaca: Cornell University Press, 158–78.

Berlin, Isaiah 1972: *Karl Marx: His Life and Environment*. London: Oxford University Press.

Bienvenue, R.M. 1983: 'Comparative colonial systems: the case of Canadian Indians and Australian Aborigines'. *Australian-Canadian studies: An Interdisciplinary Social Science Review*, I, 30–42.

Bjorklund, Ulf 1987: 'Ethnicity and the welfare state'. *International Social Science Journal*, 111, 19–30.

Black, Cyril 1966: *The Dynamics of Modernization*. New York: Harper and Row.

Blackstock, Paul and Hoselitz, Bert (eds) 1952: *The Russian Menace to Europe: A Collection of Articles, Speeches, Letters and News Despatches by Karl Marx and Frederick Engels*. Glencoe: Free Press.

Blauner, Robert 1972: *Racial Oppression in America*. New York: Harper and Row.

Blommaert, Jan and Verschueren, Jef 1991: 'The pragmatics of minority politics in Belgium'. *Language in Society*, 20 (4), 503–31.

—— 1992: 'The role of language in European nationalist ideologies'. *Pragmatics*, 2 (3), 355–75.

Boas, T. 1911/1963: *The Mind of the Primitive Man*. New York: Macmillan.

Bonacich, Edna 1973: 'A theory of middleman minorities'. *American Sociological Review*, 38, 583–94.

Borrie, W.D. 1959: *The Cultural Integration of Immigrants*. Paris: UNESCO.

Boston, Thomas D. 1988: *Race, Class and Conservatism*. Boston: Unwin Hyman.

Bottomore, T.B. 1971: 'Class structure in Western Europe'. In M.S. Archer and S. Giner (eds), *Contemporary Europe: Class, Status and Power*, London: Weidenfeld and Nicolson, 388–407.

Bracey, John H. jun., Meir, August and Rudwick, Elliot (eds) 1970: *Black Nationalism in America*. Indianapolis: The Bobbs Merill Company, Inc.

Braithwaite, E.K. 1967: 'The "coloured immigrant" in Britain'. *Daedalus*, 96 (2), 496–511.

Brandt, Conard, Schwartz, Benjamin and Fairbank, John 1952: *A Documentary History of Chinese Communism*. London: Allen and Unwin.

Brass, P. 1974: *Religion, Language and Politics in North India*. Delhi: Vikas Publishing House.

Brazean, Jacques and Cloutier, Edouard 1977: 'Inter ethnic relations and the language issue in contemporary Canada: a general appraisal'. In Milton J. Esman, (ed.), *Ethnic Conflict in the Western World*, Ithaca: Cornell University Press, 204–27.

Brubaker, Rogers 1992: *Citizenship and Nationhood in France and Germany*. Cambridge: Harvard University Press.

Bullock, Charles S. and Lamb, Charles M. (eds) 1984: *Implementation of Civil Rights Policy*. Monterey: Brooks/Cole.

Bulmer, H. 1986: 'Race and Ethnicity'. In R.G. Burgess (ed.), *Key Variables in Sociological Investigation*, London: Routledge and Kegan Paul.

Cahnman, Werner J. 1944: 'Religion and nationality'. *American Journal of Sociology*, 49 (4), 524–9.

Carr, E.H. 1945: *Nationalism and After*. New York: Macmillan.

Carr, Edward 1966: *The Bolshevik Revolution*, vol. I. Baltimore: Penguin Books.

Chalk, Frank and Jonassohn, Kurt 1990: *The History and Sociology of Genocide*. New Haven: Yale University Press.

Cheles, Luciano, Ferguson, Ronnie and Vaughan, Michalina (eds) 1991: *Neo-Facism in Europe*. London: Longman.

Cherry, Robert 1989: *Discrimination: Its Economic Impact on Blacks, Women and Jews*. Lexington: D.C. Heath and Co.

Chesler, M. 1976: 'Contemporary sociological theories of racism'. In P. Katz (ed.), *Towards Eliminating Racism*, New York: Plenum, 21–71.

Chiswick, Barry 1983: 'The earnings and human capital of American Jews'. *Journal of Human Resources*, 18, 313–35.

Coleman, James S. 1958: *Nigeria, Background to Nationalism*. Berkeley: University of California Press.

Comaroff, John 1991: 'Humanity, ethnicity, nationality: conceptual and comparative perspectives in the USSR'. *Theory and Society*, 20, 661–87.

Commission of the European Community (CEC) 1979: *The Perception of Poverty in Europe*. Brussels: EEC.

—— 1989: *Eurobarometer* (30), Special number on Racism and Xenophobia. Brussels.

—— 1988–93: *Eurobarometer* (annual survey).

Connor, Walker 1984: *The National Question in Marxist-Leninist Theory and Strategy*. Princeton: Princeton University Press.

—— 1994: *Ethnonationalism: The Quest for Understanding*. Princeton: Princeton University Press.

Conover, P.J., Crewe, I. and Searing, D. 1990: *Conceptions of Citizenship among British and American Publics: An Exploratory Analysis*. Colchester, Essex: University of Essex, Department of Government, 1–33 (manuscript).

Curtin, Philip D. 1967: *The Atlantic Slave Trade*. Madison: University of Wisconsin Press.

Dahl, Robert A. 1971: *Polyarchy: Participation and Opposition*. New Haven: Yale University Press.

Dahrendorf, Ralph 1994: 'The changing quality of citizenship'. In Bart Van Steenbergen (ed.), *The Condition of Citizenship*, London: Sage Publications, 10–19.

Davidson, Roderic H. 1948: 'The Armenian crisis, 1912–14'. *American Historical Review*, 53, 483–505.

Davis, A.Y. 1981: *Women, Race, and Class*. New York: Random House.

Davis, Horace B. 1967: *Nationalism and Socialism: Marxist and Labour Theories of Nationalism*. New York: Monthly Review Press.

Dawidowicz, Lucy S. 1975: *The War Against Jews, 1933–1945*. New York: Holt, Rinehart and Winston.

—— 1976: *A Holocaust Reader*. New York: Behrman.

Despres, Leo 1967: *Cultural Pluralism and Nationalist Politics in British Guiana*. Chicago: Rand McNally.

Deutsch, K.W. 1953: *Nationalism and Social Communication: An Enquiry into the Foundations of Nationality*. New York: John Wiley and Sons.
—— 1969: *Nationalism and its Alternatives*. New York: Alfred A. Knopf.
Deutscher, Isaac 1949: *Stalin: A Political Biography*. New York: Oxford University Press.
—— 1971: *Marxism in Our Time*. Berkeley: Rampart Press.
Devos, George and Ross, L. Romanucci (eds) 1975: *Cultural Continuities and Change*. Palo Alto: C.A. Mayfield.
Diamant, Alfred 1959: 'Is there a non-western political process? Comments on Lucian W. Pye's "The non-western political process" '. *Journal of Politics*, 21 (1), 123–7.
Disraeli, B. 1926: *Sybil or The Two Nations*. London: Oxford University Press (The World Classics no. 291).
Dobkowski, Michael N. 1979: *The Tarnished Dream*. Westport: Greenwood Press.
Dollard, John 1937: *Caste and Class in a Southern Town*. New York: Harper and Brothers.
Draper, T. 1970: *The Rediscovery of Black Nationalism*. New York: Viking Compass edition.
Durkheim, E. 1893: *The Division of Labour in Society*. New York: Free Press.
Duster, Troy 1990: *Backdoor to Eugenics*. New York: Routledge and Kegan Paul.
—— 1991: *Diversity Project*. Berkeley: University of California: Institute of Social Change.
Dzyuba, Ivan 1968: *Internationalism or Russification?* New York: Pathfinder Press.
Elias, Norbert 1989: 'The retreat of sociologists in the present'. *Theory, Culture and Society*, 4 (2 and 3), 223–48.
Emerson, Rupert 1962: *From Empire to Nation: The Rise and Self-assertion of Asian and African Peoples*. Boston: Beacon Press.
—— 1964: *Self-determination Revisited in the Era of Decolonisation*. Cambridge (Mass): Harvard University Press.
Eriksen, Thomas Hylland 1991: 'Ethnicity versus Nationalism'. *Journal of Peace Research*, 28 (3), 263–78.
Esman, Milton J. 1977: 'Scottish nationalism, North Sea oil and the British response'. In Milton, J. Esman (ed.), *Ethnic Conflict in the Western World*, Ithaca: Cornell University Press, 251–86.
Essed, Philomena 1991: *Understanding Everyday Racism*. Newbury Park: Sage Publications.
Essien-Udom, E.U. 1962: *Black Nationalism: A Search for an Identity in America*. Chicago: The University of Chicago Press.
Falk, Richard 1994: 'The making of global citizenship'. In Bart Van Steenbergen (ed.), *The Condition of Citizenship*, London: Sage Publications, 127–40.
Farley, Reynold 1984: *Blacks and Whites: Narrowing the Gap?* Cambridge: Harvard University Press.
—— 1985: 'Three steps forward and two back? Racial changes in the social and economic status of Blacks'. In Richard D. Alba (ed.), *Ethnicity and Race in the USA*, London: Routledge and Kegan Paul, 4–28.
Fassmann, Heinz and Munz, Rainer 1992: 'International migration in Western Europe'. *Population and Development Review*, 18 (3), 457–80.

Fernandes, Florestan 1969: *The Negro in Brazilian Society*. New York: Columbia University Press.

Fischer, Andrea 1992: 'Lifting the Golden Curtain'. A paper presented at the seminar 'Social Responses to Political and Economic Transformations in East and Central Europe', Prague, 29–31 May 1992, 1–9 (manuscript).

Fishman, Joshua A. 1968: 'Some contrasts between linguistically homogeneous and linguistically heterogeneous polities'. In Joshua A. Fishman, Charles A. Ferguson and Jyotirindra Das Gupta (eds), *Language Problems of Developing Nations*, New York: John Wiley and Sons, 53–68.

Francis, E.K. 1976: *Interethnic Relations: An Essay in Sociological Theory*. New York: Elsevier.

Franklin, John Hope 1967: *From Slavery to Freedom: A History of Negro Americans*. New Delhi: Areind.

Fraser, Nancy and Gordon, Linda 1994: 'Civil citizenship against social citizenship? On the ideology of contract versus charity'. In Bart van Steenbergen (ed.), *The Condition of Citizenship*, London: Sage Publications, 90–107.

Frazier, Franklin E. 1957: *The Negro in the United States* (revised edition). New York: Macmillan.

——— 1962: *The Black Bourgeoisie*: New York: Collier.

Freyre, Gilberto 1946: *The Masters and the Slaves: A Study in the Development of Brazilian Civilization*. New York: Alfred Knopf.

——— 1959: *New World in the Tropics: The Culture of Modern Brazil*. New York: Alfred Knopf.

——— 1963: 'Ethnic democracy: the Brazilian example'. *Americas*, 15, 1–6.

Furnivall, J.S. 1939: *Netherlands India*. Cambridge: Cambridge University Press.

——— 1948: *Colonial Policy and Practice: A Comparative Study of Burma and Netherlands India*. Cambridge: Cambridge University Press.

Gable, Gerry 1991: 'The far Right in contemporary Britain'. In Luciano Cheles, Ronnie Ferguson and Michalina Vaughan (eds), *Neo-Fascism in Europe*, London: Longman, 245–63.

Geertz, Clifford (ed.) 1963: *Old Societies and New States: The Quest for Modernity in Asia and Africa*. New York: The Free Press.

Gellner, Ernest 1983: *Nations and Nationalisms*. Oxford: Basil Blackwell.

Gerth, H. and Mills, C.W. (eds) 1948: *From Max Weber: Essays in Sociology*. London: Routledge and Kegan Paul.

Giddens, Anthony 1981: *A Contemporary Critique of Historical Materialism*. London: Macmillan.

——— 1985: *The Nation-State and Violence*. Cambridge: Polity Press.

Gililov, S. 1972: 'The worldwide significance of the Soviet experience in solving nationalities question'. *International Affairs* (Moscow), 7, 56–63.

Glazer, Nathan and Moynihan, Daniel P. (eds) 1975: *Ethnicity: Theory and Experience*. Cambridge: Harvard University Press.

Glenn, Edmund S. 1970: 'Two faces of nationalism'. *Comparative Political Studies*, 3 (3), 347–66.

Goldberg, Nathan 1947: *Occupational Pattern of American Jewry*. New York: JTSP University Press.

Gordon, Milton M. 1964: *Assimilation in American Life: The Role of Race, Religion and National Origins*. New York: Oxford University Press.

——— 1978: *Human Nature, Class and Ethnicity*. New York: Oxford University Press.

Greenfeld, Liah 1992: *Nationalism: Five Roads to Modernity*. Cambridge: Harvard University Press.

Greenfeld, Liah and Chirot, Daniel 1994: 'Nationalism and agression'. *Theory and Society*, 23 (1), 79–130.

Grimes, Barbara F. (ed.) 1988: *Ethnologue: Languages of the World*. Dallas: Summer Institute of Linguistics.

Grosby, Steven 1991: 'Religion and nationality in antiquity: the worship of Yahweh and ancient Israel'. *European Journal of Sociology*, 32, 229–65.

Grossholtz, Jean 1964: *The Philippines*. New York: Little, Brown and Co.

Gusfield, Joseph R. 1967: 'Tradition and modernity: misplaced polarities in the study of social change'. *American Journal of Sociology*, 72, 336–51.

Habermas, Jürgen 1992: 'Citizenship and national identity: some reflections on the future of Europe'. *Praxis International*, 12, 1–19.

Hagen, S. 1978: 'Race, politics and the coup in Fiji'. *Bulletin of the Concerned Asian Scholars*, 19 (4), 2–18.

Handlin, Oscar 1957: *Race and Nationality in American Life*. New York: Doubleday and Co. Inc. (Anchor Books edition).

Hanham, H.J. 1969: *Scottish Nationalism*. London: Faber and Faber.

Harris, A. 1936: *The Negro as Capitalist*. Philadelphia: American Academy of Political and Social Science.

Harris, Marvin 1974: *Patterns of Race in the Americas*. New York: W.W. Norton and Company.

Hasenbalg, Carlos A. n.d.: 'Race Relations in Brazil'. Rio de Janeiro (manuscript).

Hechter, Michael 1975: *Internal Colonialism: The Celtic Fringe in British National Development 1536–1966*. London: Routledge and Kegan Paul.

—— 1985: 'Internal colonialism revisited'. In E. Tiryakian, and R. Rogowski (eds), *New Nationalisms of the Developed West*, Boston: Allen and Unwin, 15–26.

Hertz, Frederick 1944: *Nationality in History and Politics*. New York: Oxford University Press.

Heyd, Uriel 1950: *Foundations of Turkish Nationalism: The Life and Teachings of Ziya Gokalp*. London: Luzac.

Hitler, Adolf 1939: *Mein Kampf*. New York: Reynal and Hitchcock.

Hobsbawm, Eric 1983: 'Mass producing traditions: Europe'. In Eric Hobsbawm and Ranger Terene (eds), *The Invention of Tradition*, Cambridge: Cambridge University Press, 263–307.

—— 1990: *Nations and Nationalism since 1780 – Programme, Myth and Reality*. Cambridge: Cambridge University Press.

Hobsbawm, Eric and Terence, Ranger (eds) 1983: *The Invention of Tradition*. Cambridge: Cambridge University Press.

Horowitz, Donald H. 1985: *Ethnic Groups in Conflict*. Berkeley: University of California Press.

Hughes, Arnold 1981: 'The Nationstate in Black Africa'. In Leonard Tivey (ed.), *The Nation-State: The Formation of Modern Politics*, Oxford: Martin Robertson, 122–47.

Husbands, Christopher T. 1988: 'Extreme rightwing politics in Great Britain: the recent marginalisation of National Front'. In Klaus Von Beyme (ed.), *Right Wing Extremism in Western Europe*, London: Frank Cass, 65–79.

Hutnik, N. 1985: 'Aspects of identity in a multi-ethnic society'. *New Community* 12 (2), 298–309.

Huttenbach, Henry R. 1990: 'In support of Nagorno-Karabakh: social com-pon- ents of the Armenian nationalist movement'. *Nationality Papers*, 18 (2), 5–14.

Ianni, Octavio 1970: 'Research on race relations in Brazil'. In Magnus Morner (ed.), *Race and Class in Latin America*, New York: Columbia University Press, 256–78.

Jain P.C. 1989: 'Indians Abroad: a current population estimate'. *Economic and Political Weekly*, 17 (80), 227–304.

Jarvenpa, Robert 1985: 'The political economy and political ethnicity of American Indian: adaptations and identities'. In Richard D. Alba (ed.), *Ethnicity and Race in the USA*, London: Routledge and Kegan Paul, 24–48.

Jennings, Ivor 1956: *The Approach to Self-Government*. Cambridge: Cambridge University Press.

Jiobu, R.M. 1990: *Ethnicity and Inequality*. New York: State University of New York Press.

Johnson, Douglas 1991: 'The new Right in France'. In Luciano Cheles, Ronnie Ferguson, and Michalina Vaughan (eds), *Neo-Fascism in Europe*, London: Longman, 234–44.

Jordon, T.G. 1988: *The European Culture Area: A Systematic Geography*. Cam-bridge: Harper and Row (second edition).

Kautsky J.H. (ed.), 1962: *Political Change in Underdeveloped Countries: National-ism and Communism*. London: Wiley and Sons.

Keating, Michael and Jones, Barry 1991: 'Scotland and Wales: Peripheral assertion and European integration'. *Parliamentary Affairs*, 44 (3) 311–24.

Kellas, James G. 1990: 'The Constitutional Option for Scotland'. *Parliamentary Affairs*, 43 (4): 426–34.

—— 1991: *The Politics Of Nationalism and Ethnicity*. London: Macmillan.

Kerning, C.D. (ed.) 1973: *Marxism, Communism and Western Society: A Com-parative Encyclopedia*, vol. VI. New York: McGraw Hill.

Keys, Charles F. 1966: 'Ethnic identity and loyalty of villagers in Northeast Thailand'. *Asian Survey*, 7, 362–9.

Klugel, James R. and Smith, Eliot R. 1986: *Belief about Inequality: America's View of What Is and What Ought to Be*. New York: Aldine de Gruyter.

Kohn, Hans 1932: *Nationalisms and Imperialism in the Hither East*. London: Routledge.

Kolakowski, L. 1978: *Main Currents in Marxism*, vol. II. Oxford: Oxford University Press.

Kolinsky, Martin 1981: 'The nationstate in Western Europe: erosion from "above" and "below" '. In Leonard Tivey (ed.), *The Nation-State*, Oxford: Martin Robertson, 82–103.

Kornhauser, W. 1960: *The Politics of Mass Society*. Glencoe: Free Press.

Legum, Colin 1967: 'Color and power in the South African situation'. *Daeda-lus*, 96 (2), 483–95.

Lemerchand, René 1970: *Rwanda and Burundi*. New York: Praeger Publishers.

—— 1993: 'Burundi in comparative perspective'. In John McGarry, and Brendan O'Leary (eds), *The Politics of Ethnic Conflict Regulation: Case Studies of Protracted Ethnic Conflicts*. London: Routledge and Kegan Paul, 151–71.

Lenin V.I. 1934: *Selected Works*, vol. II. Moscow: Co-operative Publishing Society of Foreign Workers in the USSR.

Lerner, Max 1957: *America as a Civilization* (2 vols). New Delhi: Allied.

Lestchinsky, Jacob 1946: 'The economic development of Jews in the US'. In *The Jewish People: Past and Present 1870–1914*, vol. I, 391–406.

Lewis, Bernard 1961: *The Emergence of Modern Turkey*. Oxford: Oxford University Press.

Liebman, Arthur 1979: *Jews and the Left*. New York: John Wiley and Sons.

Lijphart, Arend 1980: *Democracy in Plural Societies: A Comparative Exploration*. New Haven: Yale University Press (second printing).

Lincoln, Eric C. 1967: 'Color and group identity in the United States'. *Daedalus*, 96 (2), 527–41.

Little, Kenneth 1967: 'Some aspects of color, class and culture in Britain'. *Daedalus*, 96 (2), 512–26.

Lorwin, Val R. 1971: 'Segmented pluralism: ideological cleavages and political cohesion in the smaller European democracies'. *Comparative Politics*, 3, 141–75.

Lowenthal, David 1967: 'Race and color in the West Indies'. *Daedalus*, 96 (2), 580–629.

Luthy, Herbert 1957: 'The passing of the European order: colonialism and the cargo cult'. *Encounter*, 9 (5), 3–12.

Lutz, J.M. 1990: 'Diffusion of nationalist-voting in Scotland and Wales: emulation, contagion, and retrenchment'. *Political Geography Quarterly*, 9 (3), 249–66.

Macpherson, C.B. 1974: *The Political Theory of Possessive Individualism: Hobbes to Locke*. New York: Oxford University Press.

Marable, M. 1980: 'Black nationalism in the 1970s: through the prism of race and class'. *Socialist Review*, 10 (2–3), 57–108.

Marshall, T.H. 1965: *Class, Citizenship and Social Development*. New York: Anchor Books.

Marx, Karl 1932: *Capital, the Communist Manifesto and Other Writings*. New York: The Modern Library.

—— 1977: Collected Works, vol. VII. Moscow: Progress.

Marx, Karl and Engels, Frederich 1964: *German Ideology*. Moscow: Progress.

Mauzy, Diane 1993: 'Malaysia: Malay political hegemony and coercive consociationalism'. In John McGarry and Brendan O'Leary (eds), *The Politics of Ethnic Conflict Regulation*, London: Routledge and Kegan Paul, 106–27.

Mazrui, Ali A. 1978: 'Negritude, the Talmudic tradition and the intellectual performance of Blacks and Jews'. *Ethnic and Racial Studies*, 1 (1), 19–36.

McGarry, John and O'Leary, Brendan (eds) 1993: *The Politics of Ethnic Conflict Regulation: Case Studies of Protracted Ethnic Conflicts*. London: Routledge and Kegan Paul.

McLean, Scilla 1980: 'Development? The Kalinga, Bontoc and the Isneg of the Philippines'. In Georgina Ashworth (ed.), *World Minorities in the Eighties*, Sunburry: Quartermaine House Ltd., 38–41.

Mead, Lawrence 1986: *Beyond Entitlement: The Social Obligations of Citizenship*. New York: Free Press.

Meier, August and Elliot, Rudwick 1975: *CORE: A Study in the Civil Rights Movement, 1942–1968*. Urbana: University of Illinois Press.

Meisler, Stanley 1976: 'Holocaust in Burundi, 1972'. In Willem A. Veenhoven (ed.), *Case Studies on Human Rights and Fundamental Freedom*, vol. V. The Hague: Martins Nijhoff, 227–32.

Miles, Robert 1989: 'Migration Discourse in post-1945 British Politics'. *Migration*, 6, 29–53.

Mitra, Subrata 1988: 'The National Front in France: a single-issue movement?' In Klaus Von Beyme (ed.), *Right Wing Extremism in Western Europe*, London: Frank Cass, 47–64.

Montagu, Ashley (ed.) 1964: *The Concept of Race*. New York: Free Press.

Morgan, Kenneth O. 1971: 'Welsh Nationalism: the historical background'. *Journal of Contemporary History*, 6 (1), 153–71.

Moynihan, Daniel P. 1993: *Pandemonium: Ethnicity in International Politics*. Oxford: Oxford University Press.

Muiznieks, Nils R. 1995: 'Ethnopolitics and citizenship in post-Soviet Latvia'. A paper presented to the seminar 'Citizenship, Nationality and Ethnicity'. Collegium Budapest, 19–20 May 1–23 (manuscript).

Murray, David 1980: 'Indians in Fiji'. In Georgina Ashworth (ed.), *World Minorities in the Eighties*, Sunburry: Quartermaine House Ltd., 41–7.

Mutesa II, Kabaka, Edward Sir 1967: *The Desecration of My Kingdom*. London: Constable.

Myrdal, Gunnar 1944: *An American Dilemma: The Negro Problem and Modern Democracy*. New York: Harper and Row.

—— 1956: *An International Economy*. New York: Harper and Brothers.

Nagel, Joane and Snipp, Matthew C. 1987: 'American Indian Tribal Identification and Federal Indian Policy: the reflection of history in the 1980 census'. Paper presented to the annual meeting of the American Sociological Association, Chicago, 17–21 August (manuscript).

Nairn, Tom 1981: *The Break Up of Britain: Crisis and Neo-Nationalism* (second, expanded edition). London: Verso.

Nash, Manning 1989: *The Cauldron of Ethnicity in the Modern World*. Chicago: Chicago University Press.

Nayyar, Beldev R. 1966: *Minority Politics in the Punjab*. Princeton: Princeton University Press.

Nehru, Jawaharlal 1952: *The Taming of Nations*. New York: Macmillan.

Nielsson, Gunnar P. 1985: 'States and "Nation-Groups": a global taxonomy'. In Edward A. Tiryakian and Ronald Rogowski (eds), *New Nationalisms of the Developed West*, Boston: Allen and Unwin, 27–56.

Nisbet, Robert A. 1966: *The Sociological Tradition*. London: Heinemann.

Nogee, Joseph 1972: *Man, State and Society in the Soviet Union*. New York: Praeger.

Norton, E.H. 1985: 'Restoring the traditional black family'. *New York Time Magazine*, 2 June.

Oommen, T.K. 1967: 'The rural urban continuum re-examined in the Indian context'. *Sociologia Ruralis*, 7 (1), 30–48.

—— 1983: 'Sociology in India: a plea for contextualisation'. *Sociological Bulletin*, 32 (2), 111–36.

—— 1989: 'Ethnicity, immigration and cultural pluralism: India and the United States of America'. In Melvin L. Kohn (ed.), *Cross-National Research in Sociology*. Newbury Park: Sage Publications, 279–305.

—— 1990a: *Protest and Change: Studies in Social Movements*. New Delhi: Sage Publications.

—— 1990b: *State and Society in India: Studies in Nation-Building*. New Delhi: Sage Publications.

—— 1992a: 'Reconciling pluralism and equality: the dilemma of "advanced" societies'. *International Review of Sociology* (new series), 1, 141–72.

—— 1992b: 'Restructuring development through technological pluralism'. *International Sociology*, 7 (2), 131–9.

—— 1994a: 'Race, ethnicity and class: an analysis in interrelations'. *International Social Science Journal*, 139, 83–93.

—— 1994b: 'State, nation and ethnie: the processual linkages'. In Peter Ratcliffe (ed.), *Race, Ethnicity and Nation: International Perspectives on Social Conflict*. London. University College London Press, 26–46.

—— 1994c: 'Religious nationalism and democratic polity: the Indian case'. *Sociology of Religion*, 55 (4), 455–72.

Ostegaard, Geoffrey 1981: 'Resisting the nationstate: the pacifist and anarchist traditions'. In Lenord Tivey (ed.), *The Nation-State*, Oxford: Martin Robertson, 171–96.

Otite, Onigu 1975: 'Resource competition and inter-ethnic relation in Nigeria'. In Leo A. Despres (ed.), *Ethnicity and Resource Competition in Plural Societies*, The Hague: Mouton Publishers, 119–30.

Parole, Apolimar B. 1969: *Facts and Issues on the Pilipino Language*. Manila: Royal Publishing House.

Perlo, Victor 1988: 'Deterioration of Black economic conditions in the 1980s'. *Review of Radical Political Economics*, 20 (2 and 3), 55–60.

Petersen, William 1975: 'On the Subnations of Western Europe'. In Nathan Glazer and Daniel P. Moynihan (eds), *Ethnicity*, Cambridge: Harvard University Press, 177–208.

Pettigrew, Thomas F. 1964: *A Profile of the Negro American*. Princeton: D. Van Nostrand Co. Inc.

—— 1973: 'Attitudes on Race and Housing: a social-psychological view'. In Amos H. Howley and Vincent P. Rock (eds), *Segregation in Residential Areas*. Washington: National Academy of Sciences, 21–84.

Pinkey, Alphonso 1984: *The Myth of Black Progress*. Cambridge: Cambridge University Press.

Pi-Sunyer, Oriol 1985: 'Catalan nationalism: some theoretical and historical considerations'. In Edward A. Tiryakian and Ronald Rogowski (eds), *New Nationalism of the Developed West*, Boston: Allen and Unwin, 254–76.

Premdas, Ralph R. 1993: 'Balance and ethnic conflict in Fiji'. In John McGarry, and Brendan O'Leary (eds), *The Politics of Ethnic Conflict Regulation*, London: Routledge and Kegan Paul, 251–74.

Pye, Lucian W. 1958: 'The non-Western political process'. *Journal of Politics*, 20 (3), 468–87.

Redfield, Robert 1955: *The Little Community*. Chicago: University of Chicago Press.

Reece, J. 1979: 'Internal colonialism: the case of Brittany'. *Ethnic and Racial Studies*, 2 (3), 275–92.

Rejai, Mostafa and Enloe, Cynthia H. 1969: 'Nation-states and state-nations'. *International Studies Quarterly*, 13 (2), 140–58.

Richmond, A.H. 1987: 'Ethnic nationalism: social science paradigms'. *International Social Science Journal*, 39 (1), 3–18.

Roff, William R. 1967: *The Origins of Malay Nationalism*. New Haven: Yale University Press.

Roosens, Eugeen H. 1989: *Creating Ethnicity*. Newbury Park: Sage Publications.

Rose, A.M. 1969: *Migrants in Europe*. Minneapolis: The University of Minnesota Press.

Rose, Richard 1970: *The UK as a Multi-National State*. Glasgow: University of Strathclyde.

Rustow, Dankwart A. 1968: 'Language, modernization and nationhood: an attempt at typology'. In Joshua A. Fishman, Charles A. Ferguson and Jyotirindra Das Gupta (eds), *Language Problems of Developing Nations*, New York: John Wiley and Sons, 87–105.

Samuel, R. (ed.) 1989: *Patriotism: The Making and Unmaking of British National Identity* (3 vols). London: Routledge and Kegan Paul.

Saunders G. (ed.) 1974: *Samizdat: Voices of the Soviet Opposition*. New York: Monad Press.

Schopflin, George 1993: 'The rise and fall of Yugoslavia'. In John McGarry and Brendan O'Leary (eds), *The Politics of Ethnic Conflict Regulation*, London: Routledge and Kegan Paul, 172–203.

Seton-Watson H. 1977: *Nations and States: An Enquiry into the Origins of Nations and the Politics of Nationalism*. London: Methuen.

Shils, E. A. 1956: *The Torment of Secrecy*. London: Heinemann.

Skinner, William G. 1963: 'The Chinese minority'. In Ruth Mcvey (ed.), *Indonesia: Human Relations Area Files*. New Haven: Yale University Press.

Slater, Miriam 1969: 'My son the doctor: aspects of mobility among American Jews'. *American Sociological Review*, 34, 351–73.

Smiley, Donald V. 1977: 'French-English relations in Canada and consociational democracy'. In Milton J. Esman (ed.), *Ethnic Conflict in the Western World*, Ithaca: Cornell University Press, 197–203.

Smith, Anthony D. 1971: *Theories of Nationalism* (first edition). London: Duckworth.

—— 1973: 'Nationalism and religion: the role of religious reform in the genesis of Arab and Jewish nationalism'. *Archives de Sociologie des Religions*, 35, 23–43.

—— 1979: *Nationalism in the Twentieth Century*. Oxford: Martin Robertson.

—— 1981: *The Ethnic Revival in the Modern World*. Cambridge: Cambridge University Press.

—— 1986: *The Ethnic Origins of Nations*. Oxford: Basil Blackwell.

Smith, Donald E. 1963: *India as a Secular State*. Bombay: Oxford University Press.

Smith, M. G. 1965: *The Plural Society in British West Indies*. Berkeley: University of California Press.

—— 1971: 'Some developments in the analytic framework of pluralism'. In L. Kuper, and M.G. Smith (eds), *Pluralism in Africa*, Berkeley: University of California Press, 415–58.

Smith, W.C. 1957: *Islam in Modern History*. Princeton: Princeton University Press.

Snipp, C. Matthew 1987: *The First of this Land*. New York: Basic Books.

Snyder, Louis L. 1976: *Varieties of Nationalism: A Comparative Study*. Hinsdale: The Dryden Press.

Sowell, T. 1981: *Ethnic America: A History*. New York: Basic Books.

Speiser, E.A. 1960: 'People and nation of Israel'. *Journal of Biblical Literature*, 79, 157–63.

Stalin, Joseph 1935: *Marxism and the National Question: Selected Writings and Speeches*. New York: International Publishers.

—— 1940: *Marxism and the National and Colonial Question*. Moscow: Foreign Language Publishing House.

—— n.d.: *Marxism and Linguistics*. New York: International Publishers.

Steinberg, S. 1981: *The Ethnic Myth*. Boston: Beacon Press.

Steiner, Eugen 1973: *The Slovak Dilemma*. Cambridge: University of Cambridge Press.

Sturzo, Don Luigi 1946: *Nationalism and Internationalism*. New York: Roy Publishers.

Tabouret-Keller, A. 1968: 'Sociological factors of language maintenance and language shift: a methodological approach based on European and African examples'. In Joshua A. Fishman, Charles A. Ferguson and Jyotirindra Das Gupta (eds), *Language Problems of Developing Nations*, New York: John Wiley and Sons, 107–18.

Tannebaum, Frank 1947: *Slave and Citizen: The Negro in the Americas*. New York. Knopf.

Tilly, Charles 1973: 'Do communities act?' *Sociological Inquiry*, 43, 209–40.

—— 1975: 'Reflections on the history of European statemaking'. In Charles Tilly (ed.), *The Formation of National States in Western Europe*. Princeton: Princeton University Press.

—— 1993: *European Revolutions, 1492–1992*. Oxford: Blackwell.

—— 1994: 'States and nationalism in Europe, 1492–1992'. *Theory and Society*, 23, 131–46.

Tinker, Hugh 1974: *A New System of Slavery: The Export of Indian Labour Overseas, 1830–1920*. London: Oxford University Press.

Tiryakian, Edward. A. and Rogowski, Ronald (eds) 1985: *New Nationalisms of the Developed West*. Boston: Allen and Unwin.

Tishkov, Valery A. 1991: 'The Soviet Empire before and after Perestroika'. *Theory and Society*, 20, 603–29.

Tivey, Leonard (ed.) 1981: *The Nation-State: The Formation of Modern Politics*. Oxford: Martin Robertson.

Tocqueville, A. de 1956: *Democracy in America* (2 vols). New York: Knopf.

Touraine, A. 1977: *The Self-Production of Society*. Chicago: University of Chicago Press.

—— 1985: 'Sociological intervention and the internal dynamics of the Occitanist movement'. In Edward A. Tiryakian and Ronald Rogowski (eds), *New Nationalisms in the Developed West*, Boston: Allen and Unwin, 157–75.

Trotsky, L. 1922: *Between Red and White*. London: Communist Party of Great Britain.

Trudeau, Pierre Elliot 1968: *Federalism and the French Canadian*. Toronto: Macmillan of Canada.

United Nations Development Programme (UNDP) 1991: *Human Development Report, 1991*. Oxford: Oxford University Press.

Van den Berghe, P.L. 1970: *Race and Ethnicity*. New York: Basic Books Inc.

—— 1971: 'Pluralism and Polity: a theoretical explanation'. In L. Kuper and M.G. Smith (eds), *Pluralism in Africa*, Berkeley: University of California Press 67–81.

—— 1978: *Race and Racism: A Comparative Perspective*. New York: John Wiley and Sons (second edition).

—— 1983: 'Australia, Canada and the United States: ethnic melting pots or plural societies'. *ANZJS*, 19 (2), 238–52.

Van Dijk, Teun 1987: *Communicating Racism*. Newbury Park: Sage Publications.

—— 1993: 'Principles of critical discourse analysis'. *Discourse and Society*, 4 (2), 249–84.

Van Gunsteren, Herman 1994: 'Four conceptions of citizenship'. In Bart Van Steenbergen (ed.), *The Condition of Citizenship*, London: Sage Publications, 36–48.

Van Steenbergen, Bart 1994: 'Towards a global ecological citizen'. In Bart Van Steenbergen (ed.), *The Condition of Citizenship*, London: Sage Publications, 141–52.

Vasil, R. 1984: *Politics in Bi-Racial Societies.* New Delhi: Vikas Publishing House.

Vilar, P. 1980: Spain and Catalonia. *Review*, 3 (4), 527–77.

Von Beyme, Klaus (ed.) 1988: *Right Wing Extremism in Western Europe.* London: Frank Cass.

Waldinger, Roger 1986: 'Immigrant enterprise: a critique and a reformulation'. *Theory and Practice*, 15, 249–85.

Wallas, Graham 1921: *Human Nature in Politics.* New York: Alfred Knopf.

Wallerstein, Immanuel 1979: *The Capitalist World Economy.* Cambridge: Cambridge University Press.

—— 1991: 'Social conflict in post-independence Black Africa: the concepts of race and status-group reconsidered'. In Etienne Balibar and Immanuel Wallerstein (eds), *Race, Nation, Class*, London: Verso, 187–203.

Watters, R. F. 1969: *Koro: Economic Development and Social Change in Fiji.* Oxford: Clarendon Press.

Weber, Eugen 1976: *Peasants into Frenchmen: the modernisation of rural France, 1870–1914.* Stanford: Stanford University Press.

Weber, Max 1948: *From Max Weber: Essays in Sociology.* London: Routledge and Kegan Paul.

—— 1968: *Economy and Society: An Outline of Interpretive Sociology*, vol. I. New York: Bedminister Press.

Whiteley, W. 1971: *Language Use and Social Change.* London: Oxford University Press.

William, Liddle R. 1970: *Ethnicity, Party and National Integration.* New Haven: Yale University Press.

Wilson, W. J. 1978: *The Declining Significance of Race.* Chicago: Chicago University Press.

—— 1987: *The Truly Disadvantaged.* Chicago: Chicago University Press.

—— 1994: 'Citizenship and the innercity ghetto poor'. In Bart Van Steenbergen (ed.), *The Condition of Citizenship*, London: Sage Publications 49–65.

Woodward, C. Vann 1966: *The Strange Career of Jim Crow.* New York: Oxford University Press (second revised edition).

Working Party of Aboriginal Historians 1988: 'Aboriginal History in the Bicentennial History 1788–1988: a celebration of our resistance to colonialism'. *Australia 1939–1988*, 3, 21–5.

Worsley, Peter 1984: *The Three Worlds: Culture and World Development.* Chicago: Chicago University Press.

Wright, A.W. 1981: 'Socialism and Nationalism'. In Leonard Tivey (ed.), *The Nation-State*, Oxford: Martin Robertson, 148–70.

Yamskov, A. N. 1991: 'Ethnic conflict in the Transcaucasia: the case of Nagorno-Karabakh'. *Theory and Society*, 20, 631–60.

Yancey, L. William, Ericksen, Eugene and Richard, Juliani 1976: 'Emerging ethnicity: a review and reformulation'. *American Sociological Review*, 41 (3), 391–403.

Young, Crawford 1976: *The Politics of Cultural Pluralism*. Madison: The University of Wisconsin Press.

Young, Nigel 1967: 'Prometheans or troglodytes? The English working class and the dialectics of incorporation'. *Berkeley Journal of Sociology*, 12, 10–18.

Zernatto, G. 1944: 'Nation: the history of a word'. *Review of Politics*, 6, 351–66.

Znaniecki, Florain 1952: *Modern Nationalities*. Urbana: The University of Illinois Press.

Index

UWE, BRISTOL LIBRARY SERVICES